Powerful Principles of Instruction

STEPHEN L. YELON

Michigan State University

Longman *Publishers USA*

Powerful Principles of Instruction

Longman, 10 Bank Street, White Plains, N.Y. 10606

Associated companies:
Longman Group Ltd., London
Longman Cheshire Pty., Melbourne
Longman Paul Pty., Auckland
Copp Clark Longman Ltd., Toronto

Acquisitions editor: Laura McKenna
Production editor: Linda Moser
Editorial assistant: Matt Baker
Production supervisor: Richard Bretan
Compositor: ExecuStaff Composition Services

Library of Congress Cataloging-in-Publication Data

Yelon, Stephen L.
  Powerful principles of instruction / by Stephen L. Yelon.
      p. cm.
  Includes bibliographical references and index.
  ISBN 0-8013-1643-X
  1. Teaching. 2. Learning. 3. Teachers. I. Title.
  LB1025.3.Y45 1996
  371.71'02—dc20   95-10866
                                               CIP

1 2 3 4 5 6 7 8 9 10-VMA-9998979695

This book is for my daughters

Debbie and Lisa

who teach others in formal and informal ways; may they continue to do so. I appreciate all they have taught me about good teaching. This book is also for all my students, colleagues, and clients who have taught me well, especially masters and doctoral instructional design students and colleagues, undergraduate teacher education students and colleagues, educational psychology teaching fellows and colleagues, medical fellows and medical education colleagues, colleagues at SWRL (Southwest Regional Laboratory) for Educational Research, friends in the Office of Training of the United States Secret Service, professors from all departments of Michigan State University with whom I have worked under the auspices of the Learning and Evaluation Service, and physicians, nurses, lawyers, judges, police officers, accountants, engineers, and farmers with whom I have worked outside the university. This book is something for you to use, to think about, to argue with, and most of all, to add to and revise.

"Not only is there an art in knowing a thing, but also an art in teaching it."

Cicero

Contents

Preface

PURPOSE

This book is about principles. It is organized according to ten principles that are applied by effective instructors and trainers and are the basis for most practical instructional methods. Each principle is itself potent, but the combination of principles provides a powerful framework.

My purpose is to remind or inform you of these powerful instructional principles and to show you how you can convert them into practical procedures. Although I describe many practical procedures in the book, I emphasize principles because they are so fundamental and powerful. As Stephen Covey (1989) explains in his book *The Seven Habits of Highly Effective People,* principles are basic ideas that guide human decisions and actions. They are so basic that it would be ludicrous to think about acting without attending to them. But as Covey explains, principles are neither practical procedures nor situationally specific. They are broad and general guidelines.

I derived both the instructional principles and the procedures in this book from observations of teachers, reviews of research on teaching, and classical and contemporary theories. My belief is that most experienced instructional designers, theoreticians, and researchers in education would readily agree with the validity of these principles.

Does this text encompass all the powerful principles that excellent teachers use? Of course not. I believe it contains those that can make a tremendous difference in the design of instruction so that students will learn and want to use what they have learned. Does this text contain all that teachers must know and be able to do? No, but it does contain the basis for a great deal of a teacher's thoughtful and analytic decision making and problem solving. When applying the principles in this text in ways shown in chapter 12, teachers demonstrate a potent comprehensive strategy for planning, conducting, and evaluating instruction.

The procedures in each chapter enhance the understanding of the principles. They show concretely and practically what the principles mean. If, however, you put all the procedures together, you won't get a complete set of teaching methods. Teaching is not made up of a set of techniques; rather, it is a craft based on many sets of powerful principles.

Instructional principles can be quite practical. These ideas can help you and other potential or practicing teachers or trainers in at least five ways:

1. Instructional principles can help you understand why a certain type of instruction should work, and why it might not work. These principles will help you do the analytic thinking needed to predict the results of your instruction.
2. Instructional principles can help you design new courses in a creative and flexible manner. You don't have to rely only on traditional instructional development techniques or standard instructional methods. Principles give you the basis to judge the value of the traditional approach and to create your own procedures.
3. Instructional principles can help you to identify the causes of instructional problems and to find the solutions. You can revise courses carefully and purposefully.
4. As a unit, the ten instructional principles provide you with a mental checklist to review all aspects of your instruction systematically.
5. Instructional principles can serve as a common vocabulary for you and your colleagues so that you may easily communicate and solve instructional problems.

AUDIENCE

I wrote this book for those of you who are studying to become elementary school, high school, or college teachers, or to become technical or professional trainers. It is ideal for students of instructional design and for teachers and trainers who are anxious to do better.

Two general groups of courses lend themselves to the use of this text. First, undergraduate and graduate students in general educational methods, secondary methods, or applied instruction classes will find this text an interesting addition and contrast to their primary text. Although elementary teachers can benefit from these principles, most examples in this text are placed in post–elementary school settings. Second, undergraduate and graduate instructional design classes, teaching assistant training classes, seminars for college teachers, adult education classes, and "train the trainer" programs will find that this text complements the existing design texts.

This book should be useful either as a primary or supplementary text in several course areas:

- General educational methods
- Secondary methods
- Secondary educational psychology
- College teaching
- Principles of teaching
- Teaching practicum
- Applied teaching
- Instructional design
- Adult education
- Training of college teaching assistants
- Training of trainers
- Seminars for educators on improving teaching
- Seminars for training professionals to teach

In addition, consumers of instruction, both students and parents, can learn what to look for in the instruction they receive.

ORGANIZATION

The structure of this book is unusual. Following an introduction, each chapter is dedicated to one simple but broad and powerful principle. The principles are well established and are the basis for most instructional methods. They provide a solid framework for thinking about teaching. You can apply the principles one at a time as you learn them, or combine all of them to form a whole approach. I demonstrate several combinations in the last chapter. This approach represents one example of a flexible structure for viewing and thinking about instruction. Whatever your style of teaching, you can apply the principles and this framework to your lessons, units, courses, and programs, on all levels and in most subjects. Although I explain many procedures related to each principle, the generality of each principle allows you to discover and create your own procedures.

Because this text is arranged by principles, I address important educational topics within the context of the appropriate principle. For example, consider the topic of *assessment*. When discussing the motivational principle meaningfulness (chapter 2), I explain how to assess student motives. In chapter 3, on prerequisites, I talk about preassessing and adjusting to students' knowledge; and in chapter 4, on open communication, I explain how teachers might explicitly reveal what is going to be tested. In the chapter on essential content (chapter 5), I mention how concepts, facts, principles, and skills are tested differently. In discussing active appropriate practice (chapter 9), I explain how student preparation must be related to the test. Finally, in chapter 11, on consistency, I show how a final exam must reflect the objective and be consistent with all other parts of instruction. In a similar fashion, I cover topics such as motivation, attention, and teaching concepts, facts, principles, and physical and mental skills.

Every chapter begins with an overview containing a brief definition of the principle and a small set of guidelines for instructional practice. Each guideline is a practical, general rule to follow and represents a major section of the chapter. Each subheading refers to a more specific technique discussed in a subsection of the chapter. So in the overview you can find all the major suggestions in one place, and you have a map to find your place in the chapter.

The content is accessible and easy to comprehend. In the body of each chapter I use a conversational style to describe the principle. I give you specific practical ideas so that you can apply the principles right away, and so that you gain full understanding of each principle. I also set aside many examples. I select fitting, real, and interesting examples and tell many of them as stories to bring the principles to life. They describe common mistakes to avoid or illustrate practices to follow. The wide variety of examples will help you generalize and gain full meaning of the principles. Because I list steps and set aside examples, you can, if you wish, read the major explanations quickly to get the gist of the chapter.

As you will note in the cases throughout the text and in the uses of the principles proposed in the last chapter, the principles can be applied to all forms of teaching: direct instruction, self-instruction, problem-based learning, cooperative learning. The only limiting factors in the use of the principles are teachers' understanding of the principles and their creativity in applying the principles.

At the end of each chapter I include a final word to sum up the chapter. I follow with functional activities in which you can relate each principle to your circumstances. I have used these activities with many groups in workshops and courses. By performing these activities, you will gain a deeper understanding of the principle, in a way consistent with real teaching or training practice. After the activities I list selected further readings so you can read more about the principles and procedures mentioned in the chapter.

Appendix A is a checklist divided into sections by principle. As you learn each principle, you can use parts of the checklist to observe teaching, to create or critique instructional plans, or to evaluate an instructional session.

In the last chapter I describe how to apply the principles and unleash their power. Here you will see how all the principles can be used to teach a lesson. I emphasize the flexible, sensible application of the principles, so you won't be tempted to use any particular set of procedures as "the approach." In the end, you will see the logic in applying the principles in your own creative manner. After all, this book is about principles.

Here is a summary of this book's features:

- The text structure is a unique and powerful framework.
- The writing is clear, concise, conversational, and easily accessible to the reader.
- Each chapter is well organized with overviews, guidelines, and summaries.
- Appendix A is a useful tool for observation, planning, and evaluation.
- Important lists of ideas are noted.
- A multitude of personal anecdotes and examples from a wide variety of educational settings support each principle.
- Practical procedures, which accompany each principle, are explained and illustrated.
- Each chapter ends with useful activities that call for application of the principles and procedures.
- Each chapter contains many issues that provide ample opportunity for discussion and practice.
- The text is adaptable to a variety of teaching approaches.

ACKNOWLEDGMENTS

I appreciate the generosity of the the National Society for Performance and Instruction for allowing me to adapt portions of articles from their two journals for use in this text. Each article is reprinted with the permission of The National Society for Performance and Instruction. The section appearing on pages 62–69 on choosing appropriate strategies to adjust to differences among students is adapted from Yelon, S. L. (1985), "Making decisions about pretesting: It's not a simple matter," *Performance and Instruction, 24*(9), 12–14, copyright © 1985. The section on pages 203–208 about purposefully selecting student learning activities and implementing them is adapted from Yelon, S. L. (1995), "Active learning: A taxonomy of training activities," *Performance and Instruction, 34*(5), 38–41, copyright © 1995. The section on pages 242–244 about use of the MASS model to promote transfer is adapted from Yelon, S. L. (1992), "M.A.S.S.: A model for producing transfer," *Performance Improvement Quarterly, 5*(2), 13–23, copyright © 1992.

I am grateful to the following individuals for their help:

Josie Csete, Yuk Fai Cheong, John Lightner, Debbie Yelon, and Lisa Yelon gave me excellent advice about the ideas and the structure of the text. Debbie Sleight, Bryan Holland, and Lisa Payne provided technical assistance, while Kimberly Nichols helped with the graphics. Thanks to Fran Yelon for the birthday gift of a portable computer on which this whole text was composed. Thanks are not enough for Fran's careful and patient editing of the manuscript, which was a true act of love. Bea Reed helped me enjoy the process of writing. Fred Lopez, Chris Clark, and Don Hamachek encouraged me to get the job done, and thanks to Evelyn Oka and Jack Smith for sources. Thanks to the staff of the Cappuccino Cafe in East Lansing, Michigan, for letting me write in such pleasant surroundings. Thanks also to my colleagues who reviewed the text and encouraged me to publish this book:

Susan Adler, University of Missouri–Kansas City

James Dick, University of Nebraska at Omaha

Diane H. Jackman, North Dakota State University

Jonathan K. Parker, Huntington College

Bruce D. Smith, University of Cincinnati

M. Kay Stickle, Ball State University

David B. Young, University of Maryland–Baltimore County

chapter 1

Introduction

OVERVIEW

Four Common Attributes of Excellent Teachers
Ten Powerful Instructional Principles
The Principles versus Procedures Debate
How to Read This Book to Achieve Its Objective

For more than 30 years, I have been helping teachers to improve their teaching. I have worked with all kinds of teachers—preschool, elementary school, high school, and college teachers. But mostly I work with professionals who teach other professionals, such as doctors, nurses, lawyers, judges, police officers, scientists, accountants, and farmers.

I have worked with these teachers in individual consultations, workshops, seminars, and courses. Frequently I give them advice, and in telling them how they should teach, I exhibit a certain degree of arrogance. The message seems to be, "I know something you don't know." Consequently, every once in a while, one of them gets fed up, grabs me by the tie, and says, "If you are so smart, then tell me, what is an excellent teacher?" I respond by rattling off the early research on the characteristics of excellent teachers. "Good teachers are open, they are warm, they are flexible. . . ." But when I finish my list, nothing changes. I look down, and I notice that the person grabbing my tie has not let go. So I ask, "How come you haven't let go?" And the grabber says, "Because you haven't told me what I can do differently tomorrow from what I do today." Back in 1969, I got tired of people grabbing my ties and bending my collars, and I decided to do some case studies with my colleague Lawrence Alexander to discover the characteristics of excellent teachers. Many things I have seen and read since then have confirmed what we found.

To discover the characteristics of excellent teachers, of course, I had to find excellent teachers. Friends and colleagues recommended a group of six teachers who had been selected for an excellence in teaching award at Michigan State University. Although they had received the award, I wanted to see if they met our criteria for excellence. Did their students learn? Did their students learn to a high standard? Did their students want to use what they had learned? These teachers did indeed meet our criteria.

After identifying this set of fine teachers, I had to discover what they had in common. Lawrence Alexander, Geoffrey Yager (our graduate assistant), and I observed and interviewed them, observed and interviewed their students, and looked at their tests and course materials. We videotaped and did careful analyses of their behaviors.

What did these excellent teachers have in common? At first I was quite disappointed, as we couldn't figure out what made them special. We started with two hypotheses. First, we thought perhaps the excellent teachers would stand out as great experts in their subject matter, but on the surface that didn't seem true; they were as well qualified as any teacher on campus. Second, we thought that excellent teachers had outgoing personalities, but that wasn't a common characteristic either. In fact, the excellent teachers were quite different from one another. Let me give you an example. One of the teachers we interviewed would jump up to the chalkboard and draw maps of South America in response to our questions. It was nearly impossible to get him to sit down. His behavior was in stark contrast to another fine teacher who moved no more than a fraction of an inch during the entire interview.

Well, what was it? What did these teachers have in common? Four common attributes emerged after careful examination, which we came to believe in then, and I continue to believe in even more strongly now.

FOUR COMMON ATTRIBUTES
OF EXCELLENT TEACHERS

First, we found that excellent teachers are concerned about their subject matter. They believe with a religious fervor in what they teach. As one teacher expressed it, "It is in the students' benefit to know this content. It is imperative for their well-being that they know this." What did he teach? The history of South America during World War II! He was so enthusiastic that by the time I was finished with the interview, I wanted to study the history of South America during World War II.

Second, excellent teachers are concerned about their students. Although some have large classes where you might think it difficult to reach all students, these teachers want all of their students to learn. They also believe that their students are capable of learning.

Third, excellent teachers like the job of teaching. Excellent teachers enjoy passing on what they know to students and derive pleasure from seeing novices become experts. They enjoy the process of analyzing, planning, creating, delivering, and improving their instruction. It is fun for them. They integrate play with their teaching. I believe that this attitude is likely to lead to teaching that is beautiful, elegant, poetic, and touching.

Finally, excellent teachers put into practice ten powerful instructional principles. They apply what they know about motivation, learning, and transfer to make their instruction effective.

TEN POWERFUL INSTRUCTIONAL PRINCIPLES

Here are the ten powerful principles that I believe excellent teachers apply. Think of the best teachers you have observed. As you read these short descriptions, ask yourself how their teaching corresponded to these principles.

> ### Ten Powerful Instructional Principles
> 1. *Meaningfulness.* Motivate students by helping them connect the topic to be learned to their past, present, and future.
> 2. *Prerequisites.* Assess students' level of knowledge and skill and adjust instruction carefully, so students are ready to learn the material at the next level.
> 3. *Open Communication.* Be sure students find out what they need to know so they can focus on what to learn.
> 4. *Organized Essential Ideas.* Help students focus on and structure the most important ideas, to be able learn and recall those ideas.
> 5. *Learning Aids.* Help students use devices to learn quickly and easily.
> 6. *Novelty.* Vary the instructional stimuli to keep students' attention.
> 7. *Modeling.* Show students how to recall, think, act, and solve problems so that they are ready to practice.
> 8. *Active Appropriate Practice.* Provide practice in recalling, thinking, performing, and solving problems so that students apply and perfect their learning.
> 9. *Pleasant Conditions and Consequences.* Make learning pleasing, so that students associate comfort with what is learned; and make learning satisfying, so that students keep learning and using what is learned.
> 10. *Consistency.* Make objectives, tests, practice, content, and explanation consistent, so that students will learn what they need and will use what they have learned outside of the instructional setting.

Some of the excellent teachers acted consciously in applying these principles: They knew what they were doing and why they were doing it. Others acted unconsciously: They kept trying techniques until they found the ones that worked. These teachers could not necessarily explain why their techniques worked, but they kept trying techniques because they cared about their subject, their students, and their job of teaching.

THE PRINCIPLES VERSUS PROCEDURES DEBATE

Some say that teachers need *principles* to establish, maintain, or improve their teaching. Others would argue the point, referring to teachers who cannot articulate underlying principles; they say that to achieve improved teaching, instructors must learn teaching *procedures*. Procedural advocates say that principles are merely expressions of theory, ivory tower stuff, pie in the sky. Theory is not enough to improve a person's teaching. To be effective, teachers must learn procedures such as how to present lessons, make examples, use media, and write lesson plans.

Advocates of using principles to improve teaching counter by saying that procedures are not enough. What if a teacher learns a procedure, but finds that it is inappropriate for a situation or that, when put to use, the procedure does not work? In these cases, the teacher must apply instructional principles. With principles, a teacher can manufacture a new procedure that fits a situation or can troubleshoot a procedure to make it work. In fact, only by applying principles can teachers know what to look for in a defective procedure.

Who is right: those who advocate procedures or those who advocate principles? Both are, because both procedures and principles are needed to create a competent practitioner. To be able to operate, you must learn to use procedures. But you must also be able to apply principles to be a flexible, intelligent, and adaptive practitioner. This book will help you learn both principles and procedures, first by defining and explaining each principle in detail, then by describing sample procedures that are based on each principle. By seeing how varied procedures conform to the principles, you will get a broader understanding of the principles.

You may be tempted to adopt an interesting procedure without knowing the principle on which it is based. Many teachers observe the consequences of blind adherence to technique when they see colleagues doing exactly what a teachers' edition of a text suggests, even though the method is ineffective in their particular situation.

ADOPTING PROCEDURES WITHOUT UNDERSTANDING THE UNDERLYING PRINCIPLES

My wife, Fran, was a fine nursery school teacher; she taught little tykes 3 to 4 years old. Because she was a good role model, aspiring teachers would frequently come to observe her class. Each day I would pick Fran up at the end of her teaching day. One day I slipped into the classrooom. As I slid against the wall, I bumped into an observer. I said "Hello," and turned to watch my wife finish the day's work. Fran had a routine to mark the day's end. She noted it was time to go and then put a record on the record player. As soon as the children heard the music, one child would grab a broom and start sweeping; another would grab the large metal coat rack and drag it in from the hallway. And another child would bring all the large wooden building blocks to the block corner. All this time the observer was mesmerized; her eyes were practically hanging out on her cheeks. She turned to me and said with all sincerity, "I have got to get a copy of that record!" Can you imagine this pathetic teacher putting on the record and waiting for magic to happen? All she knew is what she saw. She didn't understand the principles that were the basis for the procedure, nor did she see the development of the procedure over time. To be effective, she needed the principles as well as the procedure.

USING BASIC PRINCIPLES RATHER THAN IMITATING ANOTHER'S TEACHING STYLE

Once a teaching assistant said that she was going to teach using my presentation style. She was going to employ the combination of techniques I use when explaining. I asked whether she meant that she was going to use the principles I talk about. "No," she said, "I am going to present the way you do." So, in her next class she talked fast, gestured a lot with her hands, made faces, and stuck her neck out just as I do. When I next saw her, she reported that she had the worst teaching day of her career. Her students thought that she had had a nervous breakdown and she said that she felt dreadfully uncomfortable. She realized then that you cannot adopt another person's style in teaching, just as you cannot take on another person's personality in everyday life. She realized that she needed to apply the principles of instruction to her teaching and allow her own genuine style to emerge.

I ask my students this question at least once a semester: "True or false: If you want to succeed, do exactly what I say and only what I say?" The braver and wiser students say false. They realize that they will have to adapt what they learn to the situation and that they may find better principles as well as better procedures than I recommend. They know that I think of this list of principles as one of many ways to express the underlying ideas.

In sum, this is one set of principles that you can use as a guide to make decisions about the design of varied instructional arrangements and teaching approaches. According to the principles, you could design and arrange the situation so well that students learn by themselves, from one another, or from the materials you have provided. There is no one right way to teach, no one set of procedures that is best. You may successfully present information to students using direct instruction, arrange for students to work together to seek information using cooperative learning, ask students to respond to problems in problem-based learning, or provide computer-based materials for students to use in independent learning.

HOW TO READ THIS BOOK TO ACHIEVE ITS OBJECTIVE

My hope is that you will be able to apply the instructional principles used by excellent teachers to your own instruction. Specifically, I hope that with your own chosen segment of instruction, you will be able to state and carry out plans for teaching, according to the principles.

To achieve the objective of this book, you must practice using the principles. As you read, continuously ask yourself: Where have I seen this principle in use? Where have I seen it violated? How might I make the best use of it in my domain? As you read the varied illustrations from training, grade school, high school, and higher education, think: How can I make that apply to my instruction? Complete the activities at the back of each chapter. Use the checklist in Appendix A to observe, plan, and evaluate teaching. As soon as you are able, adopt at least one or two ideas and use them to teach someone in either a formal or informal setting. Even if you already use some of these ideas, try to apply one or two to a new area as soon as you can. Give the ideas a fair chance. If they don't work the first time, figure out a way to make them work.

ACTIVITIES

These two introductory activities have you consider the attitudes, procedures, and principles displayed by excellent teachers that you have observed. Consider doing the activities by yourself or in a group. If you do these activities with several others, start by having each individual answer the question and then post all contributions so all the members of the group can see them. Cluster similar responses and discuss the result. Are these behaviors worthy of imitation? Are there common principles for varying procedures?

1. What behaviors reflect the attitudes of fine teachers? Think of some of the best teachers you have had. Don't think just about school or training programs; think about folks at home, people in religious institutions, leaders in clubs, and coaches for sports. How did they show you they
   a. cared about their subject?
   b. cared about you as a learner?
   c. liked teaching?
2. What did those fine teachers do that you thought exemplified good teaching procedures? List those in a column on the left side of a page. Then look back at the brief definitions of the ten principles. As you understand the definitions, which principle(s) do you think the teacher was following when performing the procedure you listed? List the principles in a second column. This activity may show that although excellent teachers use varying procedures, they adhere to certain common principles.

chapter 2

Meaningfulness

OVERVIEW

Help students make a connection between a topic to be learned and the students' past experiences, present situations (needs, interests, values), and future goals to motivate the students to learn, as well as to use their newly acquired knowledge.

Guideline 1: Use Four Steps to Help Students Make Meaningful
Connections Systematically
> Assess Your Students' Motives
> Discover the Connection between Your Topic and Your
> Students' Motives
> Help Make the Connection between Your Topic and Your
> Students' Motives
> Make the Connection and Check the Results

Guideline 2: Continuously Help Students Make Meaningful Connections
> Make Meaningful Connections before Instruction
> Make Meaningful Connections at the Start of Instruction
> Make Meaningful Connections throughout Instruction
> Make Meaningful Connections at the End of Instruction
> Make Meaningful Connections after Instruction

Students are not automatically interested in learning whatever you have to offer. You have to help make the topic interesting by showing students how it is relevant for them. If students are unable to make the connection between the topic and themselves, they simply dismiss the topic. I have heard students say:

- Why should I care?
- What does this have to do with me?
- What's in it for me?
- This is not relevant.
- Of what use is this?

STUDENTS ARE INTERESTED IN A TOPIC WHEN THEY VIEW IT AS RELEVANT

One fall I was asked to present some ideas about teaching during the orientation of teaching assistants for two departments. I did the same thing for each group and got astoundingly different responses.

In both workshops, after I presented an instructional principle, I gave an exercise. I asked the new teaching assistants to work in pairs to apply the instructional principle to their domain. In the first group, I waited a moment to let them get started. As I moved around the room, I noticed that they weren't applying the principle. In fact, they weren't doing anything. I asked if they understood the instructions and they said they did. I urged them to respond, but they didn't. In contrast, as soon as I gave the instructions to the second group, the teaching assistants paired off and began talking about their applications. I could barely get them to stop the exercise when it was time to regroup.

What made the difference? In the first case, even though classes were to start in a week, the assistants had not yet received their assignments. They didn't know if they were going to be lab technicians, test markers, or teachers. They knew that only 20 percent of them would be given teaching assignments. They were betting and hoping that they would not be selected to teach. The ideas I presented about teaching had little meaning for them. But, in the second case, the teaching assistants had been notified of their instructional responsibilities before the summer. The department sent them a syllabus and a text that they would use in the fall. The day before my presentation, each assistant had done a practice lesson and received frank feedback about his or her shortcomings. All were nervous about their compe-tence and hungry for any ideas that would help them in their classrooms the following week. The ideas I presented were just what they wanted. No wonder the two groups responded differently. Only for one group were the ideas I presented meaningful.

Your students, too, will become interested in learning something new that you have to offer when they believe that it will help them avoid their problems, understand their experiences, contribute to their interests, correlate with their values, and fulfill their goals. Remember that they will have to perceive a personal connection to the topic you present. And if you reinforce that meaningful connection throughout the course, your students are also likely to stay interested enough in the topic to want to use it outside of instruction. To motivate your students to learn and to use what they have learned, help them relate what is to be taught to their experiences, interests, values, and aspirations (Keller, 1983, 1987; Rogers, 1983).

You may think that the most fundamental thing you can do to apply the principle of meaningfulness is to derive your instructional objectives and content from needed real-world performance. In a way, that is true. If you understand the connection between what you teach and the real world, and if you structure your course to foster those connections, it may be relatively easy to communicate the relevance of what you teach to your students' experiences, interests, and aspirations. Furthermore, if there is a clear connection between what you teach and the real world, it should be easier for students to see its personal meaning.

But students will not automatically make the connection just because you provide realistic learning conditions and behaviors. A learning situation with real conditions and behaviors is not necessarily a meaningful one. What some teachers may call relevant or *authentic instruction* may relate strongly to real-world situations and performances but may not relate to students' experiences, interests, or aspirations. Medical students who want to be neonatologists but who intern in a cardiology unit, for example, may not automatically make the connection between their needs and what is offered. The attitude might be, "I can see the relevance of the internship to someone, but not to me." You can try to entice me to learn to do what a store manager does through a simulation, but if I don't see any relevance of those skills and ideas to my situation, I will not be motivated to take part. In cases where students do not see the personal meaning in very realistic instructional settings, an instructor has to help them see the relationship between the situation and their interests.

BRINGING MEANING TO THE INSTRUCTIONAL PROGRAM

Students who wanted to be trained to become pastry chefs were required to take a class on fish preparation in a restaurant. Some students complained about wasting their time learning something that they would not use as pastry chefs even if it took place in an operating restaurant. But they changed their minds when the teacher showed how they would be using prepared fish in many pastry and bread dishes and how they needed to know the methods of fish preparation as well as ingredients of fish dishes to make complementary breads and pastries. He showed how each type of cooking is related to all other types.

Students in a business school, who wanted to become managers, were required to take an accounting class where they were to keep accounts for a simulated company. Students said they would rather take more management courses than an accounting course. "After all," they said, "we are not going to become accountants." But they became more interested when the teacher explained how, as managers, each of them would have to analyze the company's accounts, understand what their company's accountants were talking about, and contribute to the making of certain schedules. "Intelligent managers know all the workings of business," said the teacher.

As these examples imply, you must relate even the most realistic field experiences, apprenticeships, and simulations to your students' interests. *Instruction becomes meaningful only when students perceive it as meaningful.* Students must perceive and understand that course objectives and content are directly related to a productive real-world performance that they need to explain their experience, promote their interests, and fulfill their aspirations.

When are you, the instructor, most responsible for applying the principle of meaningfulness? You should help your students make the connection when

- your course is required, rather than desired.
- your course takes considerable student energy and persistence because of its difficulty and length.
- potential stumbling blocks may frustrate your students during the course.
- students come to the course with negative attitudes about the subject.
- students can't make connections by themselves because (a) they don't have enough experience with the real world to be able to make connections between the topic and actual situations, or (b) they don't have enough skill in the subject to do so.
- the connection is not readily apparent to them.
- the idea or skill being taught is controversial and its use may be disputed.

In most other cases, your goal is to have students take responsibility for their own motivation—which could help produce self-motivated learners.

Before explaining how to apply the principle of meaningfulness, I should warn you that some teachers resist using this principle. I have heard some teachers say, "I am here strictly to explain and clarify. I am not here to motivate or entertain." Applying the principle of meaningfulness to motivate students does not mean entertaining them. It does mean, under certain conditions, helping students see the importance of a topic so they will want to continue to learn and to apply what they have learned. You will not have to sing, dance, or juggle in order to motivate your students.

GUIDELINE 1: USE FOUR STEPS TO HELP STUDENTS MAKE MEANINGFUL CONNECTIONS SYSTEMATICALLY

What will you have to do to motivate your students? Help them to make meaningful connections. But how can you help students make meaningful connections? Did you notice how the question was phrased? It said, "How can you *help* students make meaningful connections?" The question was not, "How can you *make* the subject meaningful for the students?" You can't make it meaningful for them; they have to do it for themselves. But you can help them see the connections.

Even though you may see the relationship between your students' lives and the topic, your perception may not be communicated to your students or understood and accepted by them. If they don't already see the connection, you have to do something to help them make the connection for themselves. How do you help students see the connections? The general approach is to find their motives and then appeal to those motives, assuming that your instruction or training is designed to help students learn what they need to be able to perform as they must in the real world. Consider the following four steps for applying the principle of meaningfulness:

1. Assess your students' motives.
2. Discover the connection between your topic and your students' motives.
3. Help make the connection between your topic and your students' motives.
4. Make the connection and check the results.

Assess Your Students' Motives

Find your students' interests, experiences, needs, aspirations, fears, and concerns as early as you possibly can. If you know who your students will be in advance of the course and can contact them, investigate their motives before the course starts. Otherwise, find out as much as you can at the start of the course and at the beginning of each unit.

When you assess students' motives you are beginning the process of *continuous asessment.* Before instruction you need to know what your students want and need to learn as well as what they know. During instruction, be aware of what students are learning. And at the end of instruction, assess what students have learned. Look for more about assessment throughout this text in applications of the principles of prerequisites, open communication, essential content, active appropriate practice, and consistency. Assessment is everywhere and is a continuous process. Now let's focus on ways to assess students' motives.

Three Ways to Assess Students' Motives
1. Ask students about their motives.
2. Present a menu of skills and ideas to prompt students' interests.
3. Use varied modes of investigation to discover students' motives.

Ask Students about Their Motives.   You run a great risk of being misled by asking those who think they know about students' motives. Watch out for the advice of previous instructors, job supervisors, zealots, or advocates who think that everyone needs to know a topic regardless of circumstance, and experts in the field who believe they know what certain people need to learn.

ASKING STUDENTS ABOUT THEIR MOTIVES RATHER THAN ASKING OTHER PARTIES

Once I was asked to talk about instructional design to a group of medical professionals. I was told that they were an open-minded group who designed and delivered instruction for medical professionals. My advisors suggested that I present design procedures such as how to write objectives because the group would be eager to learn about them. That is what I prepared and that is what I presented with gusto.

Was I off base! These folks didn't design instruction; they were administrators who found field placements for medical students. They couldn't care a bit about my topic. It had nothing to do with their experiences, interests, or aspirations. As a consequence, they became angry and frustrated with what I was presenting and began looking for flaws in my presentation. I clearly remember one audience member belligerently asking me, "What are we supposed to pay attention to? Your handout, your transparencies, or what you are saying?" Of course, all of the media were designed to match. The participants even refused to do the exercises I had designed.

After my evening presentation, the person representing the funding agency asked me not to make my morning presentation. That evening I was shunned by all of the staff and participants (except for their instructional design professional, who complemented me on a fine presentation). Now, I always check with the students themselves about their circumstances, motives, and needs, even though I may also ask other sources who have a stake in the learning.

FINDING OUT STUDENTS' MOTIVES DURING A SESSION; IT'S NOT TOO LATE

One evening I organized a seminar for foster parents on motivation and discipline of children. These parents cared for abused, neglected, and delinquent children who were assigned to them by the probate court. In the introductory part of the seminar I presented several principles of discipline and examples of successful application. During a coffee break I asked some of the parents how they thought the session was going. They said it was OK. OK? I thought I was doing a great job, at least much better than OK. I asked what was wrong, and they said that I kept using examples in which the parents dealt with small children and that they had children a lot older than the children I was portraying. Then I remembered that children in a foster parent's care frequently change. I realized that I had assumed that these foster parents were caring for little ones. So, at the start of the second half, I asked how many of the parents were caring for little ones, medium sized ones, and big ones. Surprise! Most of them had big kids. In the second half I used examples of older children. I applied the same principles that I had applied in the first half. I also asked the parents to apply the principles to their foster children. At the end of the program, as I walked out with the foster parents, I asked them how the session went. They said that the first half was OK, but the second half was very good. They felt sure that they would be able to use the ideas from the second half the next day. If you can't find out your students' interests before an instructional session, find out during the session.

Present a Menu of Skills and Ideas to Prompt Students' Interests.
Present the menu to the students who need prompting to express their interests. Some students know exactly what they want and need to learn; others need encouragement. Ask those students to choose topics from a menu. Ask, "Which of these is most interesting to you? Why?" Or ask simply, "What do you want to learn in this area, and why do you want to learn this? How does it relate to your past, present, or future?"

Use Varied Modes of Investigation to Discover Students' Motives.   Use observation, interviews, questionnaires, and discussions.

Observe Potential Students in the Real World Performing the Tasks You Might Be Teaching.   For example, a judicial educator observed judges who were going to be in his instructional design workshop plan and conduct their classes. Then, he related his firsthand observations of their work to what he would be teaching them. Observe your potential students or other people applying the ideas that you might be teaching.

Conduct Individual Interviews with Potential Students.   When working full time in a training environment, Winnie McDermott, a trainer of trainers, would converse over lunch, in the hallways, or in offices with trainers whom she knew would soon be in one of her seminars. If she knew the names of participants who were some distance away, she would interview by phone. If the number of participants was small, she would call each one; if the number was large, she would call as many as she could until the information she was eliciting became predictable.

INTERVIEWING STUDENTS IN NATURALLY OCCURRING MEETINGS

A college teacher briefly interviews students as they obtain permission to register for his class. He continues the process during the semester by arriving early to each class and talking to students about their circumstances. When he has to conduct a workshop and meet participants for the first time at the site, he arrives early and interviews as many as he can at that time. Not only does that provide information about participants' motives that he can use in instruction, but it also can prevent problems.

TIMELY INTERVIEWS MAY PREVENT PROBLEMS ABOUT RELEVANCE

I had arrived early to set up for a repeat workshop for members of a professional society. Two people were already waiting. As I set up, I began to talk to the participants to find out their interests and what they wanted to learn from the workshop. One of them responded immediately and with vehemence, "I don't want a damned thing. In fact, I don't see why we have to have this stupid workshop anyway. I have lots of things to do that are far more important than this." I was taken aback. I asked, "Well, why are you here then?" "Because the society sent me this letter that said I had to come." This was news to me. I explained to the participant that I had assumed the workshop was voluntary. Now it seemed that it was mandatory, but no one had told me. I went over the objectives for the workshop, showing him how it could be of use to him. He agreed that it might be OK. I dealt with this issue at the start of the workshop with all of the other participants, and they accepted the circumstances. Can you imagine what might have happened in the middle of the workshop had I not inquired beforehand? I can see several participants becoming angrier moment by moment and gaining nothing from the workshop.

Distribute Questionnaires.   When there are many people involved with only a little time to get the information but some time to process the information, you can find out students' experiences, interests, and aspirations by asking them to fill out a brief questionnaire. For example, a teacher educator gives a questionnaire on the first day of his class. Not only does it ask for useful information such as phone numbers, but it also asks what teaching experience the students have had, what design procedures they have used, what they believe good instructional planning is, what questions about instructional design they want answered in the course, what they aspire to do, and whatever else they feel is important for him to know about them. All this is on one page.

Run Informal or Formal Discussions.   When you can get at least some potential students together, conduct a focus group. Begin by posing a question.

Ask for your students' experiences, interests, aspirations, needs, fears, and concerns relating to the topic you are going to teach:

- What is your experience with [the topic]?
- What don't you understand about it?
- What are you interested in with regard to it? Why?
- In what way do you predict that you might use it? Where?
- What do you want to be able to do outside of class in relation to it?
- What do you feel you need to learn about it? Why?
- What problems do you have with regard to it? Why?
- What do you do now that relates to it?
- What are you afraid of or concerned about regarding it? Why?
- What questions do you have about it?
- What seems to be wrong with it?
- What would you like to understand better about it?
- How do you use it now? Is that satisfactory?
- What results do you want? What results are you getting now? Why?

As students talk, post their responses on a chalkboard, flipchart, or overhead projector. Save the answers. For example, during the winter, teacher educators conducted a focus group for a school system to plan for a special course to be offered the following summer. They asked the teachers, their potential students, what teaching problems they wanted to solve. The teachers suggested several, which the educators wrote on the chalkboard. Some examples were how to teach multiplication more effectively and how to handle children who fight. The educators then asked each teacher to choose the top three problems and, after tallying, found the highest priority items among all the teachers. They converted those into the summer seminar goals.

As you can see, you can assess students' motives in the natural course of your encounters or with minimal effort outside your usual routine. The process should give you substantive information to use in the second step: discovering the connection between your topic and your students' motives.

Discover the Connection between Your Topic and Your Students' Motives

Suppose you have information about your students' experiences, interests, needs, aspirations, fears, and concerns. Now comes the interesting and creative part of applying the principle of meaningfulness. Using one of two strategies, searching for connections or searching for consequences, find the connection between the topic and your students.

Search for Connections.   Consider your own experience. What are the connections between the topic and your experiences and interests? Read journals, magazines, and newspapers to see what connections may exist. Interview experienced friends and acquaintances about the way the topic relates to their lives. Ask these questions in each case:

- Where and when would students use this topic in the world outside of instruction?
- How could this topic help students explain what they have experienced?
- How could it contribute to and deepen present interests?
- How does it help students to fulfill their aspirations?
- How would this alleviate students' fears and concerns?

Don't think of applications and relations only in terms of job performance. Think of how ideas and skills help each of us to understand and cope with the everyday world. Ask where and when people might have to

- recall these ideas.
- explain these ideas.
- recognize examples of these ideas.
- predict using these ideas.
- infer a cause based on these ideas.
- take action based on these ideas.
- analyze a situation using these ideas.
- solve a problem using these ideas.

SEARCHING FOR CONNECTIONS BY ASKING THE RIGHT QUESTIONS

Once I asked professors who taught developmental psychology where and when in the real world their students would use ideas of developmental psychology, such as stages of mental development. They were stumped. I said, "First, think of how psychologists might use the stages. What would they be able to recognize that they could not before? What would they be able to do?" Little by little they realized that a psychologist would be able to recognize normal stages in a child's mental growth and any deviations from those stages. Then they could explain their finding to the child's parents. They could also prescribe activities to foster growth or explain how and why growth had to happen naturally.

Then I asked where and when a lay person could use these ideas. The psychologists said that lay people could use these stages to perceive and understand what is going on around them. For example, when parents used the stages to observe the actions of their children, they could understand why their children act in a certain way and whether that behavior is appropriate for the developmental stage. They could analyze a magazine article about a program to accelerate mental growth and understand its strengths and weaknesses. They could understand an article about a research breakthrough in developmental psychology. They could ask their child's teacher important developmental questions about the child's behavior and about the developmental qualities of the school program. They could also read about the topic to learn more.

By the end of the discussion the professors not only understood the principle of meaningfulness, but also were surprised about how many connections they could find when they asked, "Where and when could someone use this content?"

Can students make connections themselves? Of course. Not only can they, but they do and should. In selecting topics to learn, students naturally ask a version of the question, "What topics are relevant to my experiences, interests, and aspirations?" So when students are given a topic in formal schooling or in job training, they can ask themselves a version of the question that a responsible instructor would ask: "How is this topic relevant to my experiences, interests, and aspirations?" If no answers are readily apparent, responsible students can and should search for answers.

Search for Consequences. Keep in mind that the uses of a selected topic should be relatively important, at least worthy of the time to be spent in teaching them. To help you determine importance, ask yourself about the consequences of using this skill or idea properly and improperly:

- What will happen if this content is used well? Will there be substantial desirable consequences in the students' view?
- What will happen if this content is used poorly or not used at all? Will there be substantial undesirable consequences in the students' view?

Help Make the Connection between Your Topic and Your Students' Motives

Once you have identified students' needs and related your topic to those needs, it is time to help students apply the principle of meaningfulness to make connections to the topic. By using various techniques, you can help students make connections at five times: before instruction, at the start of instruction, throughout instruction, at the end of instruction, and after instruction.

You can, then, apply the principle of meaningfulness at any time. But how is the principle applied in each phase of instruction? After introducing the fourth step to applying meaningfulness, let's consider specific techniques.

Make the Connection and Check the Results

As a human being applying a principle to help students become interested in a topic, you know that your application will not work every time. So, when you apply this and the other principles, be sure to assess whether you achieved the results you wanted. Make this part of your ongoing course evaluation. In applying meaningfulness, determine whether your students have made some connection between the topic to be taught and themselves. Ask your students, "How interesting is this unit to you? Why are you studying this? What will learning this unit do for you?" You could do this in a final questionnaire or in interviews with representative students.

Now that you have an idea of the overall strategy for applying meaningfulness, let's take a closer look at how you can help your students make connections between what you have to teach and their needs.

GUIDELINE 2: CONTINUOUSLY HELP STUDENTS MAKE MEANINGFUL CONNECTIONS

Make Meaningful Connections before Instruction

Recall that there are five periods when you can apply meaningfulness, and your goal is to apply the principle continuously throughout those five periods. Let's begin by considering how to start motivating students before instruction. The following three sample techniques used before instruction are designed to bring your students to class motivated to learn.

Make Meaningful Links.   You can apply the principle of meaningfulnes during interviews or discussions with students before the course. Explain the link between topics in the course and any student motives you note at the time. Explain to potential course participants that they will accomplish their purposes by learning what the course has to offer. If your potential students are in a formal work setting, check with their supervisors and then tell students that their supervisors expect and approve of the skills and ideas to be learned in the course.

Provide Meaningful Advertising.   When advertising the course, appeal to the motives you have found by showing students where and when they will be able to use what they will learn.

Help Students Make Meaningful Links Early.   If possible, ask potential students to commit themselves to trying the skills to be learned and to state their reasons. In addition, ask students to bring to learning sessions some personally important and relevant case, question, project, or problem to work on during the instruction. For example, I have my students develop two personally useful units of instruction during my instructional design class.

Make Meaningful Connections
at the Start of Instruction

Many techniques can be used to apply meaningfulness at the beginning of instruction. These are designed not only to connect content to students' motives but also to grab their attention. Consider these techniques "meaningful attention-getters." They may be used to start a lesson, a unit, or a course. You may apply the meaningful attention-getter to make the connection, or you may ask students to lay the foundation for making the connection. Some of these techniques may introduce direct instruction; others may begin problem-based learning and discussion.

Appendix C lists 17 specific procedures, described fully on the next several pages, that apply meaningfulness to start instruction.

1. Relate Whatever Is Taught to a Strong Student Interest.   You can create connections in two basic ways: Start with the students' interests and relate them to the subject, or start with a subject and relate that to the students' interests. In starting with the students' interests, find some interest common to all the students and use it as a central theme. For example, if a common student interest is dogs, then the teacher might have students read about dogs, write about dogs, learn about dogs in history, study dogs as a scientific topic, draw dogs, and think about mathematical questions concerning dogs (e.g., calculating the number of dogs that would be born in 10 generations of unlimited breeding, or the cost to feed a dog for a year). If you have students who are interested in successfully meeting the needs of clients, start each unit by showing how it will help students meet a client's needs. For example, when you begin a unit on objectives, tell students that by using the objectives they will devise and write, they will be able to communicate with their clients and help them evaluate their success.

2. Provide a Real Problem to Start the Unit.   Arrange for students to confront a real problem of immediate interest. The problem must be one that students can solve because they are invested at the moment. Note in these examples that the problems are not simulated, but arranged. This could be a part of problem-based instruction.

- For students learning division of fractions, the teacher divided the class into groups of five. One pizza was ordered for each group, and students had to ensure that each person got an equal share.
- For students learning geometry, the teacher assigned a wall-sized mural about class attempts at recycling. The teacher then gave the students a stack of $8\frac{1}{2}$" × 11" paper and asked them to plan how much paper they needed with a minimum of waste.
- For medical students learning diagnosis, the medical educator assigned a real case of a patient with chest pain with relatively ambiguous symptoms.

- For instructional design students learning to design printed materials, the professor assigned the creation of a recruiting brochure describing their instructional design program.
- For teacher education students learning to teach reading, the professor assigned elementary school children to tutor in reading several times per week during school hours.
- For students learning to write, the teacher asked that they write a letter to their parents about how they were doing in class (Brick, 1993).
- For students learning to do research and to write well, the teacher asked that they select a societal problem that really bothers them, find a solution based on credible sources, and then write a letter to a representative stating the solution (Burke, 1993).
- For students learning to do research, the teacher asked that they find a problem of personal interest that has an impact on a real-world audience but has no readily apparent answer. The teacher asked students to gather and analyze data and report the results to the people concerned. One student wanted to prove to her parents that she could do homework and listen to the radio at the same time, so she conducted an experiment on visualization to remember a list of words. Some students did research to find out if the fear of transition to middle school was justified (Schack, 1993).

3. Provide a Simulated Role within a Real Situation.   Sometimes you can't provide a real problem, but you can provide one in which students pursue the same steps they would if they were in a particular role in the real world. Many of the factors of real situations can be present. You present the situation and pose the problem to the students. Then, either as individuals or in groups, students carry out the tasks according to the role. Consider these examples:

- For students learning to gather, analyze, and report data, take them to a radioactive waste site (real situation) and say to them, "You are scientists [simulated role] and you are called upon to help decide how to get rid of radioactive waste. You must gather and analyze data and information, and then present your recommendations at a real conference" (Stepien & Gallagher, 1993).
- For students studying the history of World War II, say, "You are art gallery directors [simulated role] in 1930s Germany [real historical time and place] and you are ordered to rid the gallery of 'degenerate art.' What do you need to know to do that? What will happen to you if you don't? What do you decide to do and why?" (Stepien & Gallagher, 1993).
- For students learning the construction of history and the power of selecting and using sources, say, "You are historians investigating the subject 'civil rights and race relations.' You will select and interpret

sources and write a chapter of a history text on the subject" (Kobrin, Abbott, Elinwood, & Horton, 1993).

- For those studying the changes in American culture in the twentieth century, say, "Using your grandparents, parents, and peers, find out what significant changes have taken place in our country's culture since 1900."
- For students learning mathematics, present a vivid story on videotape that illustrates a problem and then say, "You are the ambulance driver and you have to get a wounded eagle to a veterinarian; time is critical. Here are maps of the area. Find the fastest route" (Bottge & Hasselbring, 1993).

4. *State the Connection: Where and When the Content Is Used.*   For students with some idea of the real world, you can simply state the use of the topic. Explain how the topic to be learned will be used and describe situations in which the idea or skill will be used. In a discussion, you could ask students how they have seen the ideas applied.

First, if you state the uses, think of the *role* that a person might play in the real world when using this content. For example, you could begin,

"As a consumer of products"
"As a technician"
"As a programmer"
"As an intelligent reader of politics"

Second, consider the real-world setting in which the person might be using this content and the time when the content will be used. Emphasize that these situations are those in which they will really find themselves. For example, you could say,

"When in a store faced with a difficult choice of products to buy"
"When in the garage confronted with a motorcycle that won't start"
"When in the computer lab given a task to program"
"When at home reading a controversial article"

Third, mention the behavior and the purpose of the real-world task. For example, you could say,

"To make a calculation and a decision to get the best buy"
"To diagnose the problem to get the motorcycle to run"
"To write a program to produce a functioning, bug-free game"
"To analyze the arguments to clarify your stand on the issue"

When you put all the pieces together you have a direct statement of where and when to use the content to be learned: "You [students] need to learn [the topic] because you will use it

as a consumer of products, when in a store faced with a difficult choice of products to buy, to make a calculation and a decision to get the best buy."

as a technician, when in the garage confronted with a motorcycle that won't start, to diagnose the problem to get the motorcycle to run."

as a programmer, when in the computer lab given a task to program, to write a program to produce a functioning, bug-free game."

as an intelligent reader of politics, when at home reading a controversial article, to analyze the arguments to clarify your stand on the issue."

If you were having students discuss the real-world applications, you would ask questions about the user's role, the setting and the behavior, and the purpose of the real-world task.

USING A DIRECT STATEMENT OF APPLICATION

One day I was interviewing a teacher with a fine reputation for motivating students. I was curious about how he did it. When I asked how he began his instruction, he became embarrased and stammered, "I kind of waste the time. I'd rather not talk about it."

"Wait a minute. I know you do a great job of motivating your students. How do you do it?"

"OK, here's the deal. I love what I teach. I teach electrical engineering, and I love everything about it. I love the diagrams we use. I love the way we think about it. I love the little chips we fool with. But I know my students don't love it. In fact, they don't know enough about it to know whether they love it or not."

"OK, I get your rationale. But you haven't told me what you do."

He said, "Here's what I do. I tell my students exactly what they have to do on the test, and then I tell them how that relates to them."

"Can you give me an example?"

"Sure. Tomorrow we are going to learn about the Schmidt trigger. I will tell my students that on the test they will have to take one apart and put it together; they will have to diagram one; and, when I give them one with a flaw in it, they will have to troubleshoot it and fix it. Then I ask some questions like, 'Have you ever seen a dawn-to-dusk light, the kind that goes on automatically at night and off automatically in the morning? The main operating mechanism in the dawn-to-dusk light is the Schmidt trigger.' I also mention that taking one apart and putting it back together, drawing one, and troubleshooting are general skills that should help them do well in their other courses. Finally, I say that troubleshooting is the way good engineers think."

Then I laughed. The teacher turned to me and said, "First you embarrass me, then you interrupt me, and now you laugh at me. I don't have to put up with this."

"No, no, I just got some insight from what you were saying."

"Like what?"

"First, you are using one of the basic principles of motivation: meaningfulness. You are connecting what you teach to the students' past, present, and future."

"Yes, but you said you had insights."

"Oh, yes. I think I know why you said you were wasting time."

"Oh, yeh? Why?"

"I think that you were worried that here you were at the beginning of your class with no hard content on the board. You were worried that your colleagues might be looking through the window in the door, and they might think that you were wasting time."

Then he smiled. "That was my anxiety. But I couldn't have put it into words."

I said, "Don't worry about them. You are light years ahead of those people. Do your students ever ask you, 'Why are we learning this?' "

"No. In fact, come to class tomorrow and you can see for yourself."

I went to his class and lab and asked as many students as I could two questions. First I asked, "What are you learning?" They all gave me the same answer: "to take one apart and put it together, draw one, and troubleshoot one."

Then I asked, "Why are you learning this?" I got different answers from each student. Some said, "This explains a lot of things I've seen." Some said, "I've got to get out of here; if this is going to help my grades in other classes, that's great." Others said, "I want to think like an engineer, and this unit will help me do it."

A direct statement of use can have a powerful impact.

Notice from the engineering example that you may have to state more than one relationship to "hook" students with varying interests. Following is an example of applying meaningfulness and considering *individual differences.*

USING MORE THAN ONE MEANINGFUL CONNECTION

Once I gave a demonstration lesson on how to tie a bowline knot. In the lesson I used several meaningful attention-getters. I showed how the knot would be useful in sailing, boating, climbing, camping, or for wrapping packages.

To debrief the observation of my lesson, I asked the observers, the students in that workshop, why I had used sailing, camping, and tying up boxes. One of the students quickly raised his hand for attention. I nodded for him to go ahead. He started to explain, "I used to be a mediocre fisherman. Sometimes I would catch a fish, but most often I would not. I would put a hook on the end of the line, put some bait on it, and toss it in the water."

I was wondering at this point if I should interrupt and ask what his fishing had to do with the number of attention-getters I used, but he continued before I could get a word in.

"But I met a good fisherman who taught me a better way. Based on what he told me, I put a hook and bait on the end of the line; I put one in the middle of the line and one near the floater. Now I catch a lot more fish. I catch the bottom feeders, the middle feeders, and the top feeders. That's why you used more than one meaningful example. You needed more than one kind of hook to catch more than one kind of fish."

He was right on target.

5. State or Show the Use and Its Payoff.   When you or your students state where and when to use a topic, add a meaningful payoff. Say, or ask the students to say, how the use of the topic will result in consequences your students wish to achieve. For example, to persuade his students that the nomenclature of weapons was important to know, a police trainer said, "In order to be safe when you are on the firing range and on duty, you have to be able to find the parts of the weapon named. If I state that you are to check the loading and ejection port for a stove-pipe malfunction or a double-feed, or to check for broken action bars, and you don't know where those parts are, or what to look for, you can't learn what I am trying to teach you and you can't do these critical tasks in an emergency. You can't become proficient with the weapon, and you might cause harm to yourself or to a fellow officer, because the weapon will not operate properly. If you don't know where to look for a part and what to look for when a weapon is functioning properly, it might not work for you just when you need it most, when an assailant is charging at you aiming a weapon. Weapon nomenclature is important to you." Then the teacher proceeded to demonstrate the consequences of not being able to find the parts and the malfunctions named. Students saw that the results could be disastrous.

6. Use a Meaningful Quote.   Use a quote or a recent news article, and then explain how it shows that students need to learn this topic. Also, ask your students to collect quotes that show a good reason to learn the content. For example, to motivate clerical staff to learn to use computers, an instructor began her training session by showing articles on transparencies and stating selected quotes, like these, which her students found:

"Word processing will reduce the boring tasks of retyping and editing. Your work will not only proceed more quickly, but will look more professional. You will also be able to spend your time on more interesting tasks."

"Most women managers began as clerical staff who became adept at using computers. They made a direct and speedy switch to management. The starting salary for these systems managers is now over 35 thousand dollars."

To motivate police officers to learn weapon safety, a trainer began his lesson by showing an article from a recent newspaper titled, "Police Officer Is Slain." He quoted, "During a training exercise a police officer was accidentally shot and killed yesterday by another officer. The officers had been close friends." He then commented, "Can you imagine how the officer who pulled the trigger felt? That is the kind of tragedy that we can avoid by knowing and practicing weapon safety."

Every time I see an article in a professional journal, magazine, or newspaper that is related to something I teach, I cut it out. I note the photo or the passage that could be used to show my students where, when, and why that topic is applied in the real world. I also enjoy exploring and collecting statements from encyclopedias of quotations. I use a daily quotation in my class, related to the theme of the class and often showing why students need to learn the topic of the day. For example, on the day my class will work on their explanations, I will post the saying "The great artist is the simplifier—Amiel." When I start the class I will say to the students, "The saying for the day is 'The great artist is the simplifier.' By simplifying your presentations you too can be a great artist as a teacher. You can make your explanations elegant and easy to understand. How can you make your presentations simpler? The trick is to group ideas together. Let me show you what that means."

7. *Use a Meaningful Generalization.*   State a generalization designed to provoke controversy because it counters experience or values, or states one side of an issue in strong terms. For example, an instructor would begin a session on parenting by asking the parents the true-false question, "There is maternal instinct operating in humans to make them good parents." He would ask, "How many think it's true? How many think it's false?" Most would say it was true. Then he would say, "Well, I think it's totally false. There is no such thing as maternal instinct operating in humans to make them good parents. But to be fair about it, here's what we'll do. Tonight we'll take a look at some studies, and then you decide which view is supported best by the evidence."

8. *Tell of Successful Applications.*   As the following vignettes demonstrate, case examples and testimonials can show students how others have benefited by applying the topic to be taught. You or your students may tell of successes.

- To begin a session on how to deal with multiple assailants, John Desmedt, a police trainer, told a true story about two of his former trainees who had been confronted by three attackers in a public park. He said, "The two former students were able to render the three attackers unconscious with two blows! How did they do it? That's what we'll learn to do today."

- John Desmedt also began a session on handcuffing by describing how a former trainee was making an arrest of a relatively large man. He resisted her, and the next thing she knew he was down on the ground handcuffed. She could not even recall how it happened. John said, "That is the degree of skill and automaticity that I want you to attain. You will see how it is possible to handcuff a subject quickly and safely using the technique I will show you today."

- To start a unit on presentation skills, to motivate students to master the format of presentation, I read a letter of a former student, Shawn Merritt, who perfected the skill of putting together a lesson. In the letter Shawn reported that he had traveled to Pennsylania for a job interview. As a final task the company representatives gave him half an hour to put together a presentation. Within 15 minutes, he had the lesson planned and had time to rehearse. When the half hour was up, he presented with confidence. The selection group later told him that it was the presentation that made the difference in deciding to hire him.

9. Tell of Likely Problems if the Ideas Are Not Applied or Understood.   Use case examples to show how students have had problems because they did not apply this content or did not apply it properly. You may state these cases, or you may have students reveal their own experiences in a discussion.

Meaningfulness implies that you build on student experiences. All experiences, even painful ones, are of value. You can build on past failures and mistakes as well as on past successes and accomplishments. Some excellent attention-getters are reminders to students of past mistakes that they would not like to repeat. The following two examples show how important it is to explain the problems students will encounter!

- An airport security trainer was teaching how to use a magnetometer. To motivate his trainees to take this skill seriously, he began his lesson by giving a true case of a terrorist who was able to get a loaded pistol past a magnetometer. He detailed the events of the terrorist's activity and the lives lost as a consequence. He said, "How could this be possible? How can you prevent these problems? If you learn the skills I will show you today, you can be a major factor in preventing these consequences."

- A health instructor wanting to motivate students to learn to reduce the fat in their diets showed his students research results demonstrating how high-fat diets increase the risk of coronary disease, colon cancer, breast cancer, and prostate cancer. He also documented benefits of a low-fat diet by showing research results that a low-fat diet can reverse coronary disease in some patients.

10. *Conduct an Activity Demonstrating Need.*   Use an activity to show that students need to learn this topic to achieve their aspirations, as in the following cases:

USING AN ACTIVITY TO INTEREST
STUDENTS IN BUSINESS

A teacher of agriculture was concerned that his students would be interested in learning only about growing crops. Since he wanted them to become interested in the business side of agriculture, too, he began the course by taking them to the offices of local agribusinesses. He had his students ask the professionals at each office what modern farmers must know about business and what happens if they don't know those things.

The students were astounded by how much they needed to know about business, and they were somewhat anxious, because they didn't understand most of the recommendations made by the interviewees. They became nervous by the tales of farm businesses that failed because the farmers did not follow good business practices. When they returned to the class, they had ideas about what they needed to know and they wanted to get started immediately. They had many questions about the recommendations they didn't comprehend. The teacher realized that a little rub against the lamp of the real world is enough at times to bring out the motivational genie.

USING ACTIVITIES TO INTEREST STUDENTS IN ANATOMY

A graduate student taking a master's degree in teaching and anatomy noticed that physical education students were not succeeding in an anatomy course. When the scores were tallied on the final exam, the premedical students, the prenursing students, and the medical technician students were all on top of the curve. The phys ed students were on the bottom. Some said that these students didn't have the abilty to do well, but the graduate student thought differently. He believed that the phys ed students had no motivation to do well in the class. They didn't know why they were taking anatomy.

As a solution, he created a special discussion section for phys ed majors. During one of the first meetings, the students heard a panel of coaches, instructors, trainers, and athletes explain how they used their knowledge of anatomy daily. Then, on lab days, instead of the usual anatomy lab where students work on cadavers, the phys ed majors attended a different sort of lab. One day they had to find and mark muscles using washable felt-tipped markers on male and female weight lifters with excellent muscular definition. They had to answer questions that made sense in terms of their aspirations: Where is the muscle likely to give under stress? How should this muscle be moved in exercise for it to become stronger?

Then they took the final exam. Yes, the premed students, the prenursing students, and the med tech students were still on top of the curve. But, so were the phys ed students. They not only did well in this class, but without extra help they continued to do well in the advanced class. They knew why they were taking anatomy.

USING AN ACTIVITY TO INTEREST
STUDENTS IN DEFENSIVE MEASURES

John Desmedt, a police trainer who wanted to motivate his students to learn defensive techniques and to put them to use quickly and surely, opened his lesson by having students punch a bag with all their might for 30 seconds. Most were exhausted before they ever reached the 30-second time limit. He explained that because they had less than 30 seconds of energy to respond to an assailant, they had to subdue the assailant quickly. The principles and techniques he would teach them would enable them to do so.

11. Ask a Puzzling Relevant Question to Show the Content Is Needed. State an unanswered relevant question that must be answered by student learning. You can use this technique for anything you teach. One approach is to think about your subject as an answer that students must know and then make up a question leading to that answer. Another approach is to attend to and focus on a question that a student asks. In either case, be sure to connect the question to students' motives. The following examples contain questions that show students need or want the answers:

- Once when an instructor was presenting a workshop on "discipline," he presented a case of a mischievous child who would stretch the patience of any adult by breaking every rule imaginable. Then he simply asked the workshop participants this question: "How would you deal with this child if she were yours, without being physically or psychologically abusive?"

- A trainer had the difficult job of orienting clerical staff members to the history and duties of their service organization. He pondered how he could make the information meaningful to them. He created a true-false questionnaire about the history and duties that was interesting because it was puzzling. But the last question was the meaningful one: "True or false—I will influence the opinion of clients I deal with by my knowledge of the organization." The question made the clerical staff realize that they had to know what everyone did in the organization to look smart and reflect well on the whole group.

- A student in a speech class raised a question that captured the attention of the group: "I heard that good speakers have charisma. What is charisma and how do you get it?" Instead of attempting to answer the question, the teacher proposed that they all explore the question and asked for suggestions about how to find the answer. Students suggested interviews with speakers and reviews of videos of great speakers, and they became strongly engaged.

12. Show a Relevant Puzzling Event.   Provide a demonstration or arrange to observe an event. Wait for students to raise questions or ask students, "How did that work?" (Berlyne, 1950, 1960; Keller, 1987). The next three situations illustrate how using a relevant puzzling event will motivate students.

USING PUZZLES TO TEACH PHYSICS—CASE 1

Theron Downes, a teacher of *packaging,* the art of making containers to hold the products we buy, began a lesson to interest his students in some physics principles applicable to the field. When the students came into class, they saw two displays the teacher had set up. The first display had a beaker of water being heated to a rolling boil. The second had a beaker of water cooled so much that there was frost on the outside of the beaker. The teacher held up two water tumblers and said to his students, "Here I have two glasses made of material that we commonly use to package all kinds of products like milk and jam. We have to be sure that our packaging will be able to endure all sorts of temperature conditions like having hot or cold liquids poured in them. We have to be able to predict what will happen to packaging materials to make good and safe choices for a product. Let's see what kind of predictions you can make about this glass, which as I said is commonly used for packaging. If I pour boiling water into one glass and pour ice cold water into the other, which one will break? Make your predictions: hot, cold, none, or both. How many said hot? cold? none? both? OK." Then the teacher turned off the burner and slid the display table out of the way. He continued, "Now let me tell you some physics principles that may help you predict what will happen. We'll come back to your predictions to see if you want to change them. Then we will conduct the test."

USING PUZZLES TO TEACH PHYSICS—CASE 2

Theron Downs began another lesson by showing his students a bottle of catsup surrounded by a transparent plastic bag. He held the bottle by its neck and tapped the cap with a rubber mallet. The bottom of the ketchup bottle fell off! He then told his students that cases were being delivered to stores with many catsup bottles having broken bottoms. He asked, "Why should that happen? What can we do to remedy this problem? Let's take a look at some physics principles. . . ."

USING PUZZLES TO TEACH PSYCHOLOGY

Once a management trainer brought a large bucket to the front of the classroom. He withdrew a ladle and took a drink of water from it, purposely dribbling a bit as he drank. Then he lifted the bucket and tossed its contents on the seated management trainees. Of course, the audience scattered. But once they recovered from the initial shock, they looked around and realized that the trainer had poured confetti and not water. After the laughter subsided, the trainer asked, "Why did you all scatter when I poured the bucket? What does that have to with working with people?"

13. Ask Which Relevant Idea Is Correct.   When you are conducting a discussion and you note that students raise issues or state conflicting ideas, take advantage of the situation and bring those ideas to the attention of the group. You may also state some relevant competing facts, procedures, or theories and then ask in some way, "Which one is most accurate?" The conflicting ideas are likely to arouse some curiosity, as they did in the following three examples:

- In a discussion about how a concept is learned, two students debated whether they learned by discrimination and reinforcement of behavior or by construction and refinement of schemata. To increase the curiousity of students about theories of learning, the instructor focused on that issue and stated, "As instructional designers you must apply learning theory. But your problem is deciding which theory to apply. In your next project you will have to design instruction to help someone learn a concept. How do you think concepts are learned? How many of you believe that we learn concepts by making discriminations among things and then by being reinforced for doing so? How many of you think that we learn concepts by getting a primitive schema of the category, which is refined over time? Let's take a look at the evidence, and let's see if your choice is supported."

- To interest his students in the causes of human behavior, a teacher of psychology brought a case of a delinquent youth before his students. The teacher said that the young man had been in trouble with the law a number of times. In most instances he had lost his temper and assaulted another person. He quit school at age 16 and had a tested IQ of 90. Before giving any further details of this case, the teacher asked the students to discuss why this young man acted the way he did. Each person stated reasons and then shared them with two other students. The teacher posted the reasons, then asked each student to decide whether the young man's behavior was caused primarily by hereditary or by environmental factors. After students had made their choices, the teacher said the class would continuously return to this case as they looked into the influence of heredity versus environment in human behavior.

- John Desmedt, a police trainer, often encountered experienced professionals in his sessions who claimed to have good ways of dealing with a resistant or combative subject. Instead of ignoring the claim or arguing against it, he used it to create curiosity. "Which approach would be better, this one or this one? Let's give them both a fair test to see what will happen."

14. *Present an Unsolved Case.* State a case, leave it unsolved, and ask "What would you do?" This technique differs from presenting real or simulated problems for students to solve right away. Here the case is presented and then *left alone* until students can bring their new knowledge to bear on it. A teacher may use this technique in direct instruction by presenting the case, explaining what is needed to solve the case, and then asking students to return to the case to apply what they had learned. A teacher using problem-based instruction may present a case and discuss it in one session, then ask individual students to learn independently, or groups of students to learn cooperatively, what they must do to identify and solve the problem in the next session.

PRESENTING UNSOLVED CASES TO PROVOKE INTEREST

Once a veterinary medical school teacher called me about a problem he was having. He wanted me to come to observe his class. I asked, "Can't you describe it over the phone?" "No," he replied, "I'd really like you to come and see what's going on."

I went to his class. The teacher began class by dimming the lights and turning on the slide projector. He proceeded to explain the slide: "Here we have a sick chicken. Let me explain how this disease works. . . ."

As he talked, I looked around the room. Some students were reading newspapers. Some were doing homework for other classes. Some were sleeping. Some were polite sleepers, shielding their eyes. Others were open snoozers. Only one was taking copious notes.

What was I to recommend? The teacher wanted some immediate changes. I suggested that he put into practice the principle of meaningfulness and a few others while still maintaining his basic style. Here is what he did.

At the start of the next class the teacher dimmed the lights and turned on the slide projector as usual. The slide was of a cow with bloat. The teacher asked, "What is the disease entity involved here and what is the pathology?" He paused. One student put down his newspaper and volunteered an answer. The teacher said, "No, that's incorrect." Another student looked up from his homework and ventured an idea. "No." Another awoke from his nap and tried, too. "No, that's not it." By this time all of the students were looking up and voicing their opinions, all of which were wrong.

The teacher flashed another slide, asked a similar question, and got similar results. The teacher stopped and said, "I have several comments to make about these examples. First, you will see examples just like this on the test. But the reason I put examples like this on the test is because any veterinarian would know about common problems like these that you will be asked about continuously by farmers in your area. You would look like quite the fool if you had no answers to these simple and common questions. So, I'll tell you what we'll do. I'll put these slides in the slide tray at the end of the sequence. Before we get back to those, I will explain what you need to know. By the end of the session we will return to the original slides, and I guarantee that you will be able to answer the questions your clients will ask you."

During the rest of the lesson the students were not exactly on the edge of their seats, but they were paying attention. At the end of the lesson, the teacher had verification that the students gained what they needed. In fact, because of the unanswered cases the teacher presented, the lesson had a nice beginning, a middle, and an ending: the unanswered puzzling cases, the informative explanation, and the return to identify and solve the cases. Later, given more time, I suggested that the teacher present similar cases and have the students seek out the information and then report back.

15. Contrast Students' Beliefs and Students' Actions with Their Self-View.   If your students are put in a psychologically uncomfortable state where they see that some of their basic ideas about themselves are in conflict with their actions or beliefs, they may change their actions and beliefs (Festinger, 1957). So, to use this technique, first show students how their self-view is at odds with their other beliefs and actions. Then show that to promote consistency they need to change their beliefs and actions. This can be done in four steps:

1. State the belief that students have now.
2. State the belief you wish students to have.
3. Discover how students view themselves.
4. Make a statement of this form:

   "How can someone like you who sees himself or herself as [self-view] believe [present undesirable belief]?"

   "A person who sees himself or herself as [self-view] believes that [desired belief]."

For example:

1. In your nutrition class, there are a number of students who believe, "If it tastes good, it must be good for your body too!"
2. You want your students to support the idea that consumption of less sugar, less fat, and more unrefined food is good for you and to act accordingly.
3. Students say they truly care about their health.
4. Say to the students:

   "How can someone like you who sees himself or herself as *truly caring about his or her health* believe *if something tastes good it must be good for your body?*"

"A person who sees himself or herself as *truly caring about his or her health* believes that *consumption of less sugar, less fat, and more unrefined food is good for you.*"

Contrasting Students' Beliefs and Actions with Their Self-View

- Speaking to science students learning how to detect flaws in scientific thinking, the professor said, "How can intelligent people like you make outlandish and flawed arguments about issues that you find so important? Intelligent people are careful about the scientific statements they make about important issues."

- To white students who thought of themselves as fair-minded, but who also believed that people of color should not be treated the same as white people, a teacher said, "How can individuals like you who think that you are fair, be unfair to people of color? A person who is fair, is fair to all."

- To motivate students who saw themselves as respected, intelligent people to change their belief that "grammar is not important to me," the teacher said, "Here are two letters, one with proper grammatical usage and one with improper usage. Which do you think appears to be written by a more intelligent person because it communicates the idea more precisely? Which impression do you want to give? People like you, who are intelligent and want to show others that you are smart, can do it in part by proper use of grammar."

- Sometimes, if you know a group well enough, you can refer to the group's self-view. Once, when trying to motivate a group of physician educators, a teacher said to them,

  "How can people like you, who see yourselves as good communicators, who have excellent ideas and experiences, who value your time, who see yourselves as up-to-date, who care about medical students, be using teaching techniques that don't communicate well, don't put your experience to its best use, are not efficient, are antiquated, are not helping students to learn? But, there is a way out. Today I will present modern techniques that will communicate your experience efficiently in a way that your students will learn."

There are also alternatives for steps 3 and 4.

3. Find an *activity* that is in contradiction to the undesired belief and in accord with the desired belief. For example, having someone teach a unit on consumption of less sugar, less fat, and more unrefined food would contradict the idea that "anything is good to eat if it tastes good."

4. Gently request students to do the activity. For example, ask students to do you a favor by helping you teach this unit on proper nutrition to younger students.

Gently Persuading Students to Act
in Contradiction to Their Beliefs

When teaching students to detect flaws in scientific thinking, a professor asked them to criticize their own flawed views written at the start of the term about an issue they picked as most important.

For students who thought of people of another ethnic group as lazy, a teacher arranged to have the two groups work together as partners on a time-consuming community project.

A social science teacher asked students to pick an issue about which they felt strongly. To help them to have a more balanced view, the teacher asked them to write a composition arguing the opposite view.

Some students believed that "math is an abstract subject and cannot be of much use." To motivate them to believe that math comprises a set of tools and is very useful, the teacher gave this assignment: List at least 20 uses of math in everyday life.

One teacher gently persuaded students to work diligently on a subject that initially was not their greatest interest. Once students invested the effort, they were more inclined to value the subject. They rationalized, "How can I, an intelligent, selective person, spend my effort and time on a subject that does not have merit?"

16. Ask Students Why They Think the Topic Is Important.   In a discussion or as an assignment, ask students to make the connection. Ask students directly how the topic is relevant for them. For example, a counseling professor, Fred Lopez, teaching a course on theories of career counseling, asked his graduate students about problems in their own career development and in their counseling of others about career choices. The students said that these problems would be helped if they learned more about career counseling theories.

In another example, trainers simply asked their students to pose questions they want answered from the session and state why they want those questions answered. The reason was often more interesting than the question.

17. Give a Case or an Activity and Ask Students How the Topic Is Relevant for Them.   The case or activity provides a helping link for students. For example, my daughter Lisa's history teacher, Letha Collins, gave her students a list of quotations about why people should study history. The students were asked to identify the quotations they believed and those they did not and explain why. They were also to make their own statement about why people should study history. My daughter's was, "Our society needs to learn the mistakes of the past so they do not become the mistakes of the future."

Seventeen ideas, and more to come. But don't worry, these are all possibilities for you to return to, think about, and adapt to your own circumstances.

At least one of these choices is likely to be just right for you. And as you may have noticed, these techniques can be applied to a number of approaches to teaching: lecture, discussion, or problem-based learning.

Make Meaningful Connections throughout Instruction

Although applying meaningfulness is very useful at the start of instruction, to motivate students to learn a given topic, it should also be applied continuously during instruction. Following are seven sample techniques to make connections throughout instruction:

Use Real-World Meaningful Examples.   Show your students or have your students tell of the uses and rewards of the desired performance through real-world examples.

Find Out When to Use Ideas and Why.   As each skill or major idea is learned, tell your students or have them find out when they should use the skill or idea and what they will gain by its use.

Relate Content to Student Experiences.   Have students act out or describe cases drawn from student interviews and observations done before instruction. Explain or have the students discuss the consequences of using or not using the skill in each case. Relate explanations or have students relate what is learned to their particular experiences and problems.

Relate Content to Areas Not Experienced.   Project your students into examples, cases, and problems they may not have experienced. Employ phrases such as "Have *you* ever seen . . ." and, "Suppose *you* were. . . ."

Have Students Make Personal Connections.   Call on your students to present their cases, problems, or questions. Encourage them to learn actively and independently and assume responsibility for motivating themselves. Have them continuously connect what they are learning to their background and knowledge (Corno & Rohrkemper, 1985).

Use Meaningful Demonstrations and Practice.   Link practice and demonstrations during instruction directly to the students' needs by making them as realistic as possible. Conduct simulations whenever the objectives require them and whenever resources allow. Pose questions or present examples about typical problems in your students' world. Take these problems directly from interviews and observations done before the course.

Have Students Choose Topics and Projects.   When course requirements include a project, allow students a choice of topic and a choice of medium.

Make Meaningful Connections at the End of Instruction

The two sample techniques for use at the end of instruction are designed to send students from class motivated to continue to learn and to apply what they have learned.

Return of the Meaningful Attention-Getter.   Employ any of the techniques used as an attention-getter to finish the instruction with a flourish. For example, at the end of instruction you could have students discuss why a skill was important to learn and why it is important to apply.

Employ Action Planning.   Ask students to commit themselves to try the skills they have learned and to state their plans of where, when, and how they will operate in the real world. Ask them to specify what obstacles they expect and how they will overcome them. If students came to class with a personally important and relevant case, question, project, or problem, ask them to show how they will apply what they have learned to it. For example, at the end of each week-long session of a year-long medical fellowship, mentors hold a half hour meeting with each participating physician and ask how each will apply what has been learned that week to the assigned research or curriculum project. The mentors ask for an exact accounting of steps to be taken and then check for any time schedule or resource problems that may interfere with the process. If there are possible roadblocks, the mentor and medical fellow derive a plan to work around or remove the roadblocks.

Similarly, at the end of a workshop on how to use stories in training, the workshop leader, Sivasailam Thiagarajan, asked participants to pretend that they meet at an airport several years later. They were each to outdo their fellow participants by using stories to describe their accomplishments.

Make Meaningful Connections after Instruction

The two sample techniques used after instruction are to keep students motivated to apply what they have learned.

Communicate with Graduates.   To continue to promote the application of newly acquired skills, visit or write to graduates to remind them to connect what they have learned in class to real-world settings. For example, a teacher sends letters and makes calls to some of his former students reminding them of what they have learned. He does so in a way that hopefully is not seen as nagging. He asks how he might help them now, and then inquires about what they have applied, how hard it was to do, what roadblocks they encountered, and how they worked around the obstacles. Many of the students respond that by talking about what they have learned, they are reminded of an idea that they can apply to their present circumstance.

Influence Supervisors.   For those in work settings, ask supervisors to encourage, enforce, and reward the application of what has been learned (Alderman, 1988).

A FINAL WORD

With so many intructional procedures from which to choose, using the principle of meaningfulness becomes an interesting and creative endeavor, and you should be able to find ways of applying meaningfulness to your teaching situation. Remember that you can use the principle to motivate your students before, during, or after instruction. Applying meaningfulness is easier when you have derived your goals, objectives, and content from your students' needs; nonetheless, your students might not see it that way. You must help them make the connection.

Yes, people may reluctantly learn things that don't mean anything to them; they will memorize the content and spout it back on the test. But their heart won't be in it. They may choose not to use the content and may even learn to dislike it. But that need not be the case in your teaching if you make the effort to discover your students' interests and make the creative connection between your topic and their interests. You will find as much pleasure in the process of applying meaningfulness as in the rewards you will reap when students are motivated to learn your subject.

You will also find that meaningfulness together with several other principles supplies a useful set of *motivational principles* (Keller, 1987). When teachers apply meaningfulness properly, students are interested in what is taught; they think it is relevant to them. When teachers apply novelty well, students pay attention to the information and the activities that will help them learn—they are engaged. When teachers use pleasant conditions and consequences, students are satisfied with what they have learned; they are intrinsically motivated (Cameron & Pierce, 1994). And when teachers provide challenging appropriate practice with complete feedback, students gain confidence.

ACTIVITIES

Even after a thorough reading of this chapter, you are likely to find that putting the knowledge to use is difficult. It takes practice to be able to apply the principles. Although it is possible to do each application alone, you may benefit from discussing the activities with a partner or in a small group. When working in a group, consider collaborating on an activity or presenting your independent work for critique.

These activities are designed so that you can either apply the principle and the procedures in the chapter, make connections among the ideas in this chapter and other chapters, or reflect on the relationship of this principle to your teaching. The first four of these activities call for creative applications of meaningfulness that will help in teaching. In the fifth activity you are to apply the principle by evaluating instruction. Activities 6 and 7 ask you to make connections between the principle and other ideas, and activity 8 encourages you to think about the principle as you plan to teach.

1. Create a meaningful attention-getter as you would to start a lesson, unit, or course.
    a. Begin by thinking of a subject you might teach.
    b. Think of the students you might teach and their experiences, interests, and aspirations.
    c. Think of how your subject relates to your students' experiences, interests, and aspirations.
    d. Refer back to any of the 17 techniques to create a discussion, activity, or statement that will appeal to those motives to start the lesson.
    e. Think of at least one approach that is more teacher controlled and one that is more student controlled.
2. Take any procedure for applying meaningfulness at the start of instruction and describe how it could be used in different styles of teaching: by the teacher explaining, by students discussing, by students working together to learn, or by students working independently.
3. Think of a particular course, unit, or lesson that you might teach. List five ways you can help your students make connections to their experiences, interests, and aspirations *throughout* instruction.
4. For that same course, unit, or lesson describe at least two ways to help students make meaningful connections at the *end* of instruction.
5. Use the portion of the checklist in Appendix A that refers to meaningfulness to observe a teacher, plan a lesson, or evaluate some recent teaching.
6. In what ways could you take into account students' individual differences when applying the principle of meaningfulness?
7. How is the application of meaningfulness part of the process of student assessment? Assess yourself and one person you know to find what each of you needs to learn or wants to learn.
8. Reflection (These are questions to ask yourself about your instruction. They are ideas to ponder as you plan and carry out your instruction. Add your own.)
    a. How can I connect the topic I teach to my students' past, present, and future?
    b. What are my students' motives? How can I find out?
    c. Is there a payoff for students in learning this topic? When? Where?
    d. What quotation or news article points out the use of this topic?
    e. What case examples show the use of this topic? What unsolved cases could be solved?
    f. What questions, puzzles, or competing theories can be answered using the topic?
    g. What assignment could have students relate the topic to their interests?
    h. How can I capitalize on my students' questions and natural curiosity?
    i. How can I use meaningfulness in varying modes of instruction?

FURTHER READING

Ames, R., & Ames, C. (Eds.). (1989). *Research on motivation in education: Vol. 3. Goals and cognitions.* San Diego: Academic Press.

Barell, J. (1995). *Teaching for Thoughtfulness* (2nd ed.). New York: Longman. (*Note:* This book contains interesting examples of use of meaningful attention-getters in the context of problem-based instruction geared to enhance thinking skills.)

Blumenfeld, P., Soloway, E., Marx, R., Krajcik, J., Guzdial, M., & Palinscar, A. (1991). Motivating project based learning: Sustaining the doing, supporting the learning. *Educational Psychologist, 26,* 369–398.

Brophy, J. (1983). Conceptualizing student motivation. *Educational Psychologist, 1,* 200–215.

Corno, L. (1993). The best laid plans: Modern conceptions of volition and educational research. *Educational Researcher, 22,* 14–22.

Corno, L., & Kanfer, R. (1993). The role of volition in learning and performance. In L. Darling-Hammond (Ed.), *Review of research in education* (pp. 301–341). Washington, DC: American Educational Research Association

diSessa, A. A. (1990). Social niches for future software. In M. Gardner, J. Greeno, F. Reif, A. Schoenfeld, A. diSessa, & E. Stage (Eds.), *Toward a scientific practice of science education* (pp. 301–322). Hillsdale, NJ: Lawrence Erlbaum. (*Note:* This chapter discusses ways to connect future software to students' interests.)

Dweck, C. S. (1986). Motivational processes affecting learning. *American Psychologist, 41,* 1040–1048.

Keller, J. M. (1983). Motivational design of instruction. In C. M. Reigeluth (Ed.), *Instructional design theories and models: An overview of their current status* (pp. 383–436). Hillsdale, NJ: Lawrence Erlbaum. (*Note:* Read this excellent review and synthesis of the literature on motivation to learn more about the basis for meaningfulness.)

Keller, J. M. (1987). Strategies for stimulating the motivation to learn. *Performance and Instruction Journal, 26*(8), 1–7. (*Note:* Keller's ARCS model includes practical technique; see the section on relevance.)

Keller, J. M. (1987). The systematic process of motivational design. *Performance and Instruction Journal, 26*(9), 1–8.

Keller, J. M., & Kopp, T. (1987). An application of the ARCS model of motivational design. In C. Reigeluth (Ed.), *Instructional theories in action: Lessons illustrating selected theories and models.* Hillsdale, NJ: Lawrence Erlbaum.

Okey, J. R., & Santiago, R. S. (1991). Integrating instructional and motivational design. *Performance Improvement Quarterly, 4*(2) 11–21.

Pintrich, P. (1993). Beyond cold conceptual change: The role of motivational beliefs and classroom contextual factors in the process of conceptual change. *Review of Educational Research, 63*(2), 167–199.

Visser, J., & Keller, J. M. (1990). The clinical use of motivational messages: An inquiry into the validity of the ARCS model of motivational design. *Instructional Science, 19,* 467–500.

Wlodkowski, R. J. (1991). *Enhancing adult motivation to learn.* San Francisco: Jossey-Bass. (*Note:* Chapters 3 through 5 show how to use meaningfulness with adult learners.)

chapter 3

Prerequisites

OVERVIEW

Assess students' prerequisites so you can adjust instruction to help them refine and develop what they know.

Guideline 1: Analyze Prerequisites of Required Tasks
          Describe the Task
          Analyze the Task Description
          Decide on Essential Prerequisites
          Analyze the Essential Prerequisites Further

Guideline 2: Assess What Students Know
          Weigh the Dangers of Not Pretesting
          Weigh the Dangers of Pretesting
          Pretest Safely and Efficiently

Guideline 3: Adjust Instruction to Account for Analyzed Prerequisites and Students' Knowledge
          Choose Appropriate Strategies to Adjust to Differences
            among Students
          Use the Six Strategies to Adjust to Student Differences

Follow this dialogue to learn an important lesson about the second powerful instructional principle: prerequisites.

TEACHER TO CLASS: You know what a frasm is, don't you?

STUDENT: A what?

TEACHER: A frasm. You mean to tell me you don't now what a frasm is? Uh oh! I'm in big trouble here. The rest of my presentation is based on your knowing what a frasm is. Is a Volkswagen a frasm? A steak? A hat? A peach?

STUDENT: I don't know.

TEACHER: You don't know? Oh, I realize what's wrong here. I didn't define it. You see, if you define things, students get the idea and everything can proceed. So here is the definition of *frasm:*

A frasm

is a

splik with reebs.

Now you have it, and we can move ahead. Is a Volkswagen a frasm? A steak? A hat? A peach?

STUDENT: I still can't tell.

TEACHER: You can't tell? You don't have it? What do you need to know in order to move ahead?

STUDENT: What is a splik and what is a reeb?

TEACHER: OK, let's deal with them one at a time. First, I'll define *splik:*

A frasm

is a

splik with reebs.

|

a vegetable

or a fruit.

Yes. A splik is a vegetable or a fruit. Is a Volkswagen a frasm?

STUDENT: No.

TEACHER: Of course not. Is a steak a frasm?

STUDENT: No.

TEACHER: A hat?

STUDENT: No.

TEACHER: A peach?

STUDENT: Hmm, maybe.

TEACHER: That's wise. Better be cautious here. You can't tell for sure. What do you need to know to be sure?

STUDENT: What is a reeb?

TEACHER: OK, I'll tell you what a reeb is. I'll give you the singular and you can figure out the plural for yourself.

<pre>
                    A frasm
                     is a
                splik with reebs.
                   | |
           a vegetable   a seed smaller than,
           or a fruit.   or equal to, an
                             apple seed.
</pre>

Yes. A reeb is a seed smaller than, or equal to, an apple seed. Now let that work its way into your brain. Now you have it. Is a Volkswagen a frasm?

STUDENT: Obviously not.

TEACHER: Is a steak?

STUDENT: No.

TEACHER: A hat?

STUDENT: No.

TEACHER: A peach?

STUDENT: No. Although it is a fruit, its seed is too big.

TEACHER: How about an apple?

STUDENT: Yes, a fruit with seeds equal to an apple seed.

TEACHER: How about a grape?

STUDENT: Most varieties, probably.

TEACHER: An avocado?

STUDENT: No, you swallow that reeb and you die.

TEACHER: A pear?

STUDENT: Yes.

How many times have you been in front of a class, or in a class, and witnessed the following scenario: The teacher begins, "Today we are going to be talking about frasms. You all know what frasms are, don't you?" "What?" the class responds. "What was that?" Then the teacher looks at the class as if they were genetically defective and says, "Well, if I have to, I'll define it for you. Write this down: A *frasm* is a splik with reebs. Now do you all understand?" And all of the students nod, "Uh huh." Then the teacher launches into a presentation about frasms and the students have little idea of what is going on. At the end of the session the students have not learned; they are unprepared. The students are frustrated, anxious, and angry. The session was a waste of the students' and the teacher's time. The lesson is to avoid these adverse consequences, remember the frasm, and apply the principle of prerequisites.

What are prerequisites? Prerequisites refer not to previous courses on a person's transcript or records of a person's training, but rather to the ideas that a person knows before instruction takes place, although not each idea in isolation. *Prerequisites* are the ideas that a person knows as they relate to the ideas which must be learned.

Learners always have some prerequisites; that is, learners always have some knowledge that relates somehow to a new idea. However, the old ideas and new ideas may be only remotely related. Of course, most teachers wish to have learners who have mastered all of the ideas most closely related to the ideas to be taught. Some educators say that when a learner has mastered all of the ideas most closely related to the ideas they wish to teach, that learner is *ready* to learn. The learner is more likely to learn from instruction without much review. That's a nice fantasy. The reality is that few students have all the ideal prerequisites.

Am I talking about bringing all students up to par so they are ready to understand an explanation? Only in part. You must consider how you will assess and adjust to prerequisites not only when teaching by direct instruction, for example when lecturing or explaining, but also when using learner-centered instruction, such as discovery learning or cooperative group learning. It may seem simple to ask individual students or groups of students to figure out an idea for themselves. But to benefit from these approaches, students must have knowledge that allows them to learn from sources they use and they must have the skills to extract ideas from sources and to work together in groups. You will have to assess, adjust to, and monitor students' prerequisite knowledge and skill when using any form of instruction.

How do you know what ideas your students have? What do you do about the differences you may find among students? What do you do about wide gaps between what students know and what is to be taught? How can you consider students' feelings while trying to find out what they know? The principle of prerequisites implies that you carry out three teaching tasks:

1. Analyze high-priority tasks and ideas to find the most influential prerequisites.
2. Choose and administer a safe, efficient assessment of students' knowledge that elicits enough information to be worth the time spent pretesting.
3. Choose an efficient strategy to help students with varying prerequisites refine and develop their knowledge (Gagné & Driscoll, 1988).

Keep in mind that you must be sensitive to students' feelings while analyzing, assessing, adjusting to, and accounting for their prerequisites. Learners may be threatened by an antagonistic question about competence, by an assignment of "remedial" instruction, or by a comment about adjusting vocabulary for those who are uninformed. For example, before designing instruction, I suggested to a teacher that we find out what his potential students knew. The teacher took this to mean: Let's find out what students in your program don't know; let's find out how ignorant and deficient they are. The teacher was adamant about not preassessing his students, fearful of striking a fatal blow to their self-esteem. Keeping students' and teachers' feelings in mind, let's consider three guidelines.

GUIDELINE 1: ANALYZE PREREQUISITES OF REQUIRED TASKS

One way for you to find prerequisites is to look for the knowledge and skills hidden within the tasks you teach (Gagné, 1985; Gropper, 1983). Because you probably don't have enough time to analyze every task you teach, concentrate on analyzing the tasks that have the most important consequences, are performed most frequently, and are the most complex (Lakein, 1973). If you want to be even more efficient in your planning, analyze the most crucial steps and ideas in the most important tasks. Begin by describing the task and then analyzing the pieces that you find.

Describe the Task

If a task is important but not necessarily complex, find the prerequisites without a task description. Analyze the objective. For example, most of the prerequisites are clearly represented in this objective: "Recall important facts in cardio-pulmonary resuscitation such as the ratio of breaths to compressions." Study this phrase:

"the *ratio* of *breaths* to *compressions*"

For the most meaning to come from learning "the ratio of breaths to compressions," students have to know what *ratio, breaths,* and *compressions* mean. They must be able to identify examples of those three concepts. They must also know numerals and what they mean, or in other words, they must be able to recall the very elementary prerequisite of the amounts associated with numerals.

For relatively complex tasks, begin to find prerequistes by doing a *task description.* Write the steps and decisions for the task being taught in the form of a recipe. To know what to write, do the task yourself very slowly and self-consciously, or observe experts doing the task. Ask them questions: What are you looking at? What are you looking for? What are you doing? What are you thinking? What do you check to see if you have done a step correctly?

Include all parts of the task. You can enumerate the steps as in a cookbook, create a flow diagram, or use a combination of words and pictures. The steps may be physical or mental, visible or invisible. Add the cues preceding each step as well as the results of each step. State each step so specifically that someone who knows the vocabulary could follow the steps and perform the task. Be as detailed as you can. Check the task description by having an expert review the steps as he or she is performing the task.

If there is more than one good way to pursue a task, specify each as time permits. If you don't have much time, spell out one of the most basic and effective approaches. Let students know that this is a basic approach and they will be able to learn and use others later.

Following are two formats of the task description "How to Take a Blood Pressure." One format is a narrative description; the other, in Figure 3.1, is a

FIGURE 3.1   How to take a blood pressure

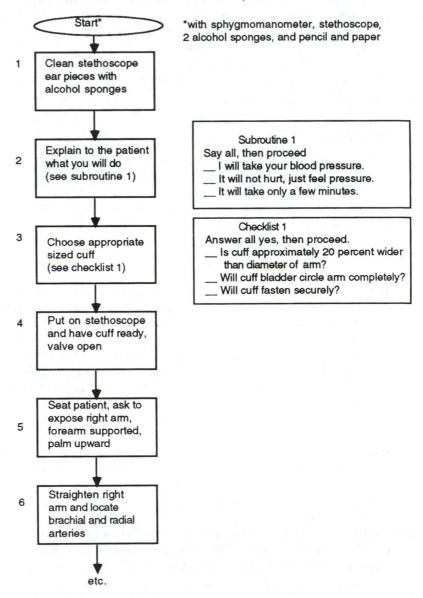

Start*

*with sphygmomanometer, stethoscope, 2 alcohol sponges, and pencil and paper

1   Clean stethoscope ear pieces with alcohol sponges

2   Explain to the patient what you will do (see subroutine 1)

3   Choose appropriate sized cuff (see checklist 1)

4   Put on stethoscope and have cuff ready, valve open

5   Seat patient, ask to expose right arm, forearm supported, palm upward

6   Straighten right arm and locate brachial and radial arteries

etc.

Subroutine 1
Say all, then proceed
__ I will take your blood pressure.
__ It will not hurt, just feel pressure.
__ It will take only a few minutes.

Checklist 1
Answer all yes, then proceed.
__ Is cuff approximately 20 percent wider than diameter of arm?
__ Will cuff bladder circle arm completely?
__ Will cuff fasten securely?

flow diagram of part of the task description. Of course, the task could also be described with pictures and words.

Narrative Task Description: How to Take a Blood Pressure

1. Gather equipment: sphygmomanometer, stethoscope, two alcohol sponges, pencil and paper.
2. Clean the stethoscope earpieces with the alcohol sponges.
3. Explain the procedure to the patient:
   a. I will take your blood pressure.
   b. It will not hurt, but you will feel some pressure.
   c. It will take only a couple of minutes.
4. Choose appropriate sized cuff so that it
   a. is 20 percent wider than patient's arm.
   b. will circle arm completely.
   c. will be secure.
5. Put on the stethoscope and have the cuff ready with the valve open, bladder ready and open on the diaphragm side.
6. Seat the patient and have the patient expose right arm, with forearm supported, palm upward.
7. Straighten the right arm and locate the brachial and radial arteries.
8. Grasp the bladder cuff with both hands, Velcro side up and tubing toward you.
9. Place bladder over middle third of upper arm so that
   a. the tubing is centered over the brachial artery.
   b. the lower edge is 2 cm over the antecubital fossa.
   c. the cuff has no wrinkles.
   d. it is loose enough to put one finger in.
10. Wrap the Velcro under the arm and then wrap the loose end around the arm.
11. Make sure that the cuff is snug, but not able to slip.
12. Close the valve.
13. Pump above systolic pressure slowly until radial artery pulse is no longer palpable.
14. Place the diaphragm of the stethoscope over the brachial artery just beneath the cuff.
15. Cradle and extend arm with the same hand.
16. Ask the patient to relax the arm.
17. Release the air from bladder at 5 mm Hg/sec.
18. Listen for the systolic reading and mentally record the reading you see on the manometer.
19. Listen for the diastolic reading and mentally record the reading you see on the manometer.
20. Completely deflate the cuff and remove it.
21. Record the measurements and tell the patient the results and explain them.

Not only do observable physical skills merit task description. You must also use task descriptions when teaching thinking skills and problem solving. That is because some students, lacking precise information about how to think, create ineffective and inefficient strategies (Whimbey & Lockhead, 1982). For example, I was convinced that my smart friends in high school could simply read complex mathematical story problems and immediately know the answer. I had no idea they read and reread the question, asked themselves questions, made little diagrams and pictures, estimated the answers, tried different approaches, and kept trying even when an initial attempt failed. I was convinced that my bright friends could read a paragraph in a text once, skim the page with their fingers, read every third word, and produce excellent interpretations of the prose. I had no idea that they read and reread every single word very slowly, figured out and made educated guesses about the meaning of unknown words, made pictures in their minds, changed those pictures as the meaning changed, checked and rechecked their interpretations. For the sake of students like me, who need some direction to create their own effective and efficient strategies, I urge you to describe thinking skills.

You may find it relatively easy to describe thinking skills that already have been specified. You will probably find it more difficult to describe to a student processes that have not been carefully formulated. Can you describe how you recognize an example of a concept, how you analyze an issue, how you apply a principle, how you write a thesis statement, how you support a topic sentence, how you compare and contrast ideas? To answer these questions and to describe these approaches to thinking, you may discover that a good strategy is to work through a specific example and write down what you think, then restate the steps in more general language. For example, here is one way I might derive a general description of how to apply theoretical principles to predict the outcomes of a given case:

Specific Thinking Step	*General Thinking Step*
Someone asks me if I think it is very likely that a learner would recall what he or she had studied if he or she just read a page of text and underlined the key ideas.	Review the case. Check the task. If it is a task of prediction, then go ahead.
Because the problem is about recall, I decide to make my predictions using a theory for explaining learning and recall: information processing theory.	Note the outcome (dependent variables) called for. Recall the kind of theory needed to predict that outcome.
I recall, in brief, the appropriate information processing principles: To store an idea, a learner must attend to relevant cues, encode them, organize them, and rehearse	Recall the principles related to the relevant outcomes. Note most care- fully the variables (independent variables) and the relationships needed to produce the outcome.

them. To be able to recall an idea on demand, a learner must practice retrieving the stored idea.

I look at the case to see if the learner has taken any actions related to paying attention, encoding, organizing, rehearsing, and recalling what has been stored.	Check the case for actions likely to produce the outcomes: those actions applying the variables needed to produce the outcome.
From the information given, the only learner action is underlining the key terms, one that implies attention to certain parts of a text. Other actions implying use of the other factors are absent.	Assess the presence, quantity, and quality of the actions taken according to the effective variables.
If underlining while reading is the only action the learner takes, then I would predict that the learner would recall relatively little of the text. If I had seen evidence of the learner encoding (making notes), organizing (structuring notes), rehearsing (repeating what was being read), and practice recalling (saying the ideas without notes), I would have predicted a better chance of recall.	If the presence, quantity, and quality of effective variables in the actions are insufficient according to the principles, predict the low likelihood of the outcome. If they are sufficient, predict the high likelihood of the outcome.

On the basis of this analysis, you could be ready to tell your students both the specific steps and the general steps. However, some thinking skills are longer and more complicated. The following is a rough example of how to analyze and evaluate a plan. It is an extension of identifying an example of a concept because the thinker is called upon to find examples of many concepts and then is required to organize and summarize the findings.

1. Read the whole plan, looking for the all the elements of a good plan.
   a. The need for the plan
   b. The purpose of the plan
   c. The method of the plan
   d. The evaluation of the plan
2. Recall the specific attributes of each of the elements of a good plan.
   a. The need states a real gap between what is and what is desired.
   b. The need documents the real gap with hard data.
   c. The purpose is structured to fill the specific need.
   d. The purpose is stated in observable, measurable terms.

   e. The method is complete: who, when, what, where, how.
   f. The method is specific and operational.
   g. The method is feasible.
   h. The method is likely to fulfill the purpose.
   i. The evaluation question relates to the purpose of the plan.
   j. The evaluation is complete: instruments, subjects, setting, and analysis.
   k. The instruments are valid.
   l. The instruments are reliable.
   m. The sample and setting are suitable for the question.
   n. The analysis is suitable for the question.
3. See that the elements and attributes of a good plan are present in the plan analyzed.
   a. Note any omission of need, purpose, method, or evaluation.
   b. Check the attributes of any elements present (e.g., Is the method feasible?).
   c. When attributes fit or not, note how they fit or don't fit (e.g., Why is it or isn't it feasible?).
4. Write a draft acccording to the sequence of the plan.
   a. Describe the element.
   b. Describe the section analyzed.
   c. State what was good and how.
   d. State what was OK and how.
   e. State what was poor and how.
   f. Summarize the overall quality.
5. Check the written draft of the analysis.
   a. Check the draft for ease of reading.
   b. Check the draft for clear comparisons.
   c. Check the summary to see whether or not it fits the data.
   d. Rewrite and recheck.

Remember, we are describing a complex task, for example, a physical or mental skill, so that we can find the content embedded in its steps and decisions. Now, let's turn our attention to the next step in the process.

Analyze the Task Description

A complete and explicit task description points out all of the necessary decisions and subskills for a task. You know just by inspecting the task description on taking a blood pressure reading that a performer must decide on the correct cuff and be able to place the cuff correctly. However, to draw out the hidden prerequisite ideas in each step and decision, you must know what type of knowledge to look for. Robert Gagné (1985) proposed that prerequisite knowledge be classified and taught by methods appropriate to each classification. Instructional theorists such as Gagné (1985), Gropper (1983), Merrill (1983), and Farnham-Diggory (1994) proposed taxonomies for classifying knowledge. Table 3.1 is my taxonomy, a composite that I find useful when analyzing tasks. Study Table 3.1 carefully because these ideas will appear throughout the rest of the book.

Look for Subskills. Look for related series of steps, or *subskills,* within the task. To do the whole task, students will have to perform many of these. Ask: What are the smaller skills and decisions making up the larger task? For example, consider the first few steps in taking a blood pressure. Students must master each of these subskills:

- How to clean the earpieces
- How to explain the process to a patient
- How to choose the appropriately sized cuff

TABLE 3.1 Search for these types of knowledge

Type of Knowledge	Brief Definition	How Students Display Knowledge	Example
Skill	A series of steps.	Perform the skill.	Take a blood pressure.
Rule	A command to act a certain way.	Follow the rule.	Clean equipment before using on a patient.
Principle	A relationship among factors.	Apply the principle (i.e., control, predict, infer cause, explain, troubleshoot, vary the task based on new conditions).	Use of sterile equipment will avoid the spread of infection.
Fact	A statement describing or defining people, places, things, events, behaviors, and processes that have occurred, are occurring, or generally do occur.	State the fact(s) without prompts.	The definitions of systolic and diastolic readings. The steps to take blood pressure.
Concept	A category of experience bounded by a definition and given a name.	Identify a previously unobserved example of the category and explain the reason for recognition.	Properly placed stethoscope. Presence of radial arterial pulse.
Attitude	A willingness to act a certain way (positive attitude).	Voluntarily, intensely, and persistently expend time, energy, or money in acting toward a certain type of object, person, or process.	Concern for patients. Precision in measurement.

Look for Rules.   Look for implied commands to act a certain way. Think of rules that students must follow as they do the task. Ask: What rules are implied in this step or series of steps? What "dos and don'ts" are implied by this part of the task? Consider the following step in taking a blood pressure:

"Clean the stethoscope earpieces."

To take a blood pressure properly, a performer must follow this implied rule:

• Before you use any intrusive equipment, clean it.

Also consider the step,

"Explain to the patient what you will do."

To take a blood pressure properly, a performer must follow this implied rule:

• Before you do any procedure, explain it to the patient.

Look for Principles.   Look for relationships among factors that students may apply as they do this task and others. A principle has three parts:

1. An independent variable (an antecedent factor)
2. A relationship
3. A dependent variable (a consequent factor)

Even though many principles are correlational rather than causative, it may still be helpful to think of the independent variable as the factor that is manipulated, the *cause,* and the dependent variable as the result of that manipulation, the *effect.* For example, sterile treatment of a wound (independent variable, the cause) will increase the likelihood (relationship) that the wound will heal (dependent variable, the effect.) Students may use principles in many ways:

To control (we want to promote healing)
To predict (under these circumstances this wound should heal)
To infer cause (this wound didn't heal possibly because . . .)
To troubleshoot (to find the cause of the spread of infection, let's check sterilization . . .)
To adjust the task to changing conditions (we don't have alcohol, but we do have something else to use for sterilization)

One way to find principles is to look for relationships between rules and their consequences. Rules are prescribed, presumably because they lead to desirable results, or at least to the avoidance of undesirable ones. In this kind of principle, the rule is the independent variable and the consequence of the rule or its reason is the dependent variable. Because you already have rules, inspect each one and ask: Why should students do this step or make this decision as it should be done? What is the consequence of doing the step according to the rule? How could you state the general principle to be followed? What cause and effect, or correlational relationship, is implied by this rule? Could students use the principle to troubleshoot problems or adjust the task to changing conditions? Look at the step about cleaning the earpieces and its implied rule:

"Before you use any intrusive equipment, clean it."

You may derive a principle by adding the consequence of following the rule:

- Sterilize equipment that will come in contact with vulnerable areas of the body (independent variable), to avoid (relationship) the spread of infection (dependent variable).

Also consider the step about explaining the process to the patient and its corresponding rule:

"Before you do any procedure, explain it to the patient."

You may derive a complex principle by asking, Why follow that rule?

- Explain procedures to patients before doing them (independent variable)
  a. to gain (relationship) a patient's confidence (dependent variable),
  b. to reduce (relationship) anxiety (dependent variable), and
  c. to ensure (relationship) the accurate completion of a procedure (dependent variable).

Look for Facts. Look for statements about anything that students must recall as part of the task: lists, steps, definitions, names, general facts. Ask: What must students recall to do this step or make this decision? What definitions, locations, lists, names, amounts must they remember? For the step about putting on the stethoscope, a performer must recall certain simple facts, such as

- which is the front of the stethoscope.

For the step of locating the brachial and radial arteries, a performer must recall

- the locations of the brachial and radial arteries.

For the steps about listening for the systolic and diastolic readings, a performer must recall

- what those terms mean, and what the differences are between the two readings.

For the steps to record and explain the results, a performer must recall

- the way to record these readings and what the readings mean.

For the entire skill, a performer must recall

- the sequence of the steps.

Look for Concepts.   Look for categories of items, processes, and behaviors that students must recognize while doing the task. Ask generally: What categories must students identify to do this part of the task? Look at the key terms noted in the task. Notice any "frasms"? What categories to identify are implied by key terms? What cues must students recognize while performing? What criteria must students use to judge a performance or a product? The main question is: Will students have to spot an example of this category as they proceed successfully through the task? In doing the first four steps about preparing the equipment and the patient to take a blood pressure, a performer must identify examples of these cues and criteria when he or she sees them:

- Proper equipment
- Clean stethoscope
- Properly explained procedure
- Appropriately sized cuff

From the subsequent measurement steps, a performer must recognize examples of many categories of cues and criteria when he or she sees or hears them, such as:

- Properly seated patient
- Properly placed cuff
- Properly placed stethoscope
- When a radial artery pulse is present or absent
- The systolic reading
- The diastolic reading

Look for Attitudes.   Look for a positive attitude, a willingness to perform a certain way. First ask: Do students need to display a certain attitude in doing this task? Does willingness to act in a certain way play a role in any of the steps? If so, look for indicators of willingness: voluntarily acting in a certain way, acting with intensity, persisting to act in that way, and giving up personal resources like time, energy, and money. To prepare a patient to take a blood pressure and to explain the process to a patient, a performer must be willing to demonstrate the attitude of

- concern for the patient's physical and emotional well-being (voluntarily, intensely, and persistently give up personal time and energy to ensure a patient's welfare).

To do all the subsequent steps of checking a blood pressure, a performer must be willing to display the attitude of

- being precise in measurement and recording (without coercion, time after time, carefully measuring and double checking).

Prerequisite attitudes are sometimes neglected. You know how important attitudes are for the proper performance of a task if you have ever tried to teach swimming to a person who is afraid of the water. Sometimes students' attitudes may prevent them from learning. I found this once when I worked with teachers of manipulative therapy, an approach to curing certain physical ills by moving parts of the body. The teachers were using acceptable skill-teaching techniques, but the students were not learning. When interviewed, the students revealed that they had no faith in the procedures. Their attitude was, "Teach me, I dare you!" The lesson I learned was to look for prerequisite attitudes in tasks students must learn.

Decide on Essential Prerequisites

Although there may be ideas embedded within a task, your students may not need to know them all in order to do the task. One way to decide what is an essential prerequisite (Aaronson, 1983; Gagné, 1985) for a given task is to ask: What would happen if a student did not know this idea and tried to do the task? For example, I can drive a car and operate a computer without knowing the principles behind the rules I follow.

For some tasks there are good reasons for students to understand why they are performing as they do and to know the related ideas. If your students know the principles behind what they are doing, they are more likely to be able to solve problems that arise when doing the task. If they learn the rules, facts, and concepts as part of the task, they may also use those ideas to learn related tasks. So, ask: Which of the ideas that you found does a person have to apply during the task to be successful? You may use a combination of professional judgment and empirical testing to answer that question.

Five Questions to Ask to Decide on Essential Prerequisites
1. Which of the rules must the performer recall and follow to complete the task successfully?

2. Which of the principles must the performer understand in order to explain, troubleshoot, or adjust to new conditions?
3. Which of the related facts must the performer write, state, or bring to mind while doing the task?
4. Which of the concepts must the performer apply by identifying examples during the task?
5. Which of the attitudes must the performer display by showing willingness to act as the task progresses?

Analyze the Essential Prerequisites Further

You may wish to further analyze the most critical rules, principles, facts, and concepts. You may use the same approach described at the start of this chapter in the case of the "frasm." Look for concepts, like "spliks and reebs," embedded in the statements of the most important rules and facts and in the definitions of the most important concepts and principles. For example, if a principle was defined as, "For every action there is an equal and opposite reaction," then the embedded concepts that you would consider as prerequisites might be *action, reaction, equal,* and *opposite.*

There is also the question about how well or how much students must understand in order to learn and to perform. Will the general idea suffice, or do they need the most technical understanding of the idea? Jerome Bruner (1960) stated that it is possible to teach most ideas at a simplified level to students who are not perfectly ready for them. He suggested revisiting those ideas as students are ready for the more complex explanations. I have found that students who enter my advanced instructional theory course without the knowledge of learning theories and instructional design still learn, but that those with the prerequisites learn more. Consider the analogy of going on a tour of an art museum. If you haven't much knowledge of art history, you will still learn something; but if you have the facts, concepts, and principles of art history, you will learn much more. Think about the degree of technical accuracy for the most important ideas that a performer needs. Should you look for that degree in your students? If your students do not have that degree of technical knowledge, should you take the time now to teach it in depth, or should you teach the idea in a simple form and revisit it later as needed?

GUIDELINE 2: ASSESS WHAT STUDENTS KNOW

Once you have analyzed your task description and found the hidden skills, ideas, and attitudes, you will know what prerequisites to assess. Decide first if you should pretest at all. If you have good evidence of relevant student knowledge from previous courses or units, you needn't pretest. If you have no time to administer a pretest and make any adjustments, then why pretend? Admit you can't. Make due now with a review of your students' likely prerequisites and negotiate for more time under similar circumstances to pretest. There are three steps to assessing what students know:

1. Weigh the dangers of not pretesting.
2. Weigh the dangers of pretesting.
3. Pretest safely and efficiently.
   a. Pretest formally or informally, but in a nonthreatening way.
   b. Use an efficient pretest strategy.

Weigh the Dangers of Not Pretesting

Suppose you decide not to find out what individual students know in advance of teaching. Instead you might teach what you believe is important, what the curriculum prescribes, or what prerequisites you think meet the needs of the "average student." What problems might you encounter if you do not preassess students' knowledge?

If you teach a lesson without finding out what students know, you run the risk that students will leave the lesson without achieving the objective. As a student, do you remember finishing some classes and wondering what you had learned that day? If as a teacher you do not account for students' prerequisites, then there is a good chance that your students will finish a lesson relatively untouched by any new ideas or skills. They are unlikely to integrate new ideas into their repertoires. How can you help students connect new ideas to old ideas if you don't explore the old ideas?

Furthermore, if you teach a lesson without finding out what students know, your students are likely to become frustrated and angry. Do you recall ever sitting through a presentation without even comprehending what was being said? Do you recall an instructor ever assuming what you knew and what you believed? He or she may have said, "I assume that you all have read about DNA, I assume that you all know what a gene is." How did you feel? Did you sit there and wait for the session to end? Most adults would not tolerate that; they would get up and leave. Some students and trainees have little choice. Fears of looking stupid and group norms to behave like a "good smart student" make it virtually impossible for someone to interrupt and say, "Excuse me, I don't know what you are talking about. Could you please explain some of the basic terms you have been using so that I can fit them into what I know?" Most people suffer in silence and try to get help after the class. Some complain. Some simply give up.

If you do not account for prerequisites, you will discover significant gaps in your students' knowledge on their first assignments or their first tests. When you consult with students about their test performance, you have a second chance to account for your students' prerequisites. But many instructors miss this opportunity; they ignore what students know and merely explain the content again. Under those circumstances some ambitious students will use tutors and friends to help them learn. For example, my daughter recognized early one semester that her instructor explained physics without assessing student prerequisites. The result was that, given her prerequisites, she didn't understand what he was saying. So she did not attend class, but asked her friends who were physics majors to teach her what she needed to know. That was an excellent coping strategy, but not why she paid tuition.

If you do not account for prerequisites, you also stand a chance of boring students by teaching things they already know. Then, when you reach ideas they do not know, they may not be listening.

When teachers do not assess prerequisites, they seem to be subscribing to the theory that the way to teach is to open the empty heads of students and pour in the knowledge. But students' heads are not empty, and the new ideas will not automatically flow from the teacher's head into the students'.

Weigh the Dangers of Pretesting

Suppose you decide to find what students know before you teach. What are the tradeoffs to doing that? What will it cost you to pretest?

First, it takes time to find out what students know. In that time you could be explaining, demonstrating, and providing practice. If you are like most instructors, you have barely enough time to teach and test. But if you do find out what students know, you may realize that you need even more time, as well as materials and tutors, to adjust to students' prerequisites.

Second, it is difficult to assess students without making them feel dumb. Some people are hurt emotionally when they reflect on the results of tests that show their relative strengths and weaknesses. Some people are very sensitive about this issue.

Third, it is hard work to find out what students know and to adjust to those findings. Some instructors would rather not find out what their students know. They just teach what they want to teach and don't adapt at all. Suppose you find that some of your students have only partial understanding of a concept, such as "First Amendment Rights," on which you must build. Consider that some of your students have a distorted notion of a principle, such as supply and demand, that they must learn to apply. Imagine that some of your students have never heard of facts such as those relating to the Boer War that you will use as an example. You know that in each of those cases, if you gallop ahead, you will be leaving those students behind in the dust. You feel compelled to do something about it, and that takes work.

Fourth, it is sometimes difficult, and often time-consuming, to analyze the prerequisites of a course. Consider how many ideas you may teach in a single lesson. How many unknown concepts like the "frasm" are embedded in that lesson? Think about just the crucial ideas. How long might it take to analyze those ideas to find the hidden "spliks" and "reebs"?

Fifth, the purpose of assessing prerequisites is to find accurate ideas on which to build, as well as deviations from expert knowledge. It is tempting to look only at errors and overlook the accurate knowledge that a student demonstrates. Once in an airport, I overheard a woman say to a companion, ". . . and we had prunes. You know what prunes are, don't you? Prunes are plums that you have cooked up. First, they are plums and after you cook 'em, they're prunes." Of course I said nothing aloud, but I focused only on what I considered to be an error and said to myself, "What! Boy, that's completely off base." I didn't consider the accurate elements. If by the terms *plum* and *prune* she was referring to the same fresh fruit that I know as a plum and its dried version I know as a prune, then by her comment I might conclude that she knew (a) plums and prunes are related, (b) prunes were once plums, and (c) plums undergo a process to make them prunes. It seemed that the only erroneous element was the process: cooking instead of drying. She knew a lot more than I first gave her credit for. If I were her teacher, I would have the task of building on what she knew and helping her refine the idea she had about the process of changing a plum to a prune.

Finally, if you pretest but do nothing with your findings, you may gain little in student learning and lose time and credibility. If you pretest, you have to be prepared to do something about your findings.

The Pretesting Dilemma
1. If you don't pretest,
    a. students may not achieve the objective.
    b. students may become frustrated and angry.
    c. you may have to reteach after inadequate performance on assignments and tests.
    d. students may be bored.
2. If you do pretest,
    a. you use time for explaining, demonstrating, and providing practice.
    b. students may feel dumb because of their showing on the pretest.
    c. you may have to work hard to find out what students know.
    d. you may have to spend time analyzing the prerequisites of the course.
    e. you may focus only on what students don't know.
    f. you will have to be prepared to do something about the findings.

Pretest Safely and Efficiently

If you have weighed the advantages and disadvantages and have decided to pretest, you must begin to think about testing safely and efficiently (Yelon, 1985).

Pretest Formally or Informally, but in a Nonthreatening Way.   You may be able to pretest in a formal way, such as the nurse educator who gave his student nurse practitioners a short, written, formal pretest about the location of organs in the thorax. He did so just before teaching them how to do a clinical assessment of the midsection. You may remember teachers who began a formal pretest by saying something of the sort, "Now we'll find out who is well prepared

in anatomy; who belongs here and who doesn't; who has done what they should and who hasn't." Many students remember such statements and the associated embarrassment. To prevent these consequences, assess prerequisites in a non-threatening manner and phrase your questions accordingly.

Compare choices *a* and *b* in each of the questions that follow. Which do you think would be less threatening?

    a. Here's a situation. Tell me what you would do.
    b. Here's a situation. How do people do this?
    a. What do you mean by _____ ?
    b. What do people believe _____ means?

If you asked your students "What would *you* do?" and your students were wrong, *they* would look foolish. But if you asked your students "How do *people* do this?" and they were wrong, they wouldn't necessarily look foolish because they were just reporting what other people do. Now look at these questions. Are they threatening?

    Have you ever heard of _____ ? What did you hear?
    Here is a list of topics. What did you hear?
    What questions do you have about _____ ?

Maybe not. If you didn't hear the right thing or have questions, who can blame you?

I know teachers who use true-false statements gently to assess their students' prerequisites as they proceed through a presentation. They will introduce a section with a true-false question such as "True or false: It is best to study with no distractions, sight or sound." If students give the correct answer, then the teachers give students the short version of that segment. If students give the wrong answer, then they give them the full version of that part of the lesson. Some teachers outline whole presentations using questions.

Sometimes the time and place of pretesting are what makes it more or less threatening. Pretesting in informal circumstances reduces its threat. When they can, some teachers will meet for coffee or lunch with students before or during a course. In casual discussion they can learn a good deal about their students' ideas. A medical educator, Bill Anderson, calls physicians who are going to be in his courses and completes a simple assessment on the phone. When he is able, at the request of his potential students, he observes them perform.

On the questionnaire at the start of each course that asks for demographics, I add questions about prerequisites. Then, during the course, I organize "talk sessions" or group office hours in which I encourage students to ask and answer questions about what we have done. But I also take the opportunity to ask questions and encourage them to ask questions to assess what they know about the next unit. I do the same thing when I come early to class.

Pretesting in a nonthreatening manner does not imply testing in an invalid manner. Do not use a pretest question such as, "Do you know how to insert an intravenous needle?" Even when students do not know the answer, it is too tempting to say, "Sure I know how!" There are too many reinforcing consequences: the student is off the hook; the student is not embarrassed; the teacher is satisfied and doesn't bother the student anymore. And nobody knows the difference until the instruction builds on that knowledge or until the student is accountable.

Instead, ask students to give you evidence that they know the idea or skill. Have them show you the skill. If it is not possible or it is too dangerous for you to have the students demonstrate the skill, then look for an approximation to the skilled performance. A student should give reasonable evidence of understanding, such as explaining the steps of the skill in detail. (Note how this approach is used in the top-down strategy discussed below.)

Use an Efficient Pretest Strategy.   Pretesting will take time and energy that could be used for other purposes. The idea is to gain a proportional amount of useful information for the time you and your students spend pretesting. There are four strategies that you may consider.

1. Pretest When You Need the Information.   I could suggest simply that you pretest in a timely fashion, but there is a conflict about the purpose of timely pretesting that makes it a bit more complicated. One side of the conflict argues to pretest just before you are ready to teach, so the ideas assessed will be fresh in the students' minds and aid their learning. The other side argues to test in advance of teaching so that you may better adjust your plans to meet students' needs. One solution is to divide the instruction into units, separated by enough time to make adjustments in design. Pretest at the end of one unit for the next, leaving some time to make adjustments. If you do pretest before a course or at the start of a course, you will probably have to review the relevant prerequisites before each unit.

2. Test Top-Down.   If you suspect that you have some students who know how to do the task now, you can test top-down, assessing your students' ability to do the task to be learned. *Warning!* A top-down pretest is potentially dangerous. Imagine someone saying, "OK, let's see what you know about driving a tank. Hop right in." Because pretesting should be safe as well as efficient for students, do top-down testing when the task is not dangerous, or ask a series of questions to filter out students who don't know the task well enough to attempt the total performance safely.

> ***A Series of Questions to Avoid the***
> ***Dangers of Top-Down Pretesting***
> **1.** Here's a situation. Can you do this? (If yes, go on.)
>   "Can you fly a plane?"
> **2.** Here's a situation. Tell me what you would do. (If satisfactory, go on.)
>   "Suppose you wanted to turn, what would you do?"

3. Watch this performance. What was good? What was not? (If OK, go on.)
   "Watch how I descend toward the airport. Give me a critique."
4. Here's a simulated situation. Show what you do. (If OK, go on.)
   "Pretend we were given new coordinates. Show me what you would do."
5. Here's a real situation. Show what you do.
   "We have new coordinates. Show me what to do."

In analyzing the results of a top-down pretest, you can use your task description and task analysis to diagnose errors and misconceptions.

3. Test Bottom-Up.   If you have no clue as to what your students know, you could test bottom-up, working from the most basic ideas to the most advanced. Do this also if the ideas you are testing are critical to the task, and if these ideas will be useful for learning other tasks. Of course, bottom-up pretesting will take considerable time and effort, not only to make the pretest, but also to administer and score it.

4. Focus Your Pretest.   If you suspect that students know certain critical ideas but not others, focus your pretest by testing only for ideas you think they have and lack. That would be most efficient; it would be relatively quick and easy and worth the time spent considering the information gained. For example, a police trainer I know hesitated for years to give a pretest to his students to check their knowledge of the law. He didn't have time to develop the pretest, so he kept teaching ideas he suspected that his students knew. Finally he had some time to make a pretest consisting of the most important laws his recruits had to know, and he administered it. Using what he learned, he was able to save about 4 hours of valuable training time. He found that the saving of one-half day's training time was worth the time he invested in a focused pretest.

GUIDELINE 3: ADJUST INSTRUCTION TO ACCOUNT FOR ANALYZED PREREQUISITES AND STUDENTS' KNOWLEDGE

Once you have scored the pretest, you will need a strategy to respond to the results. Through use of each of the strategies, you will help students shape, refine, develop, and redirect existing ideas so they gradually become clearer, more elegant, and more functional.

Choose Appropriate Strategies to Adjust to Differences among Students

Choose an appropriate combination of strategies to deal with the individual differences you find. There are six strategies to deal with *individual differences:*

1. *Self Care.* Direct students toward resources, so they can bring themselves up to par to learn from whole-group instruction.
2. *Individual Care.* Work with individual students, helping them refine their ideas and work toward the learning objective.
3. *Small-Group Direct Instruction.* Form small groups of six to ten students who have similar ideas, gaps, and misconceptions and teach them by direct instruction.
4. *Facilitated Small-Group Learning.* Form small groups of students who have similar ideas, gaps, and misconceptions and have students discover methods to approach the task to be learned from their peers' responses.
5. *Review by Whole-Class Instruction.* With the whole class, review the most essential prerequisites and then move on to explain new ideas.
6. *Counseling to Other Resources.* Advise students to use other learning opportunities.

You may combine any of these strategies, and you may adjust to differences all at once or as needed. Table 3.2 outlines when to use each of these strategies based on the range of knowledge in the class, the context of instruction, the resources available, the ratio of students to resources, and the nature of the content. Refer to the table as you read the text explanations of each strategy. Simply read across the table. For example, the strategy of self-care is appropriate when you find that your whole class misunderstands a few key ideas, when you are only moderately committed to getting every student to achieve the goal, when your students can take care of their own studies, when you are quite limited in your resources, and when the goal is important but possible to achieve because it is simple, safe, and routine.

Use the Six Strategies to Adjust to Student Differences

This process of using various strategies to adjust to what your students know is an example of considering and accommodating *individual differences.*

1. Use Self-Care.   You might think that self-care is no care: no careful analysis of prerequisites, no pretesting, and no adjustment to prerequisites. The teacher makes a guess about where to start and moves on.

In contrast, the self-care strategy is based on careful analysis and pretesting of prerequisites. You direct students toward resources that they can use to bring themselves up to par on prerequisites. Use this strategy when you find that

1. students lack only a few ideas or have a few misunderstandings closely related to the ideas to be learned.
2. students know how to and are willing to refine any misconceptions on their own.
3. the subject is not overly complex and is based on accessible, authoritative sources so there is a good chance your students will be

TABLE 3.2 Choose the strategy to adjust to prerequisites you find

Adjustment Strategy	Range of Present Knowledge in Class	Context of Instruction	Resources Available	Ratio of Students to Resources	Nature of Content
Self-Care	Students in the whole class lack or misunderstand a few key ideas.	Moderate commitment to all students achieving. Your students can take responsibility to study on their own.	You have one teacher and one room.	You have many students and few resources.	Simple, safe, but important goal. One way to do this task. Students' present ideas are close to the goal.
Individual Care	A wide range of knowledge in the whole class.	High commitment to all students achieving. Your students can take responsibility to study on their own.	You have many staff monitors and tutors. You have individualized materials. You have space for media labs and tutorials.	You have few students and many resources.	Complex, important, and possibly dangerous goal. One or more ways to do the task. Some students' present ideas are close to goal, some are not. Subject matter does not change much.
Small-Group Direct Instruction	Groups of students with similar knowledge.	High commitment to all students achieving. Students are not concerned about being separated into groups.	You have staff to teach each group. You have materials for each group. You have space for each group by level or type of knowledge.	You have a moderate amount of students and moderate resources.	Complex, important, and possibly dangerous goal. One way to do this task. Some students' present ideas are close to goal, some are not.

Facilitated Small-Group Learning	Groups of students with similar knowledge.	High commitment to all students achieving. Students are not concerned about showing their ideas and being challenged.	Excellent facilitator. Well-chosen group activities. You have considerable time for instruction.	You have many students and few resources.	Complex, important, but not dangerous goal. Many ways to perform this task. Students' present ideas are close to goal. Part of the goal is understanding from personal discovery and learning to learn.
Review by Whole-Class Instruction	Students misunderstand or lack a few key ideas.	Medium commitment to all students achieving. Capable independent learners.	Excellent instructor. Accurate specification and testing of present knowledge.	You have many students and few resources.	Moderately complex, important, but not dangerous goal. Students' present ideas are close to the goal.
Counseling to Other Resources	Widely varying differences among students.	High commitment to all students achieving.	There are classes preceding and following this class.	You have many students and few resources.	Complex, important goal. Goal far from some students. Goal far surpassed by some students.

SOURCE: Yelon, S. L. (1985). Making decisions about pretesting: It's not a simple matter. *Performance and Instruction, 24*(9), 12–14. Reprinted with the permission of the National Society for Performance and Instruction, copyright © 1985.

able to gain the ground they need independently and without becoming overwhelmed.

4. the subject is not dangerous (i.e., if your students do not master an essential prerequisite on their own, there is likely to be little harm during practice).

5. you have to cope with few resources for the number of students you must serve.

USING SELF-CARE

Imagine that you have to plan a whole college curriculum. You have several constraints, such as students of all ages and spread all over the country, and no campus. You will have to do most of your teaching via correspondence. You will have a little help from radio and television, supplemented by a summer school. Talk about problems of handling individual differences! This is a small part of the true story of the Open University in Britain (Lewis, 1973).

Part of every correspondence unit was a page of prerequisite ideas, both concepts and principles, that looked something like this:

Assumed from General Knowledge	Introduced in a Previous Unit	Unit No.	Developed in This Unit	Page No.	Developed in a Later Unit	Unit No.
Natural gas	Periodic	7.8	Polarization	9	Carbohydrate	13
Flint quartz	table		Valence	12	Protein	13
Melting	Covalent	8	shell		Polysaccharides	13
point	and ionic		Structural	15	Enzymes	15
Boiling	compounds		isomers		Polymers	13
point	Electronic	7	Double,			
etc.	structure		triple,			
	etc.		and			
			multiple			
			bonds			
			etc.			

Students were responsible for using their encyclopedias and dictionaries to find the ideas listed in the first column. They were also responsible for looking back at the ideas introduced in previous units. They were alerted to ideas introduced in this unit and ideas mentioned here, but developed later. The students at Open University did well, in part because they were directed toward the prerequisites that they needed to learn and review.

2. Employ Individual Care   When you provide individual care, you adjust the content, pace, and even the mode of instruction to each student according to his or her prerequisites. One way to provide individual care is with self-contained teaching modules. You could provide modules in the form of text: ordinary prose, prose organized into charts and diagrams for quick and easy reading, or programmed text with explanations and built-in activities. You could also base your modules on audiotape, videotape, computer, or interactive video. You could provide individualized modules as independent work or homework; you could assign them as "seatwork" in the classroom or in the lab. A self-contained module is a good idea if the content is not likely to change much over time, if you have the time and money for development, and if the students are responsible enough to carry on with the self-instruction.

USING INDIVIDUAL CARE

An excellent example of an individualized approach is a soil science teaching lab I observed. A student entered the lab and requested a unit from the lab supervisor. The student sat down and viewed a mediated presentation—slide tape, videotape, or interactive video. Based on what she learned in the unit, she went to the side of the room and used the chemicals provided to test soil samples. Finally, she checked the results with the lab supervisor. Because she was correct, she proceeded to another unit. Some students finished the course in weeks, some in months, depending on where they started the sequence and how fast they were able to go.

The most powerful way to provide individual care is to tutor each student. You, an assistant, or a peer could be the tutor. Use a tutorial when you have a wide range of student knowledge in the class and an important, consequential objective. You will be able to do this when you have enough trained staff to be tutors for your students, and when you have adequate materials for tutors to use. You can make small contributions to individual care by coming early to class and asking and answering questions about prerequisites or having a specific time before a lesson when students can E-mail or call with questions.

3. *Provide Small-Group Direct Instruction.* You may want to group students whose prerequisite knowledge and skills are approximately the same. Anyone who has taught a technical class, like the applications of computer software, realizes the need for groups. In any computer class you may note that one group in the class is typing away doing what they were shown; another group is sitting at the console weeping over their lack of understanding; and another group is anticipating what you will say next and repairing the machine in their spare time. Most people in these circumstances realize that they need to group students into beginning, intermediate, and advanced classes. Of course, for each group you need instructors, materials, time, and class space. The students must be assured about the purpose and the meaning of being grouped. Anticipate and discuss with students any possible negative connotations of being in the "beginners" group.

4. *Apply Facilitated Small-Group Learning.* You may want to have students help one another learn just as it is done naturally in good study groups. Use this approach when you are teaching relatively safe skills that can be done in more than one way, and when you want students to learn how to learn from their own experience. You do so by arranging an activity that requires the task to be learned. The task should be the next logical objective, considering the students' prerequisites.

USING FACILTATED SMALL-GROUP LEARNING

For students who knew addition and were learning multiplication, the teacher set a realistic activity of finding out how much money they would have by the end of vacation if they got $4.25 per hour and worked 150 hours. She asked her students to solve the problem independently and be ready to explain how they did it. She chose some students to demonstrate and explain their solution, answer questions, and argue their approaches. When a student was explaining his or her solution, the teacher encouraged those listening to ask questions and help clarify the approach. She used excellent facilitative skills: She was able to find interesting solutions among the ones produced independently; she promoted discussion; and she kept quiet about her solution. She also allotted considerable time.

5. Review by Whole-Class Instruction.   A review is relatively simple and greatly underestimated. The approach is to explain the most important prerequisites to the whole group. A good review can prevent holding students back from learning something of interest to them because of some suspected lack of prerequisites.

USING WHOLE-GROUP REVIEW

Bloom (1984) reports a study by one of his students in which teachers in a second-term algebra class and a second-term French class reviewed carefully and selected prerequisites for an experimental group. On common mastery exams, 80 percent of the students in the experimental group exceeded 50 percent of the students in the control group. Bloom asserted that review of prerequisites was one of the most influential factors in instruction.

You could provide a review just preceding an explanation of new ideas. To do so, note the most influential prerequisites that will be needed by students to understand your explanation. During the explanation, just before you are about to use one of those ideas, ask a question to see if students understand the idea well enough to proceed. Be ready to explain and illustrate the idea if students do not know it. Then, after explaining the idea, ask the question again to be sure you can go ahead.

You could also review at the start of a lesson or at the end of a previous lesson, or conduct a special preparation session before an important class. For example, instead of holding a typical recitation section during which the leader reviews what has been said in an explanation, consider a session before the explanation to reveal what will be said. You could ask students to read a piece outside of class before a lesson, or you could give students self-checking tests with sources to learn what they lack or misunderstand.

> ### THE NEED FOR A WHOLE-CLASS REVIEW
>
> Once I was observing a class where the teacher was talking about nematodes. When the class was through I asked one of the students near me what a nematode is. He looked at me quizzically and said, "A toad named Nemo?" When the student went to the lab and saw examples of nematodes, he understood. "Oh I see, a nematode is a grub like the kind that eats my peach tree." Had the teacher sequenced the lesson so that the lab preceded the lecture, the student may have gained more from the lecture. In sequencing your lessons, consider what ideas might be better learned first in order to understand others.

6. Counsel to Other Resources.   Counsel students who are so far from the objectives that, given your resources, you are unable to help them finish successfully, and talk to students who already have achieved the objectives. Refer them to classes preparatory to and continuing from your class. Be sure to base your recommendations on good evidence.

A FINAL WORD

Here we are again in the process of *continuous assessment.* In addition to finding out students' interests before a segment of instruction, you also find out what they know by pretesting. Then you adjust your instruction to acccommodate what you find. You will follow that pattern again as you provide feedback for practice and as you respond to student test performance. Look for more on the process of assessment in chapters 4, 5, 9, and 11.

How should you accommodate differences in your students' prerequisites? Analyze the tasks you are teaching for their prerequisites, find out what your students know, and adjust your teaching using a systematic strategy. Consider the range of knowledge in the class, the context of instruction, the resources available, the ratio of students to resources, and the nature of the content. Then choose the most appropriate strategy: self-care, individual care, small-group direct instruction, facilitated small-group learning, review by whole-class instruction, or counseling to other resources. By doing so you will trade incomplete learning, bored students, and confused students for students who make solid progress toward competence.

ACTIVITIES

These activities will take you through the process of describing what is to be learned, deriving the essential content, pretesting, and adjusting the instruction to the pretest results. Whether you do each step individually, with a partner, or in a small group, write out your responses so you can use the results of each activity in the next one.

1. Describe a physical task and a mental task.
   a. Choose a physical skill that you might teach, such as how to print a document using a computer, how to measure with a ruler, or how to arrange the equipment for an experiment. Create a step-by-step task description either as an outline or as a flow diagram. Test your task description to assess whether a person can perform properly.
   b. Choose a thinking skill such as finding the main idea in a paragraph, solving a math story problem, creating a plan to make a product, finding and stating the point of a story, identifying an example of a concept, applying a principle to explain a case, inferring the cause of an event, predicting an event, or writing a paragraph. Create a step-by-step task description either as an outline or as a flow diagram. Test this one, too. What was the same and what was different about describing the two tasks?

2. Analyze critical steps of the tasks you described for their component prerequisites. Look for and list *subskills* (a series of steps to do), *rules* (commands to be followed), *principles* (relationships among factors to apply), *facts* (statements to recall describing or defining people, places, things, events, behaviors, processes, in the past or present), *concepts* (categories of experience to identify bounded by a definition), and *attitudes* (a willingness to act a certain way).

3. Choose the essential prerequisites. Look over the content list and circle those that a student must absolutely learn to be able to do this task.

4. Choose one important rule, fact, concept, principle, or attitude from the essential prerequisites. Express the idea fully in a definition or proposition. Then list all of the *concepts* hidden in the definition. Indicate which of these concepts students must know to understand the defined idea.

5. State how and when you might pretest for the essential ideas or skills you have listed. State your arguments for and against using this particular pretest.

6. Suppose you had pretested and found some students who knew all of what they needed of the essential prerequisites, some who had a few ideas, and some who had none. Describe a specific situation, then state specifically what you would do.

7. Which of the following techniques to adjust to students' prerequisites have you used or observed: self-care, individual care, small-group direct instruction, facilitated small-group learning, review by whole-class instruction, counseling to other resources? How successful was each technique? How did each approach accommodate individual differences? How well did each take into account the students' feelings?

8. Suppose you were teaching students how to use computers. Some students have considerable experience in using computers, some know the basics, and some don't know how to turn on one. What would you do to help each student gain from your course?

9. Reflection
   a. How can I present at my students' level so they are ready to learn?
   b. How can I find out what my students know at the start in a way worth the time to do it?
   c. How can I remedy the lack of prerequisites?
   d. How can I help students assess themselves and remedy their deficiencies?

FURTHER READING

Anderson, R. (1984). Role of the reader's schema in comprehension, learning, and memory. In R. Anderson, J. Osborn, & R. Tierney (Eds.), *Learning to read in American schools: Basal readers and content texts* (pp. 243–257). Hillsdale, NJ: Lawrence Erlbaum. (*Note:* This chapter explores how prerequisites contribute to learning.)

Bransford, J. D. (1984). Schema activation and schema acquisition: Comments on Richard C. Anderson's remarks. In R. Anderson, J. Osborn, & R. Tierney (Eds.), *Learning to read in American schools: Basal readers and content texts* (pp. 259–272). Hillsdale, NJ: Lawrence Erlbaum.

Farnam-Diggory, S. (1994). Paradigms of knowledge and instruction. *Review of Educational Research, 64*(3), 463–477. (*Note:* The author asserts a knowledge typology based on contemporary cognitive psychology as well as experimental paradigms that resemble facts, concepts, principles, skills, and images. See what you think.)

Gagné, R. M. (1985). *The conditions of learning and theory of instruction.* New York: Holt, Rinehart & Winston. (*Note:* Gagné offers ideas about internal conditions and several types of learning contributing to a task.)

Lienhardt, G. (1992, April). Research on learning tells us about teaching. *Educational Leadership, 49,* 20–25. (*Note:* Worthy of special attention are the sections on multiple kinds of knowledge and prior knowledge and their implications for instruction.)

Resnick, L. B. (1987). Constructing knowledge in school. In L. S. Liben (Ed.), *Development and learning: Conflict or congruence?* (pp. 19–50). Hillsdale, NJ: Lawrence Erlbaum.

Smith, J. P., diSessa, A. A., & Roschelle, J. (1993). Misconceptions reconceived: A constructivist analysis of knowledge in transition. *Journal of the Learning Sciences, 3,* 115–163.

Von Glaserfeld, E. (1987). Learning as a constructive activity. In C. Janvier (Ed.), *Problems of representation in the teaching and learning of mathematics* (pp. 3–17). Hillsdale, NJ: Lawrence Erlbaum.

Vygotsky, L. S. (1978). *Mind in society.* Cambridge, MA: Harvard University Press. (*Note:* Vygotsky explores his idea of the "zone of proximal development" and how it relates to prerequisites.)

chapter 4

Open Communication

OVERVIEW

Give students access to the information they need to be able to learn efficiently. Listen to students to improve your instruction.

Guideline 1: Orient Students
        Provide Objectives
        Provide Sample Test Items
        Provide Sample Final Products
        Provide an Overview
        Provide an Agenda
        Provide a Complete Package of Course Materials

Guideline 2: Provide Feedback to Students
        Respond to Students' Performance
        Respond to Students' Questions
        Respond to Students' Attitudes

Guideline 3: Respond to Students' Feedback to You
        Decide What Information You Want
        Decide on the Means for Data Collection and Write
            Questions
        Collect the Information after an Appropriate Unit
        Tally the Information
        Make Decisions for Change
        Report Back to Students
        Implement Changes

How many times have you been involved in a class where the teacher plays the game of "guess what's going to be on the test"? It goes like this: A teacher makes the announcement that there will be a test soon. As soon as the announcement is made, students raise their hands. "Can you tell us what will be on the test?" The teacher answers, "No."

You can recognize a class where the students have no idea of what to expect. The teacher walks in, approaches the desk, and says, "Good morning." And the students write it down. The teacher talks for a while. "The main concept of the position of the. . . ." The students madly write every word, fearing they might miss something that might appear on the test. As soon as the teacher leaves the desk to give an example or elaborate on a point, the students stop writing. They lean back, put their pens down, and form a glazed expression on their faces. The teacher talks on, and the students remain frozen. As the teacher swivels and turns toward the desk, a small light of alertness appears on the students' faces. The teacher takes one step toward the desk, and the students lean forward. The teacher moves a bit closer, and the students raise their pens. The teacher approaches the desk; the pens are poised. Just as the teacher reaches the desk, the pens hit the paper and the students madly write every word.

Then, when the teacher writes something on the board, the students write that down. When the teacher smiles about a point, they have to write that down; that's important. And if, heaven forbid, the teacher says, "There are four major points here. . . ." Oh, my goodness, sounds like a possible multiple-choice test question. Better write that down, too.

As you can see, most students have developed a keen lack of trust based on their experience of not being told what to expect. To counter this attitude, strive to establish and maintain open communication between you and your students. Ensure that your students know everything that will help them direct their attention as they learn. Tell your students what they are to learn and how they will be evaluated (Ausubel, 1980; Bloom, Engelhart, Furst, Hill, & Krathwohl, 1956; Davis, Alexander, & Yelon, 1974; Gagné & Driscoll, 1988; Mager, 1962; Yelon & Scott, 1970). The only exceptions are some cases such as concept or principle learning, where you do not reveal the precise test questions or the exact nature of test conditions. More about this later. Generally, *open communication* implies that you allow students access to all information they need for learning, or tell students everything they need for learning that they cannot provide for themselves.

GUIDELINE 1: ORIENT STUDENTS

What is the most critical information your students need at the start of a new learning segment? They need to know what they are required to do on the "test" and how well they will have to perform, what the main ideas are, how those ideas are organized, and the nature and length of each instructional event. There are six techniques to help orient students: provide objectives, sample test items, sample final products, an overview, an agenda, and a complete package of course materials.

Provide Objectives

At the beginning of instruction, students like to know what is to be expected of them. You can simply tell your students how they must be able to perform at the end of instruction, or you can help them to find out and decide for themselves by referring them to appropriate sources. Whichever approach you use, students need to know exactly how they, as graduates, will be required to perform after the course and how they will be tested at the end of the course. The description of the graduate's performance is the instructional *goal.* The description of the student's performance on the final exam is the instructional *objective.*

To form an objective, you or your students first derive the goal. When you form the objective, you ask: What do people in the real world have to do to show that they know this idea or skill? Then you ask: What is the best simulation of the real-world performance that you can create within the constraints of the instructional environment? Next you ask: How could you check a student's progress toward that performance at the end of instruction? When students form the objective, they ask the same questions of their sources.

In essence, when you specify an objective, you describe the test. Note that *test* refers not only to pencil-and-paper exams, but also to any measure of real-world performance that you can employ. For the test to be valid, you need to vary it according to the type of knowledge you require.

Describe the Test.   If you follow the general guideline of ensuring that students know what they must do on the final exam, you will enable them to focus their learning. Please remember that a test is not necessarily written; it could be a skilled performance in a real setting. In any case, think about what your students would like to know about the test. Tell them or have them state exactly what they will be doing on the test, what standards will be used to judge their responses, and what the criteria are for passing the test. Tell them or have them state what they will be given to work on and work with during the test and what they will be restricted from using (Mager, 1962; Yelon, 1991; Yelon & Scott, 1970). Each of the following four examples has all the essential components of a test; each could have been written by a teacher or composed by students to guide their own study.

> ***Parts of a Test***
> 1. Test conditions
>   a. What students will be given to work on
>   b. What they will be given to work with
>   c. What they will be restricted from using (if appropriate)

2. Test behavior
   a. What exactly they will be doing on the test
3. Test criterion
   a. What standards you will use to judge their responses
4. Test lower limits
   a. What the cutoff for passing the test is

Note in the following examples that the objective behaviors are always expressed as observable actions. By using these words, called *behavioral terms,* you can clearly state how you expect students to demonstrate the achievement of the goal. (Behavioral terms appear in italics in each example.)

SAMPLE GOAL AND OBJECTIVE: EXAMPLE 1

Goal	Graduates working in an automobile manufacting plant will accurately predict parts needed for just-in-time manufacturing.
Objective	
Conditions	Given written problems calling for the calculation of the number of parts needed to have on hand for manufacture; using the present parts inventory and manufacturing schedule, and a computer program called "Schedule"; without consulting with colleagues and within one work day—
Behavior	*write* a report noting the number of parts needed over the next quarter;
Criterion	according to the standard formula, and done within one work day;
Lower limits	for one set of data, with a margin of error of 20 parts.

SAMPLE GOAL AND OBJECTIVE: EXAMPLE 2

Goal	Graduates working as supervisors will assess their staff accurately.
Objective	
Conditions	Given a videotaped case of a worker performing tasks on the job, using a word processor and a list of company policies and requirements; without reviewing the videotape a second time—
Behavior	*write* an assessment of the worker and *state aloud* a summary of the assessment as if talking to the worker,
Criterion	according to the report checklist of points and qualities,

Lower limits   with no more than three deviations from the checklist in each of two cases.

SAMPLE GOAL AND OBJECTIVE: EXAMPLE 3

Goal   Graduates working as lawyers will give sound advice on contracts.

Objective

Conditions   Given a live simulated client who asks for advice about a contract, using any texts on contracts, without any restrictions—

Behavior   *state aloud* your advice about additions, deletions, and corrections that need to be made to the contract;

Criterion   according to relevant statutes and case law, so well that the client can explain what you intend to do with the contract, in one-half hour;

Lower limits   for four clients, with no errors in applications of the laws, and with only one deviation in each client's understanding.

SAMPLE GOAL AND OBJECTIVE: EXAMPLE 4

Goal   Graduates working as museum docents in a twentieth-century exhibit dealing with Michigan's role in World War II will be able to answer questions about the exhibit accurately.

Objective

Conditions   Given oral questions about any part of the exhibit of Michigan's role in World War II, using only the exhibits present, with no aids—

Behavior   *state aloud* the most accurate factual answer,

Criterion   according to the docent's guide "Facts and Figures of Michigan's Role in World War II,"

Lower limits   answering at least 80 percent of 20 questions correctly.

Depending on when you are informing students of requirements, you may tell them the goal, the whole objective, or part of the objective. Early in instruction you may tell students what they will be asked to do in the real world when they graduate and, perhaps, the behavior. Later, as needed, you may add the conditions and criteria. When students form their own objectives from sources you provide, they will probably progress from general to specific as clarification is needed.

Describing the test is another part of continuous assessment. You or your students have to figure out what they are to do on a written test, or in an activity, or on a project to show they have learned. Only then can you and your students assess progress and know that they have reached their destination.

Vary Tests and Objectives for Types of Knowledge.   There should be a "truth in teaching" law. Often instructors tell their students that they will be teaching concepts, principles, and skills, and these are what students expect to learn and be tested on. A teacher may say, for example, "I teach concepts of biology," "I teach principles of psychology," or "I teach skills of science." Yet when you inspect their tests, you find questions like these:

> List the stages in the frog's life cycle.
>
> Define positive reinforcement.
>
> State the steps for making a gel.

These questions indicate that, contrary to the teacher's pronouncements and students' expectations, the teacher is actually teaching facts, for that is what he or she is testing. After the first test, you can be sure that facts are what the students will learn. If you wish to direct your students to learn more than recall of propositions, then you must test for concepts, principles, and skills and tell your students what you are doing (Gagné, 1985). Use Table 4.1 to decide how to tell to your students what you want them to learn, and how you will test for that. In a similar fashion, if you are guiding your students to form their own objectives, be sure their objectives match their intentions. It is easy for students to fall into the same trap of forming objectives that refer only to facts.

Objectives, authored by a teacher or students or both, describe the "test." As you will see in chapter 11, if that test is an authentic assessment of performance in situations outside of instruction, students are more likely to use what they have learned. If students also see the objective and the test described as connected meaningfully to their experience, interests, or aspirations, then they are likely to want to pursue that objective. But students can't get excited about a goal unless they understand it.

Provide Sample Test Items

There are several other ways of informing students about course requirements. You can simply show samples of the test items, the cases, or the questions. You can provide a practice test to be worked on at home that is a variation of the final test.

Wait a minute! Isn't telling the students what's on the exam unethical? Isn't that making the subject so easy as to be considered spoon-feeding? Won't it narrow the students' focus so that they study and learn only what's on the test?

No, it is perfectly justifiable. Suppose that for good reason we want our students simply to recall some facts. For example, imagine that we want our students to be able to spell the 100 spelling demons in the English language or to recall the names of all parts of the brain. It doesn't seem unethical

TABLE 4.1 What to tell students about the test for different types of ideas

Type of Idea	Intent	What to Say about the Test	Example of the Test
Fact	Recall ideas.	You will state or write from memory, this group of facts ____ without aid, based on this authority ____ .	Write from memory the effects of all modern pesticides without aid, based on the text.
Concept	Recognize objects, events, or relations.	You will identify new examples among nonexamples of this category ____ based on this definition ____ .	Identify, from the new specimens given, examples of healthy plants, according to this definition of a healthy plant ____.
Principle	Predict or explain; infer cause.	You will be given a; new event to observe; you will explain or predict, or infer cause based on this principle definition ____ .	Here is a new case of a farmer treating crops. Explain the farmer's actions and predict the health of the crops, and explain your prediction, according to plant growth principles.
Skill	Perform the task.	You will perform a skill at the time it's needed, according to process standards or product standards, based on checklists of steps and qualities, or parts and qualities.	Here are seeds. You may request other items. Plant and care for them according to the plant procedure development checklist, so that 80 percent of the plants produced match the healthy plant checklist.

to say to our students, "You must remember these facts. I promise you they will be on the test." Does it make the subject easier? I think not. Will it narrow their focus? Definitely. If that is the content we want them to learn and that is how we want them to display their knowledge, then we don't want them doing something else. If we do tell students that these facts are required, the chances are good that they will study them and remember them on the test.

The same would be true for skills. If we wanted our students to write essays defending a proposition according to a set standard, what would be wrong with telling them that they will have to do just that? I bet that they would practice writing essays defending propositions according to the standard we set, and perform well on the final test. However, I would not tell the students the topic to be given on the exam; I would say that the topic assigned would be like the ones we used for practice.

What if we were teaching concepts and we wanted our students to identify examples not seen before? Suppose, for example, we wanted our students to identify a good story. Imagine telling them that they will be given several short stories they have not seen and that they will have to pick the good one and justify their choice according to the definition discussed in class. We would add that the stories on the test will be similar to the ones we analyzed in class. Is there any problem with that? No, we wouldn't violate the intent of our test. Our students would generalize from their knowledge of the concept. We wouldn't reveal the stories actually given on the test, but would tell them everything else they needed to know. Given that information, to get ready, they would probably analyze every story they could find to prepare for the exam. Our statements would narrow their focus, and that is what we would want. We wouldn't want students spending time analyzing good sentences or paragraphs when they should be analyzing good stories.

The same procedure applies to using principles to solve problems in cases not seen before. If we wanted our students to solve new problems of motivation in instruction acccording to the principle of meaningfulness, we would tell them that they would be given new cases, like those used for practice, and they would have to state a solution. We would not reveal the actual cases to appear on the test, but we would tell them everything else about the types of cases so they could direct their study.

What if there isn't time to test all the ideas and skills? If it's worth teaching, then it's worth testing. If you teach critical skills and ideas, then you should test all of them and students should know that. If there are more skills, facts, concepts, or principles than you have time to test, then decide which ones are most important and tell your students that those will be tested.

USING PRACTICE TESTS

I provide my students with practice tests on concepts and principles. Some of the items are multiple choice and some are fill-in. The practice tests inform the students what is required while maintaining the validity of the test.

Practice Test Item: Which of the Following Is an Example of Behavioral Terms?
a. Create a sentence
b. Analyze a poem
c. Write a paragraph
d. Understand a question

I tell my students that they will get items like this on the test. The question will be exactly the same, but the choice of examples will not have been discussed in the materials, the practice, or the class. Here's an example of a related test item:

Test Item: Which of the Following Is an Example of Behavioral Terms?

a. State aloud a story
b. Solve a problem
c. Derive a formula
d. Comprehend a recipe

I expect my students to do very well on the test, and they do.

Students who are not accustomed to being told what is expected of them may not believe you. Before the first test, some students may ignore the objectives and skip the practice tests. They may study all the things you have not emphasized, thinking that the test will consist of trick questions. After the first test, the light dawns.

One of my students commented to me that telling students the requirements and giving practice tests eliminates the temptation to cheat. Instead of figuring out ways to cheat, students can spend the energy on mastering the material.

Provide Sample Final Products

If your students will be expected to demonstrate their learning by creating a product of a certain quality, you can inform them about the course requirements by showing them samples of the final product and pointing out features that make them acceptable. For example, I am learning to weave baskets. I notice that all of my instructors begin their classes by showing the basket that class members will learn to make and describing what makes the sample a good quality product. One instructor mentions how evenly spaced and straight the staves are on the demonstration basket. I keep those initial comments in mind all the time I am weaving, working hard to space the staves evenly and straightening them out as I am weaving.

To explain the parts and qualities of a good product you will need a *checklist*.

USING A CHECKLIST TO COMMUNICATE QUALITIES OF A FINAL PRODUCT

Have you ever tried to teach someone to write well? One of my students, Frank Cusmano, was trying to teach writing and having some difficulty. He would assign an essay; the students would do a lousy job; and then he would spend 30 to 40 minutes apiece giving feedback. Sometimes he had more to say than the students did. He decided to tell his students exactly what he wanted them to do in the form of an objective and a checklist. He gave his students a handout, which I paraphrase here (Yelon, 1984):

You will be given a choice of topics such as "It is impossible to be a real individualist in today's society." You will write an essay of 500–700 words that will defend a clear well-defined proposition according to this essay checklist:

Essay Checklist*
A. Check the opening paragraph
  1. Do you have a proposition which is
    a. in concrete terms?
    b. a complete thought?
  2. Does the paragraph have an attention getter?
  3. Is the proposition in your opening paragraph?
  4. Do you have a transition to the next paragraph?
  5. Have you presented a statement to explain your organization?
B. Check supporting paragraphs
  1. Do you have transitions to and from each paragraph?
  2. Does each paragraph support and explain the proposition?
  3. Do you have statements in each paragraph to show an organization consistent with the initial statement?
C. Check conclusion
  1. Does the conclusion tie all ideas together?
  2. Does the conclusion reinforce the central point?
D. Check grammar and spelling
  1. Did you check the spelling of words you are not sure of?
  2. Are your sentences complete (not run-ons or fragments)?
  3. Are correct words used for meaning in context?

How did he use this tool? He explained the objective and the checklist to his students. He explained each point on the checklist, giving an example and a nonexample of each. Then, right before their eyes, he developed a rough draft of an essay using his development steps. After some work on the draft, he introduced and projected a more complete draft of that essay. He analyzed the better draft of the essay point by point, according to the checklist. He divided his class into pairs of students and gave each pair an essay to judge by the criteria. They discussed their findings. Then he assigned an essay and told them to check their own work at home against the criteria.

When the students turned in their work, he discovered that these were the best student essays of this type he had ever seen. Instead of spending 30 to 40 minutes apiece giving feedback, he spent only 10 to 15 minutes. By telling students exactly what was required, he was being efficient as well as effective. Furthermore, from then on his students believed him when he told them what was required.

---

* From Yelon, S. L. (1984). How to use and create criterion checklists. *Performance and Instruction, 23*(3), 4. Reprinted with the permission of the National Society for Performance and Instruction, copyright © 1984.

Using a checklist, you can describe most precisely to your students what you will be looking for. Consider including the criteria from your checklists on the pages your students will use for written assignments. While doing their assignments, students can't help but pay attention to the standards for their written work. Give them completed models of the required written work on which you write notes explaining what makes each example a good one (Yelon & Reznich, 1991). Figure 4.1 is a model for writing an introductory paragraph.

Of course, students can create their own checklists or revise and enhance existing ones. This forces them to attend to what makes the required process or product one of quality.

Provide an Overview

Have you ever felt lost while studying a topic? Have you ever wondered, where are we? What does this idea have to do with the rest of the ideas in the unit? To enable your students to find their way and remain on track, present an overview of the content.

Let students in on the grand scheme of the instruction. Tell them what the main ideas are and how they fit together (Ausubel, 1980). Explain how the ideas relate to one another and to the requirements. If needed, you can even show them *how* to study the subject.

FIGURE 4.1   An introductory paragraph in an article

SOURCE: Yelon, S., & Reznich, C. (1991). Creating and using annotated examples. *Performance and Instruction, 30*(4), 27. Reprinted with the permission of the National Society for Performance and Instruction, copyright © 1991.

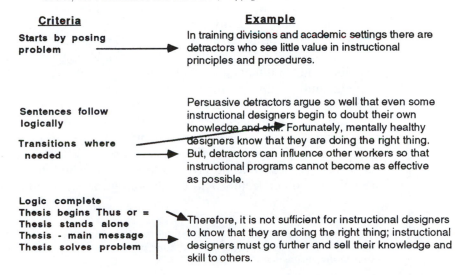

You can explain the main ideas verbally and provide a visual representation to show the organization. Use a diagram or an outline, but keep it simple (Yelon & Reznich, 1992).

A SIMPLE OUTLINE USED AS AN OVERVIEW*

Suppose you were teaching a fitness course. You could explain to your students, "There are two main parts to the course: creating fitness plans and implementing them. Here is an outline representing the main ideas and how they fit together."

Creating and Implementing Fitness Plans
I.   Creating fitness plans
    A. The base of your fitness plan: creating a healthy nutrition plan
    B. Three interrelated aspects of your fitness plan
        1. Increasing and maintaining strength
        2. Increasing and maintaining flexibility
        3. Increasing and maintaining cardiovascular conditioning
II. Implementing fitness plans
    A. Early implementation
        1. Integrating separate fitness plans for practical use
        2. Scheduling events
        3. Selecting equipment
    B. Later implementation
        1. Recording progress
        2. Adjusting schedules
        3. Maintaining motivation

"The two major topics, creating and implementing fitness plans, are of equal importance and scope but are sequenced in the order you use them. Nutrition, strength, flexibilty, and cardiovascular conditioning are related in a more complex fashion. You will need proper nutrition to maintain your strength, flexibility, and cardiovascular conditioning while your strength, flexibility, and conditioning also influence each other. For instance, you need strength and flexibility to do cardiovascular conditioning, but you need flexibility to do the exercises for strength and aerobic conditioning safely. The topics for implementing fitness plans are related by time. Early in implementation you integrate components of your separate fitness plans for practical use, then you schedule events and select equipment. As you follow plans, you record your progress, adjust your schedule on the basis of progress and other factors, and continuously maintain motivation.

---

* From Yelon, S., & Reznich, C. (1992). Visible models of course organization. *Performance and Instruction, 31*(6), 10. Reprinted with the permission of the National Society for Performance and Instruction, copyright © 1992.

"This is the order in which we will study fitness. You will create and implement your own fitness plan using each of the parts of the outline."

In the above scenario, you could also show the development of a real fitness plan and how each component fits into the overall scheme. If you taught a whole lesson at the start of a course as an overview, sometimes called an *epitome* (Reigeluth & Stein, 1983), you might have students apply what they learned from the overview. For example, you might ask the students to check existing fitness plans for the proper components or outline the major pieces of their own fitness plans.

You may supply an overview at the start of any segment of instruction. Although the fitness example you just read was for a course, you could provide an overview at the start of each unit in that course. For example, at the start of the nutrition unit you could explain the main nutrition ideas and how they fit together. And at the beginning of each nutrition lesson, such as a lesson on controlling fat in your diet, you could provide the major categories of fat and how they interrelate.

At the end of a course, each unit, and each lesson, you could use the same outline to summarize the major ideas and to integrate them with ideas from previous or future segments. You could present the visual structure as a guide and ask questions of the students to draw forth their own summary.

An overview need not be abstract. It could be an excellent example of the final product of the course, such as a completed fitness plan or a videotaped performance—a documentary of someone developing and implementing a plan. The students could take part in a simulation of the general process and make a plan on the spot; they could observe someone role-playing the fitness planning process, or listen to a testimonial of how someone made and used a plan. These would serve as concrete and common referents throughout the rest of the course.

Provide an Agenda

Are we there yet? On trips people like to know the route and how long it is likely to take. So too with an instructional journey. Be sure to tell students what will happen, when, and for how long. For example, a teacher I know provides a tentative calendar for each course and workshop that tells what students will do each period. When he presents the course calendar after an overview, the schedule makes good sense to the students because they see it as following the content structure. Each time the class meets, the teacher also posts an agenda announcing the topics of the day, such as where they are in the published course notes, any assignments that are due, or how to study for the upcoming test. He writes his daily agenda on a large sheet of paper, which he attaches to the classroom wall with masking tape, as shown in Figure 4.2. This way he wastes no time writing on the board and he has a record for the next time he teaches the course. By posting the daily agenda, he need not repeat its contents

```
┌─────────────────────────────────────────────────┐
│  Agenda CEP 808              Session 3            │
│                              Sept 15             │
│                              page in notes: 113  │
│  How to justify objectives                       │
│         explanation                              │
│         demonstration                            │
│         practice                                 │
│  Can we write complex objectives?                │
│  ───────────────────────────────                 │
│  Assignment 1: due next Monday                   │
│  Be sure to use format                           │
│  Do practice and project example                 │
│                                                  │
│  ───────────────────────────────                 │
│  Test 1 following Monday                          │
│  Check yourself on the practice test             │
│  ───────────────────────────────                 │
│  Contact teacher for second project              │
│  ───────────────────────────────                 │
│  Today's Saying: Teach students not just         │
│  what is in "the book;" teach them what          │
│  they can use in the real world.                 │
└─────────────────────────────────────────────────┘
```

FIGURE 4.2 A typical agenda

for students who straggle in late. He also has a record of the announcements he has made in case anyone claims never to have heard of an assignment change. Some other teachers use weekly newsletters or computer conferencing for the same purpose.

Can students help determine the course overview and the agenda? Of course. With proper guidance, students and teachers can collaborate on the main ideas and structure of the course and its schedule.

Provide a Complete Package of Course Materials

Open communication implies that you either provide the information students need to learn, or tell students where they can find it. One approach is to create a complete package that provides course information or directs students to sources of the information. A complete package for your students would include information about the course requirements, the ideas and skills to be learned, practice for the tests, and course procedures and instructions.

AN EXAMPLE OF THE CONTENTS OF A COMPLETE COURSE PACKAGE

As you read the following table of contents for course materials, note all the types of information available:

A. Introductory Materials
  1. Course overview
    a. Main concepts and principles
    b. Course structure or model relating all contents and units
  2. Course introduction
    a. Assumptions and philosophy of the course
    b. Goals and objectives of the course
    c. Tests and projects: contents and formats of exams and projects
    d. Grades: how computed and consolidated
    e. Calendar
      i. Class schedule
      ii. Test dates including final exam
      iii. Assignment and project due dates
    f. Class norms and etiquette
    g. Practice assignments and practice tests
    h. How to study for this course
    i. Overview of all assignments
    j. Model of all assignments consolidated in final project
    k. Materials to buy or to get (computer disks with assignment formats)
    l. Office hours and E-mail use
    m. Assistance: how, when, and where to get it
    n. Lab sessions: when, where, and how they will be held
B. Unit Number and Title
  1. Motivation: why study this topic
  2. Goals and objectives
  3. Agenda or schedule
  4. Assignment asssociated with this unit (how it fits in whole project)
  5. Annotated model of assignment
  6. Content outline to accompany explanation and demonstration
    a. Definitions of concepts and principles
    b. Outlines of facts
    c. Examples, evidence, diagrams, figures, steps, sources
    d. Short practice questions and problems interspersed
  7. Practice tests at the end (match the tests in content and format)
  8. Readings with annotations of content attached
  9. Readings to get: where and when

GUIDELINE 2: PROVIDE FEEDBACK TO STUDENTS

In addition to telling students what performance you expect, you can apply the principle of open communication by telling students how well they are meeting those expectations. There are three ways to provide your students with feedback: respond to their performance, respond to their questions, and respond to their attitudes.

Respond to Students' Performance

Imagine getting back a class project or a test. As you look through it, you find it as pristine as when you handed it in. But in the upper right-hand corner in red print you find a small notation: C++, or 76.5, or 2.8, or Good Work. You sit quietly for a long time and wonder what that little note means. It doesn't tell you what you did well, or what you did poorly, or what ideas you must refine, or what to do next. In fact, it doesn't tell you anything that you need in order to continue to learn. The principle of open communication implies that, to help students learn, the instructor gives them a complete, accurate, and honest assessment of their progress (Keller, 1987; Schon, 1987).

Information about the quality of students' performance, or *feedback,* is important because we are so ineffective in teaching. If we knew all we needed to know about teaching, we could teach perfectly the first time. There would be no need for checking a student's reception and promoting further development. But we make mistakes in our teaching; students make mistakes in their learning; and we both must refine what we do.

To apply feedback to your instruction, you will have to decide when to use it, what to say, and how to use it. Let's consider each decision.

Decide When to Use Feedback.   Feedback is not always necessary. Have you ever worked through instructional materials where the authors have provided answers to questions at the bottom of the page? Did you really struggle to answer the questions, or did you peek at the answers? When feedback is present in very well structured instruction, students may not do the practice, may not think through the questions, and as a consequence, may not remember well. When feedback is not immediately accessible, alternatively, students may be forced to think, to attend, and to remember.

If you observe an error *during* performance, especially when the performance may be dangerous or when the error may be compounded, try to prompt students in a way that makes them do most of the thinking and that allows them to finish practice with as little interruption as possible. The term *prompting* is taken from the world of theater where a person backstage may whisper a forgotten line to an actor on stage so the show can go on.

When students are not aware of their results, when they are compounding an error, or when danger is likely, give students feedback *as soon as you are able after the task* is done. In cases of important errors that you have noted, remind students of what they should do *just before the next practice.* For example:

- A swimming teacher would give immediate feedback when she caught someone making an error in the crawl stroke. This way the student would not form the wrong habit by repeating the same flawed stroke many times before getting feedback.

- A trainer would give immediate feedback as soon as he saw a student incorrectly placing paper in the tray of a copy machine, so as to prevent further errors and difficulties such as jamming the machine.
- A nurse educator would give immediate feedback as soon as he saw a student making an error in filling a syringe in preparation for giving an injection.

It is possible to give feedback too quickly; therefore, it is important to avoid feedback that is so quick it discourages performance. For example, once I conducted a course via television. Students could watch a presentation at home on their televisions and then take a multiple choice quiz. Students knew that they had to answer eight out of ten questions correctly, or they had to come to campus to take an alternative form of the test to meet the minimum standards. The answer sheet was a commercially available, chemically prepared sheet on which they could indicate their answers by using a special marker.

The answers were arranged like this:

a. _____
b. _____
c. _____
d. _____

If the students were correct, a message would appear immediately as they marked the space with the special marker: a. <u>Right</u>.

If they were incorrect, they would find that out too: b. <u>Wrong</u>.

I thought this was a great idea. I would know what the students got right or wrong and how many guesses they had to make to find the right answer, and the students would know the results right away. But the students didn't like this idea. Some said it drove them crazy. If they had already answered two questions incorrectly, they approached each subsequent question with great anxiety. They told me they would rather wait until the test was over to find out what was correct and incorrect. They said that they preferred this extremely speedy feedback for practice, but not for the tests that counted.

Decide What to Say.   When you give feedback, give complete feedback. Of course, state what your students have done correctly to confirm their proper performance and to encourage them. For feedback to be complete, you must find errors and be most explicit about what's wrong, what should have been done, and what to do next. There is no doubt that this requires diagnostic thinking and a lot of time and hard work.

PROVIDING COMPLETE FEEDBACK

Each assignment given by Chris Reznich consists of two parts: practice and project. For example, students must prepare two plans, one that the teacher checks carefully and one that he looks at but does not address. The idea is that students will benefit from the feedback on the practice, and not only apply it to that practice piece, but also use the feedback to improve their projects. For the practice segment, Chris writes on their assignment what is correct as well as what is incorrect. For each part that is incorrect, he states what they must do to correct it. Because he has a moderate sized class, he is able to spend 20 minutes per student, per week on the weekly assignments.

The most useful feedback points out errors and misconceptions and helps students to correct them. The more errors you find and *help students correct,* the greater gain in your students' learning (Bangert-Drowns, Kulik, Kulik, & Morgan, 1991). I tell my students that when they see their papers returned with writing all over them, they should not worry about what errors I have found, but concern themselves with what errors I didn't find. I may do my students a disservice if I miss an error and let them believe that what they have done is fine when it isn't.

THE IMPORTANCE OF POINTING OUT ERRORS TO STUDENTS

One afternoon an international student who had taken my course appeared in my office. Because her advisor was on leave, she asked if I would help her with a problem. She said that she was accused of plagiarism by one of her instructors. I asked to look at the paper she had written. I pointed to a section written in excellent prose, which sounded nothing like the projects that she had written for me. I asked her whose words those were. She pointed to the author's name somewhere on a previous page and said they were his words. I asked if those were the words exactly as he said them in the source and she said, "Yes." I told her that was not proper citation and I could see how she had been accused. I asked if she had meant to represent those as her ideas and words, and she gave an emphatic, "No." The question that bothered me was why she was still citing sources in this manner late in her masters program. At the hearing the student produced three other papers in which she had used the same procedure for citation and for which she had received "A" grades and praise. At least three teachers had had the opportunity to find and correct this mistake, but none did. Because of the lack of feedback, she was convinced that her approach to giving credit for ideas was legitimate.

Decide How to Give Feedback.   You may provide feedback using all sorts of media. You could *write* comments on students' work or write a note about a performance. You could provide a *reference* for them to compare their work with a particular text, an answer sheet, or a picture. You could give them a *model response* such as a model essay or a best answer. You could state your comments *aloud* or provide *video* or *audio* replays. To clarify what is shown and heard, you could conduct a *debriefing* by reviewing aloud what happened and what to do next time. To encourage self-analysis, you could ask students to *review their own performance* before anyone else does. Whenever possible, rely on *natural feedback* to demonstrate the consequences of inept performance, such as the normal reactions of team members when a meeting leader interrupts them or does not post what they say.

At some times when you are giving feedback you might do most of the talking or writing; at other times you might let the student take that role. In the first case, you might state exactly what was wrong and prescribe a way to correct that. For example, you might say in response to a student's presentation, "You were looking down when speaking. You should have been looking at the audience. That would show your confidence and interest and probably hold the audience's attention better. Next time, pick out a friendly face or two and talk to those people. Then, scan around for others."

In the second case, you might lead a student to diagnose his or her own errors and figure out what to do to correct matters. You might have students check one another's work. In that situation, your job is to give up some control and stimulate students to think for themselves and further refine their ideas. You might ask the student either to consider his or her own work using these questions, or to ask these questions of a partner.

Where were you looking during your talk?

What results did you get in the audience's reaction questionnaire?

Which of those responses might be the result of your eye contact?

What responses do you want from your presentation?

How might you get those responses?

Consider using a combination of the two approaches depending on the time you have for learning and the number of students with whom you are working. Table 4.2 suggests formats of what to note and how to respond to students' errors.

When prompting is needed during a task, there are four prompting steps to follow. The steps are designed to proceed from the least intrusive to the most intrusive and to be accomplished quietly and calmly. They require the instructor to do as little as possible and to stop when the prompting has served its purpose. Suppose you observe a student in a lab improperly closing a wound with stitches. You would:

1. Stop the student. Say, "Hold it." The student knows you are reacting for a good reason and therefore stops and looks at the work. In some cases the light bulb goes on, and the student realizes the error and says, "Oh I see, I'm not going deep enough." But in other cases the light bulb doesn't go on. If not . . .
2. Describe the performance. Say, "Let me tell you what you are doing. You are inserting the needle and going to this level. . . ." Then, in

TABLE 4.2 What to note and how to respond to types of errors

	Requirement	Look for	Say	Ask
Concepts	Identify new examples based on attributes.	Missing or misused attributes applied to new examples.	The attributes of ____ are ____ . This example does have the attributes. This non-example does not have the attributes.	What are the attributes of ____? Does this example have the attributes? Does this non-example have the attributes?
Facts	Recall propositions based on source.	Missing or distorted facts.	Here are the differences between the source and your facts.	What are the differences between the source and your facts?
Principles	Predict, infer, apply, explain variables and relations in new cases.	Missing or wrong variables or relationships applied to new cases.	The principle says this is the relationship between variables ____ . In this case, this is the independent variable, and this is the dependent variable. Thus, following the principle, we would predict in this case ____ and here is why.	What is the relationship between variables in the principle? In this case, what is the independent variable? In this case, what is the dependent variable? Following the principle, what would you expect in this case and why?
Skills	Perform mental or physical steps based on process or product standards.	Missing or incorrect steps when needed.	When under these conditions, you should have done this in this way.	When under these conditions, what should you do and how should you do that?

some cases, the light bulb goes on. "Oh I see, I should be going a level deeper." If not . . .

3. Ask questions regarding the error, such as, "When closing a wound, to what level should you go?" Even before giving an answer, the student may realize the error. But, if not . . .

4. Explain briefly. Remind the student of the proper level for suturing a wound.

We are also likely to be imperfect in our feedback. What we wish to communicate is not automatically granted. Even when we have used complete feedback, it is important to check to see if students have received the messages sent. You can check by asking students to tell you what they have understood as the recommendations for improvement or, better yet, asking them to do the assignment again showing you that they have understood what needed to be improved.

Respond to Students' Questions

Another form of feedback is responding to students' questions, and open communication implies that you respond fully. Sometimes students ask questions at an inopportune moment. Sometimes the questions may move prematurely to something students may not be prepared to understand, or may confuse students by interrupting the flow of an explanation or discussion or taking the class "off the track" to some topic irrelevant to the objective. Here are two strategies for responding to students' questions, whether or not they are perfectly timed: (1) develop a policy for answering questions, and (2) create a time for asking and anwering questions.

Develop a Policy for Answering Questions.   It would be naive and impractical to suggest that you answer each question fully at the time it is asked. Instead, develop a policy for answering questions that depends on the nature of the question and its timing. Explain the policy to students early in the course and ask for their advice.

SOME POLICIES FOR ANSWERING QUESTIONS

One teacher's general policy is to fully answer all relevant questions as they are asked. A *relevant question* is on the topic and is one whose answer will increase the likelihood that students will learn what they need to achieve the objective. But if a full answer to a relevant question will tax the students because of their lack of prerequisites, then the teacher gives a short, simple answer and explains why he is doing so. He tells the questioner when the complete answer is coming or where to get more information in the interim if he or she would like to. He may ask another student to answer if that is not demeaning to the questioner.

If a question is relevant but the teacher feels that it concerns a point that has been clarified and understood by students, he then asks how many other students have the same question. If many do, he answers it. If not, he gives a brief answer and asks the student to wait until after class for a full clarification. If he has time, he sometimes asks a student to answer that sort of question because he wants students to practice explaining. He tries to do so in a way that doesn't make the questioner feel stupid. He may say, "May I ask someone to answer the question 'What is the difference between a condition and a criterion?'"

If the question is not relevant, he will say so in a kind way, either suggesting when it will be relevant, or offering to answer it privately. He might say, "Dale, that question is important, but it goes beyond what we are working on today. I would like to postpone that until Wednesday. Please remind me then. But, if you like, we can talk about that right after class today. Thanks."

He thanks students for their questions but doesn't label them necessarily as good questions. He thinks it may discourage questions because some students may not consider their questions "good ones" according to what has been asked and labeled as such.

When someone asks him a question he can't answer, he says so. He may ask if anyone else has a response. If he thinks it is important and interesting, he tells the student that he will look for an answer and he will invite that student or any others interested to join in the search. But he does not punish a student for asking a question by *requiring* that student to find the answer as an assignment.

Designate a Time for Asking and Answering Questions.   In addition to the time spent naturally and openly answering questions in class, set another time either in or out of class when students are asked to formulate and ask questions. Call for questions specifically: "Are there any questions about _____?" Then wait for students to form and ask their questions.

In larger classes when I have less time for interaction, I arrange what I call "talk sessions" for the purpose of discussing the answers to any questions, old or new, big or small, relevant or irrelevant. I find a time during the week when most students can meet. I tell them the session is optional. When they arrive, they introduce themselves to one another. Then I gather and post all of the questions. We figure out a sensible sequence and we all answer the questions. If I am the best one to answer, I do. But I direct many questions to other students. When the question is regarding an individual's assignment or project, I make the project content public and answer that question so that all listening learn a general lesson. When we run out of questions and there is still time left, I may pose questions or have the group go through a process. If I can't have a talk session, I will answer questions by coming early to class.

Respond to Students' Attitudes

Students of all ages sometimes need feedback about their behavior. You may face the difficult problem of responding to a student who is an obstacle to his or her own learning and to the learning of his or her classmates. I am talking about students who talk during another student's presentation, who talk when others are talking, who read newspapers in class, who don't do their work or don't cooperate with their team on a group project. Many people would think of these behaviors as rude and inconsiderate.

In dealing with these situations you may have to work hard not to make assumptions about the students' motives. When I make hypotheses about motives, I am usually wrong. Intervene only when the process of learning is at issue. Explain to the student what observable behaviors are taking place and what effects the behaviors are having on others. State your feelings and the effects on you. Try not to assign cause or tell the student what to do.

GIVING FEEDBACK ON ATTITUDE WITHOUT BLAMING OR DIRECTLY PRESCRIBING

In one of the first lectures in a course, Jack, a student sitting in the front row, responded aloud to each question and commented on each point the teacher made. After a few remarks by Jack, some students began turning to one another with looks of frustration; others rolled their eyes and mumbled to themselves. When Jack would make his comments, the teacher would lose her train of thought and would have to recapitulate the argument she was making. After the class she reflected on the advantages and disadvantages of having Jack continue to respond as he did. His comments were minor contributions to other comments in the class. Other students were disturbed by the interruptions. This part of the large class was intended to be an efficient presentation of basic information to prepare students for timely assignments. The presentation was slowed and was losing coherence. The teacher decided she would intervene before the next class. She called Jack.

"Hello, Jack?"

"Yes."

"This is Rose Klahr. How are you?"

"Oh, hi. I'm fine. How are you?"

"Fine, Jack. Hey, I wanted to talk with you about class."

"Sure. I really like class. I'm really excited about it."

"I think I could tell that by your responses. But I was wondering if you were aware of how people were responding to your comments?"

"No, what do you mean?"

"When you comment, people fidget, whisper to one another, and roll their eyes."

"Oh gee! OK, I'm not going to say anything then."

"Well, that's not necessary, but you may be a bit more selective about when and how you make comments and observe how others respond. Even I lost my train of thought a bit. But I want you to keep your high interest and I want you to respond. Just be judicious."

"OK, I think I know what to do. Thanks for calling me."

"Sure, Jack. See you in class."

In the next class Jack sat at the back of the class and did make a comment. But he watched the teacher's reaction and the reaction of the class. The teacher thanked him for his comment. After class Jack thanked the teacher for giving him the feedback about his behavior. He maintained his enthusiasm for the rest of the course. The teacher is still in touch with Jack, who continues to apply the content and the interpersonal skills that he learned in the class.

GUIDELINE 3: RESPOND TO STUDENTS' FEEDBACK TO YOU

Open communication implies a two-way process. Students give you samples of their work; you give students problems, questions, and assignments, and you respond to their work. But, what about students responding to the instruction they receive? Some instructors say, "OK, I'll tell my students what they need to know, but I don't want to hear anything from them about my teaching." That's like saying:

Mirror, mirror on the wall,
Who's the fairest of them all?
I don't care what truth you see.
Say the fairest one is me.

Instead of denying your faults, collect information from students about the class and attend carefully to students' statements and actions throughout instruction to discover which instructional methods are working well and which methods must be improved. Evaluation for the purpose of seeking improvement is commonly called *formative evaluation.* Getting student feedback is one way of conducting formative evaluation. Use the following seven steps to formative evaluation using student feedback:

1. Decide what information you want.
2. Decide on the means for data collection and write questions.
3. Collect the information after an appropriate unit.
4. Tally the information.
5. Make decisions for changes.
6. Report back to students.
7. Implement changes.

Decide What Information You Want

Figure out what you want to know about your instruction. Remember, formative evaluation concerns improvement. You can improve your effectiveness, efficiency, or acceptability. Do you want to assess effectiveness for purposes of improvement? Then, in addition to looking at test results for strengths and weaknesses, you may want students' views of what they are learning, how well they feel they have learned, and their degree of confidence in using what they have learned. Do you want to check efficiency? Then, in addition to collecting time management information, you may want students' reports of what they did with their time, how well their time was spent, which materials speeded or slowed the process of learning, which aids made learning harder or easier, where aids might be needed, and where time could be saved. Do you want to check acceptability? Then you may want students opinions about how well they liked the instructional methods, schedules, and materials.

Decide on the Means for Data Collection and Write Questions

You may interview a group of representative students or you may use a questionnaire to collect the information from students. You may also have students drop notes in a letter box, contact you by E-mail, or leave messages for you on a phone answering machine.

If you decide to *interview* a representative group of students, then tell them, "I want to improve my instruction. Today I want you to help me gain information to improve this class. I am going to ask some questions about the instruction, and I want you to give your frank answers. You are in the best position to know what is going well and what is not. Your feedback is important. So, don't hesitate to give your opinion even if it sounds like what others say or if it runs counter to what others say. As you tell me your answers, I will post them on the board. When you run out of things to say, I will ask you to pick the suggestions you believe are most important. This will take only 10 minutes. Take a few minutes to answer the posted questions by jotting your answer on the paper supplied. Don't put your name on the paper. I will collect them."

When the students are finished writing, say, "Here is the first question: What helped you learn in this segment?" Recognize the students one at a time. Listen to their answers and quickly post their responses. Ask for clarification. Next ask, "What hindered your learning?" Post responses. Do not defend your instruction and do not comment. Finally ask, "How would you change the instruction to remove the hindrances?" Post responses and number the suggestions.

Say to the students, "Pick your top three suggestions, the ones you most want to see used." Then ask, "How many picked number one?" Tally. "Number two?" Tally, and so on.

"Thank you for your time. I will summarize this information and present a report in class with suggestions for improvement. Thanks again."

Here are some tips for using a survey, or *questionnaire,* to collect the information. Write questions that the individual student can answer from his or her perspective: "What helped *you* learn? What hindered *your* learning? What changes would help *you* learn better?" I suggest trying the questions on some typical students to eliminate ambiguities and to be sure your intent is understood. Be sure that the answers tell you possible improvements or give you solid information on which to base decisions. Use general open-ended questions like the three just mentioned for groups of up to 50 students. You might also use scaled items, like the following samples, using a three- or five-point scale.

Using Some Scaled Formative Evaluation Questions

	Agree	Don't Know	Disagree
I need more examples to understand the points.	_____	_____	_____
The pace of presentation needs to be slowed for me to comprehend.	_____	_____	_____
I would like more explanation as to why this topic is important.	_____	_____	_____

You may use aspects of your course that concern you or that you are working on and a scale that tells you whether students want to add, delete, or keep that aspect the same. Here is a sample:

Asking about Specific Aspects of a Course

	Add	Keep the Same	Reduce
Number of examples	_____	_____	_____
Pace of presentations	_____	_____	_____
Length of assignments	_____	_____	_____
Difficulty of projects	_____	_____	_____

When you are ready to present the survey, say, "I am continuously trying to improve my course and teaching. This questionnaire is one tool that I use for that purpose. You can supply me with some useful information. Your responses will remain anonymous. I will read, tally, and study your responses to find suggestions for improvements and report back to you. Please think about this carefully and give me your thoughtful responses. Thank you for your time."

Collect the Information after an Appropriate Unit

Don't wait until the end of the course to get feedback from students; you can elicit feedback daily or weekly. An excellent time is at the end of a whole unit of instruction so that you can make adjustments on the next unit. By responding to students in this way, you share with them the control of the course. You need not restrict this feedback process to courses; you may conduct town meetings of all the students in a program.

Tally the Information

Be prepared for some shocking responses. Some students will not take the questionnaire seriously and will vent their anger about the program or their personal problems in the questionnaire. To put the nasty comments in perspective, summarize all the survey or interview data using frequencies or clustered tallies. Add a direct quotation if it brings out a point most clearly.

Using Frequencies and Clustered Tallies to Summarize Information

	Add	Keep the Same	Reduce
Number of examples	22	7	2
Pace of presentations	0	29	2
Length of assignments	0	15	16
Difficulty of projects	7	19	5

"What hindered *your* learning?" Clustered tallies with quotations:

- The instructor   1

    Quote: "You did! You drive me crazy!"

- Not enough time   12
- Too few examples   22
- My own scheduling   3
- Not knowing what was expected   12

> Quote: "I didn't know what we were supposed to do with this information."

Make Decisions for Change

When the data show a weakness, you can make a clear decision. Suppose five out of six students said give more examples in an interview, or you get frequencies like this to the survey question, "I need more examples to comprehend the ideas":

Strongly Agree	Agree	Don't Know	Disagree	Strongly Disagree
24	12	2	0	0

Your decision could be: "Be sure to give at least one example for each major idea presented," or, "Ask students a question about each idea before moving to the next one to see if they need further examples to make the idea understandable."

Your main problems in interpretation will be in dealing with inconsistent data. Then you will have to make a professional decision, noting the inconsistency and stating the reason for your judgment. Suppose half your students say go faster and the other half say go slower. You respond, "Although there is balanced evidence supporting going slower and going faster, I decided to go the same pace as I do now and check if students are ready to move ahead after an explanation and at least one example. I will check by asking you a question. If you answer correctly, I will move ahead. If you answer incorrectly, I will use the answer to diagnose the misconception and provide a better explanation. This should satisfy those who need more time to be sure they have the idea and those who like to see steady progress."

Another interpretation problem arises when you have a small amount of evidence to act a certain way. In that case be open about your awareness of the limited evidence for the recommendation and state the reason for your judgment. Imagine that 10 of 38 students want more examples. You could decide: "Although there is a small amount of evidence for this decision, I will make sure there is at least one example for each point and more than one example depending on the importance of the point. This will help all students learn. It will probably add interest to the lesson, too. The time I use for examples should be worthwhile if it eliminates some unnecessary questions during class and office hours."

What if students suggest actions that you just can't do? What if half the students ask for one thing and the other half ask for the opposite, and you can't make up your mind what to do? Josie Csete, an instructional designer, suggests using the principle of open communication by bringing the issue to the students.

If you can't do what is asked or if you can't decide what to do, say so; then, in collaboration with the students, try to find an acceptable alternative solution.

Report Back to Students

Report back to your students, showing the full range of responses. Explain what you have decided and what actions you will take. This will demonstrate that you have the courage to find your faults and correct them, a good practice to model for students.

Implement Changes

Make some changes during the session you report back. Explain to students what you are doing and why. Showing that you listen to their comments will reward students for making suggestions and perhaps give them a reason to make even better suggestions the next time you ask. If the students suggested improvements in organization, say to them, "Today I am going to use a projected outline to add some structure so you can follow along, and each of you is going to create your own diagram relating the ideas as a class activity."

LEARNING ABOUT TEACHING BY SOLICITING FEEDBACK

A teacher heard through the grapevine that his students thought he was not concerned about teaching or about students. While some teachers might not be bothered by such a rumor, this teacher did care and was hurt. He asked what he might do. I suggested that he gather some data; I recommended that he wait until a unit was complete and then ask these questions:

What helped your learning?
What hindered your learning?
What changes should we make?

I warned him that some students may have been hurt before and they may take out their anger in an anonymous questionnaire. I told him to tally the data to put individual comments into perspective. He collected the data, and some students let him have it.

What helped your learning?   "Nothing!"
What hindered your learning?   "You!"
What changes should we make?   "Cancel this class!"

He put these comments into perspective by tallying them. He listed the frequencies on a transparency and revealed them in class. He told his students that most of them thought that the videos and visuals helped greatly, that the lack of organization was a hindrance, and that greater organization would be a desirable change. He stated that he would be using one of the suggestions during that class. He showed the outline for the day and then proceeded through a well-structured session.

I interviewed some students after that session and asked what they thought of the teacher. They said he had his faults but was working hard to improve. He was a teacher who obviously cared about his job and his students. I asked them how they knew that, and they said, "He keeps asking us what would help us and what we suggest. He can't do all that we say, but he keeps on trying. He cares. And the least we can do is care enough to try and do our part."

A FINAL WORD

Instruction is not a game of hide-and-seek. Of course, students must exert considerable effort to comprehend and acquire knowledge and skill. But they need not guess at what is required of them, why it is required, and how they will proceed to meet the requirements. If you, as their teacher, know what is required, tell them. Until students are able to create their own requirements, structures, and schedules, supply them with that information and gradually teach them how to do so for themselves. Otherwise, only students with well-developed extrasensory perception will know what is happening.

Furthermore, instruction is not the practice of self-deceit. Do not follow the lesson of the three monkeys—*see no evil, hear no evil, and speak no evil.* Find out and face what is going well in your instruction and what is not; then enhance your strengths and repair your weaknesses. Little by little you can become an extremely competent instructor.

ACTIVITIES

In the following activities you have an opportunity to apply open communication in several ways. In the first activity, you can apply the principle to the start of a course. In the second and third activities, you can use the principle as part of the evaluation process. In the next three activities you can apply the idea to interaction with students via questions and discussion.

1. Prepare an *orientation* for a course you might teach.
   a. First, describe the test or final performance; in other words, state the objective.
   b. Give a sample test item, if that is applicable.
   c. If students are to produce a final product, state what sample of that product you would present and how you would do it.
   d. State the main ideas in the course as an overview.
   e. Give the major events in the class schedule in an agenda.
   f. If you have a package of course materials, describe their major components.

2. Think of a particular performance you require or an assignment you give to students. When will you provide *feedback?* What will you say? How will you give the feedback?

3. Conduct a *formative evaluation* of some teaching. This is a great activity if you are teaching now. If you are not teaching now, then find a teacher who would like to get some information about a course, unit, or lesson.

   a. State the information you want from the students about the teaching. For example: How can I improve my course materials to help students learn?

   b. State how you will collect the data. Write four open-ended questions for the students to answer to get the information you want. For example: What in the course materials helped you learn; what in the course materials hindered your learning; what could I change in the course materials to help you learn better; what is the most important idea you have learned from the materials?

   c. Collect the information from students when the instructional segment is done.

   d. Tally the information, decide on changes, and report back to your students. Make sure you implement some change that same day you report back.

4. Think of a particular topic you might teach. How might you use *questions* in applying the principles of meaningfulness, prerequisites, and open communication? Write out the questions you might use. Consider questions for

   a. meaningfulness to help students make connections to their experience, interests, and aspirations, as well as questions to provoke curiosity.

   b. prerequisites to assess known facts, concepts, principles, and skills.

   c. open communication to show students what they are to learn.

5. State your question answering policy as if you were explaining it to your students the first day of class.

6. Have you ever felt reluctant to contribute to an instructional *discussion?* Have you ever noticed someone dominating a discussion? Have you ever noticed a discussion leader who acknowledged only the people with whom he or she agreed? Why is it important to maintain open communication in a discussion? What are some rules that you could propose to maintain open communication in a discussion?

7. Reflection

   a. What can I tell my students so they may focus on the important issues in learning?

   b. How can my students get the information they need at the start of the course?

   c. How can I best tell students what is on the tests?

   d. How can I provide an overview of the content?

   e. How can I best tell students the schedule of learning activities?

   f. How can I get information from students to improve the course?

   g. How can I provide complete feedback? What's right and what's wrong to do?

   h. How can I provide feedback that is at least "neutral"?

   i. How can I get students to provide feedback to one another?

   j. How can I use a checklist to be objective?

   k. How can I have students check their own work?

FURTHER READING

Bangert-Drowns, R. L., Kulik, C., Kulik, J. A., & Morgan, M. (1991). The instructional effect of feedback in test-like events. *Review of Educational Research, 61*(2), 213–238. (*Note:* This article summarizes research on feedback.)

Dick, W., & King, D. (1994). Formative evaluation in the performance context. *Performance and Instruction Journal, 33*(9), 3–10. (*Note:* This is a good explanation of basic concepts of formative evaluation and its extension beyond the classroom.)

Gronlund, N. E. (1995). *How to write and use instructional objectives* (5th ed.). Columbus, OH: Charles E. Merrill (*Note:* This and the Mager book [1993] are good clear texts about objectives.)

Mager, R. F. (1993). *Preparing instructional objectives* (2nd ed.). Belmont, CA: Lake.

Marshall, H. (1987). Motivational strategies of three fifth-grade teachers. *Elementary School Journal, 88,* 136–150. (*Note:* The article shows how teachers communicate to students their expectations for high performance.)

Ramsey, I., Gabbard, C., Clawson, K., Lee, L., & Henson, K. (1990, May). Questioning: An effective teaching method. *Clearing House,* 420–422. (*Note:* This brief article sums up a technique related to open communication.)

West, C. K., Farmer, J. A., & Wolff, P. M. (1991). *Instructional design: Implications from cognitive science.* Englewood Cliffs, NJ: Prentice-Hall. (*Note:* Chapter 6 discusses advance organizers.)

Yelon, S., & Reznich, C. (1991). Creating and using annotated examples. *Performance and Instruction Journal, 30*(4), 26–30. (*Note:* When and how to make annotated examples as orientation aids is discussed.)

chapter 5

Organized Essential Content

OVERVIEW

Assign the most class time to well-structured important content to ease the students' mental load in comprehending and learning, and to use instructional time well.

Guideline 1: Extract Essential Content
        Choose Essential Content from the Task Description
        Choose Essential Content for the Required Facts, Concepts, Principles, and Skills
        Choose Essential Examples

Guideline 2: Organize Essential Content
        Organize Course Content
        Organize Unit and Lesson Content

Guideline 3: Present Essential Content in an Organized Manner
        Present a Course Overview
        Move from One Unit to Another within the Structure
        Present Lesson Content in an Organized, Simple Way

Meaningfulness, prerequisites, and open communication have excellent applications near the beginning of courses, units, and lessons. Of course, these principles can and should be applied throughout instruction. But what principles apply specifically to providing information to students by an explanation, a discussion, a reading assignment, or an activity? The first principle oriented to providing information is organized essential content; it relates to what information to provide and how to provide it.

WHAT IS ESSENTIAL CONTENT?

Once a teacher visited my office struggling with an arm-stretching package he was barely able to bring to rest on my desk. The teacher opened the box to reveal enough paper to fill an encyclopedia.

"What's that?" I asked.

The teacher replied, "That's the content I have to teach. But excuse me, I forgot something in the car. I'll be right back."

The teacher returned with a tiny ring box.

"What's that?" I asked.

"Well, that's the amount of time I have to teach it. I need to know how I can fit the big box of content into this little box of time."

I said, "Select the pages that have ideas that you want your students to learn by the end of the lesson and keep only those pages."

Then he asked, "But how do you decide on the ideas you want to keep?"

I thought for a moment and answered, "The secret is to specify the performance needed by your students and then give priority to the ideas essential to achieving that objective."

Time is your most precious instructional resource. There is always more content to learn than there is time to learn the content. Accordingly, you should teach efficiently and help students learn efficiently. One way of being most efficient in instruction is to select and give priority to that content which is essential for your students to learn to achieve your course objectives. Prescribe only that content which students need to learn to perform. In your explanations, discussions, or activities, give the time you have to the essentials and dispense with the unnecessary ideas. In this way, students will learn what you want them to learn. You will want to maintain the efficiency you have gained by providing the content in an organized, clear, concrete, and well-paced fashion (Clark, 1986).

GUIDELINE 1: EXTRACT ESSENTIAL CONTENT

To be a "lean and mean teaching machine," derive the essential content for your instruction. First ask: What would students have to do to demonstrate to me by the end of the instruction that they know the idea or skill? That's your instructional objective. Second ask: What should I definitely have my students learn so that they are able to demonstrate the idea or skill? That's the essential content.

Three Steps for Extracting Essential Content
1. Choose essential content from the task description.
2. Choose essential content for the required facts, concepts, principles, and skills.
3. Choose essential examples.

Please note that a central idea of this entire text is that the choice of essential content such as concepts, facts, principles, and skills influences the rest of instruction. The content influences the form of assessment. The form of assesment influences how a student must practice. The practice, in turn, influences what a student must see as a demonstration of the desired performance.

Choose Essential Content from the Task Description

Choosing essential content is just basic subtraction using the objective, the task description, and the facts, concepts, principles, and skills derived from the task analysis.

Steps to Find Essential Content

Specify what students must know.	(The objective and task description)
Subtract what students know now.	(The students' prerequisite knowledge) The subskills, rules, principles, facts, concepts, and attitudes students know now
The remainder is what you must teach.	(The essential knowledge to teach) The subskills, rules, principles, facts, concepts, and attitudes students must learn

Follow the same process shown in the chapter on prerequisites (chapter 3), but now make a distinction between prerequisite content and content to be taught. You can now decide on the essential knowledge for a program, course, unit, or lesson. The only difference is the scope of the objectives and the task descriptions.

WHAT IS "ESSENTIAL CONTENT" AND WHAT IS "NICE TO KNOW"?

Once a teacher came to me complaining about never being able to comfortably finish a topic in class. She would always run out of time. So, one way to frame the problem was to ask her how she could fit what she wanted to teach into the time allotted.

I asked her, "What do you want to teach tomorrow?"

She said, "I want the students to learn about Machiavelli. You see, I want them to be able to apply various political theories to modern problems. Machiavelli wrote about one of those theories."

"What should the students be able to do at the end of the lesson that would meet your overall objective?"

"They should be able to say who Machiavelli was, what his ideas were about, politics and power as he expressed them in *The Prince* [facts], how his ideas may have influenced Europe in his day [facts, maybe principles], and how people use Machiavellian schemes today [concepts]. Also, I want them to predict the effects of those schemes [principles]."

I asked the subtraction question. "Based on what you know of your students, do they know how to do these things already?"

"No."

"Great," I replied. "Now consider looking at your teaching notes and starring only those points which directly answer the questions you posed."

We drank some coffee as she checked her notes.

When she finished, I noticed that only one-third of the content was starred. I asked, "What would you call the starred segments of content?"

"The essentials, of course."

"What about the other ideas, for example, his hometown, his date of birth, his personal history, his wife and children, how long he lived, where he lived, his occupation, when *The Prince* was published. What are those?"

"Those are 'nice to know.'"

Two-thirds nice to know! I said, "The solution is straightforward. Keep the essentials and drop the nice to know."

"But what about all the ideas that are nice to know?"

"You could give out bibliographies, extra handouts, or hold an optional session."

The teacher hadn't decided what to do by the end of our discussion. When she returned to my office for a follow-up conference, she was pleased. She said she had taught the class keeping the essentials and sprinkling in a little "nice to know" for its motivational value. She also handed out an annotated bibliography. For the first time since she could recall, she finished the lesson on Machiavelli with 15 minutes to spare. She used the extra time for students to bring up modern examples about who was using Machiavellian principles to serve their political ends and the effects of their use.

Do you, as the teacher, derive and decide on all the content? In some forms of instruction such as problem-based instruction, you would present problems to students that you have selected as useful and meaningful. But after discussing a problem with your students for a short while, you would give them the responsibilty to select the content they must learn to be able to solve the problem. In some forms of cooperative group learning or individual independent learning, your students would set their own objectives and choose the appropriate content either by themselves or in collaboration with you. Furthermore, not all your plans would be made before instruction begins. You and your students would be able to derive essential content during instruction as students discover interests and questions that lead in unexpected directions.

Choose Essential Content for the Required
Facts, Concepts, Principles, and Skills

Once you have found the essential facts, concepts, principles, and physical and mental skills your students must learn, take the analytic microscope in a little closer using Table 5.1 to find out the essential content for teaching each (Gagné, 1985; Gropper, 1983).

TABLE 5.1 Essential content for teaching facts, concepts, principles, skills

	Facts	Concepts	Principles	Skills
Ideas	Organized set of facts	Definition of the category	Definition relating variables	Ordered, simplified steps
Examples	Vividly illustrated substantiation	Typical example Example– nonexample pairs	Evidence showing relationship of variables	Demonstration

If you want to teach *facts,* then provide an organized, vividly illustrated body of those facts through explanation, discussion, assigned readings, or a discovery activity. For example, if you want your students to be able to recall and state aloud certain events in the American Civil War, such as events in the Battle of Gettysburg, then *show* them the story of the battle. Present the events in chronological order, using a film if it is available and concrete artifacts, such as photos, letters, uniforms, weapons, equipment, and newspaper articles to substantiate the statements of fact.

If you want to teach a *concept,* then give its definition and show examples, or have the students derive the definition from the examples. As an illustration, suppose you wanted your students to be able to identify examples of good rules. You could begin by presenting a definition: "A good rule is one that is defined, reasonable, enforceable, and positive." Then give examples. If possible, present a typical and fairly memorable example that fits the definition very well:

"Walk on the dock surrounding the swimming pool."

Finally, have students point out the attributes of the example:

The swimming pool rule is *defined;* you can observe someone walking.
The rule is *reasonable;* it's not too much to ask a person to do.
The rule is *enforceable;* you can tell when someone is not walking.
The rule is *positive;* it tells what to do—walk.

Alternatively, you could present the example and ask students to tell you why it is a good example and thereby derive the definition. In either case, if you wish to emphasize certain characteristics, then have students contrast examples with nonexamples. To show that a characteristic of a good rule is that it is defined, present an example and a nonexample and have students compare them:

"*Walk* on the dock surrounding the swimming pool."
"*Be careful* on the dock surrounding the swimming pool."

If you want to teach a *principle,* then provide a definition and evidence to establish its validity, either in the form of an explanation or in the form of a discussion of the meaning of the evidence. The definition should show the relationship between the independent and dependent variables. Suppose, for example, that you want your students to be able to solve problems related to controlling fire. First, in a discussion, you could collaborate with students to define the principle:

"Combustion [dependent variable] is a function of heat, oxygen, and fuel [independent variables]."

Second, show evidence demonstrating the relationship. Give evidence supported by research studies or have your students find such evidence. Encourage students to use research evidence if they can understand the studies and if they need knowledge of research to operate in the real world. Demonstrate or have students demonstrate the relationships if you can. Show that all variables—heat, oxygen, and fuel—are necessary for combustion to occur. For example, to show that oxygen is neccessary, have students cover a burning candle with a glass jar and discuss the outcome.

If you want to teach a *skill,* then provide the ordered, simplified steps of the skill and then demonstrate those steps. Imagine that you want your students to be able to take a blood pressure. You would reduce the task description by grouping the steps and simplifying the language. You would then show each step. (*Note:* Compare the task description below with the one on page 47.)

Reduced Task Description: How to Take a Blood Pressure
A. Prepare
   1. Get equipment: manometer, stethoscope, two alcohol sponges, pencil and paper.
   2. Clean stethoscope earpieces.
   3. Explain procedure
     a. Will take blood pressure (BP)
     b. Not hurt, feel pressure
     c. Couple of minutes
   4. Choose cuff
     a. Twenty percent wider
     b. Circle completely
     c. Secure
   5. Stethoscope on, cuff ready—valve open, bladder ready and open on diaphragm side.
   6. Seat patient, expose right arm, forearm supported, palm upward.
B. Place
   1. Straighten right arm, locate brachial and radial arteries.
   2. Grasp bladder cuff with both hands, Velcro side up and tubing toward you.
   3. Place bladder over middle third of upper arm
     a. Tubing centered over brachial artery
     b. Lower edge 2 cm over antecubital fossa

     c. Cuff has no wrinkles

     d. Loose enough for one finger

   4. Wrap Velcro under arm and wrap loose end around arm.

   5. Make sure cuff snug, does not slip.

C. Inflate

   1. Close valve.

   2. Pump above systolic slowly, until radial pulse no longer palpable.

   3. Place stethoscope diaphragm over brachial artery just beneath cuff.

   4. Cradle and extend arm with same hand.

   5. Ask patient to relax arm.

D. Measure

   1. Release air from bladder 5 mm Hg/sec.

   2. Listen for systolic reading and mentally record.

   3. Listen for diastolic reading and mentally record.

   4. Completely deflate cuff and remove.

   5. Record and explain measurements.

Choose Essential Examples

You can use examples for motivating students, providing practice, giving tests, and explaining ideas. Motivational examples show the use and consequence of applying an idea. (See chapter 2 for further discussion of the use of motivational examples.)

Practice and test examples are presented as problems. When using them to teach concepts, one approach is to ask students to identify examples of a particular category: "Which of the following is a prime number?" For principles, one approach is to ask students to apply the principle to a given example: "Use the principle of survival by camouflage to explain why these herrings in the aquarium are swimming in large schools." For facts, one technique is to ask the students to recall a fact and justify it by supplying illustrative evidence: "What were the major causes of World War II? Give examples to justify your answer."

Memorable, attention-getting, and communicative examples are esssential content for explanations, discussions, and student information-seeking activities, yet they are difficult to find or produce (Yelon & Massa, 1987). A good example must be *accurate, clear,* and *attractive.* Futhermore, a single good example is often insufficient. You will need sets of good examples to help students generalize and transfer their knowledge to new situations.

Essential Examples Are Accurate.   In a presentation, discussion, or activity, examples must be accurate; that is, your examples must fit the idea to be learned. How can you tell if the examples fit the idea? When accurate, the elements of the examples are analogous to the elements of the idea. But the elements of concepts, principles, and facts differ. So the examples you use to portray each type must match the idea appropriately. Consider each type of idea.

Concepts are categories. Concept definitions limit the objects, processes, or ideas that fall into the category. People show they know a concept when they can recognize examples that belong in a category and explain why they belong. The elements of your concept's examples must clearly match the defining attributes in the concept's definition. A teacher presenting the concept *insect* might show an example of an insect such as an ant with its defining attributes clearly labeled: a separate head, three mouth segments, three thorax segments, each with a pair of legs attached ventrally, and so on. A teacher describing the concept *bird* might show an example of a bird such as an eagle with its feathers and wings clearly labeled. Figures 5.1 and 5.2 are two examples; in each, the example's elements match the concept's defining attributes. In Figure 5.1, an example of the concept *square* shows the attributes of a square: four equal sides and four right angles. In Figure 5.2, note how the example given for an *objective* matches the attributes in the concept definition: A good objective must contain one or more conditions, behaviors, criteria, and lower limits.

FIGURE 5.1   Labeled example of the concept *square*

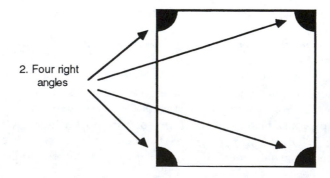

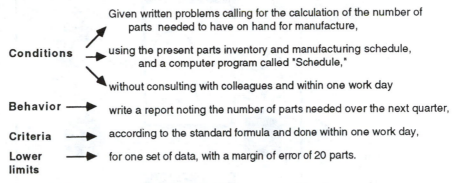

> A good objective contains
> one or more
>   conditions,
>   behaviors,
>   criteria, and
>   lower limits.

A Good Objective

Conditions
Given written problems calling for the calculation of the number of parts needed to have on hand for manufacture,

using the present parts inventory and manufacturing schedule, and a computer program called "Schedule,"

without consulting with colleagues and within one work day

Behavior → write a report noting the number of parts needed over the next quarter,

Criteria → according to the standard formula and done within one work day,

Lower limits → for one set of data, with a margin of error of 20 parts.

FIGURE 5.2   Labeled example of the concept *objective*

A *principle* is a statement defining the relationship between variables. For a principle, your example's elements must clearly match the independent variables, the dependent variables, and the relationship. Suppose you were teaching the principle, "Healthy plants require food, water, and light." You could present evidence by means of a demonstration to substantiate the principle by showing that each variable—food, water, and light—is necessary for a plant to be healthy. You might present a set of controlled demonstrations, each manipulating one variable. Figure 5.3 illustrates a demonstration to show the relationship between one independent variable, light, and the dependent variable, the health of the plant. What demonstration would you use to show water and food as necessary for plant health?

To show students that an optimal amount of water is required to keep plants healthy, you might use a demonstration like the one in Figure 5.4, which shows the consequences of too much water, an optimal amount of water, and too little water. Of course, the more sophisticated the principle, the greater the depth of explanation and discussion, and the more sophisticated the demonstrations for evidence.

Under certain conditions you should use evidence from *published scientific studies* to substantiate the principle you are teaching. Use evidence from research studies when your students

- need to substantiate their applications with documented scientific support,
- have the prerequisites to understand the studies,

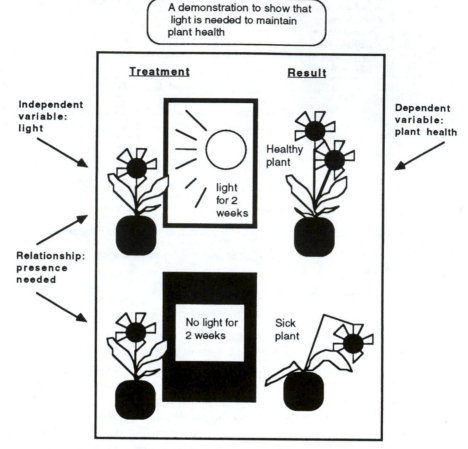

FIGURE 5.3 Demonstration of the relationship between *light* and *plant health* (principle)

- have had the concrete experiences to which the studies refer,
- have the ability to use the abstract reasoning called for, and/or
- need to be convinced by documented scientific evidence.

Also use evidence from published studies as examples of your principles when

- the evidence from the study is quite compelling,
- the conclusion of the study fits the principle exactly,
- the principle is counter to popular knowledge, and/or
- you cannot do a live demonstration within the class time and resource constraints.

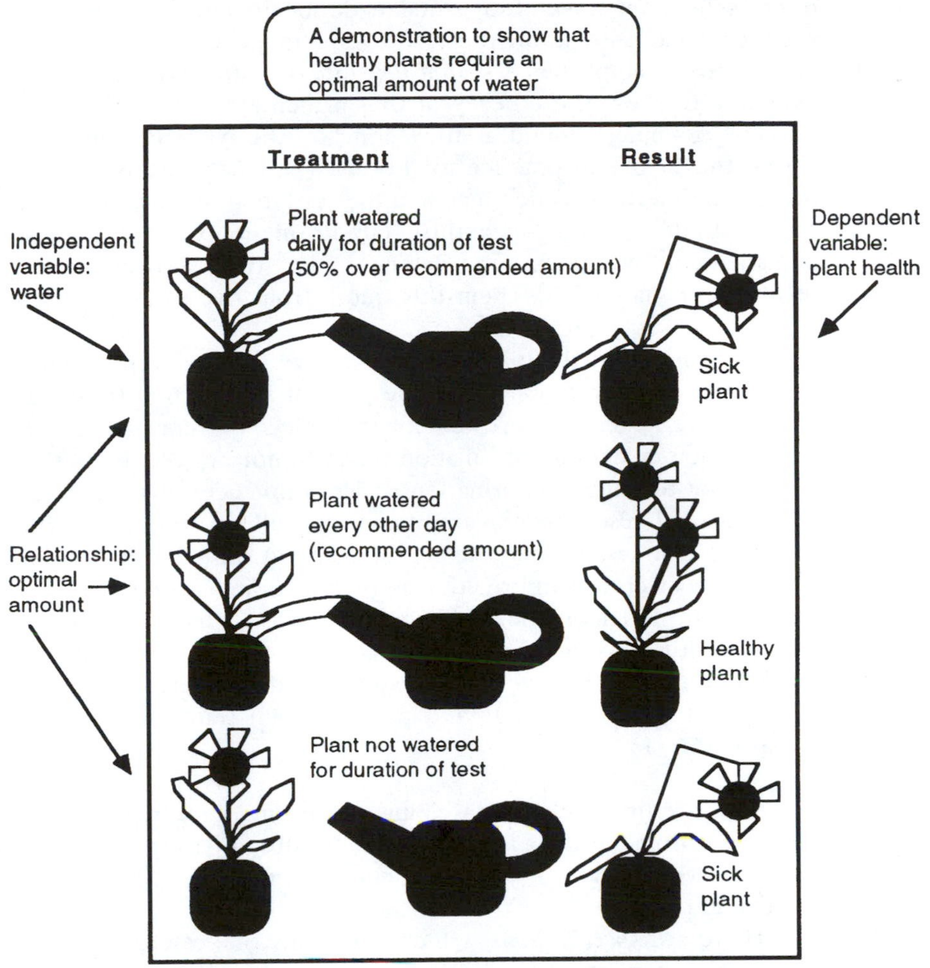

FIGURE 5.4 Demonstration of the relationship between *water* and *plant health* (principle)

I use published evidence to illustrate the principle, "Student's will perform well on a test when they have practiced what is required on the test. If recall of certain content is required and students practice recalling that content, then they will do well on the test. If application of an idea to new cases is required and students practice application to new cases, then they will do well on the test."

I use published evidence to teach that principle rather than just demonstrating it, because my students often have to justify design recommendations about practice to their clients. They are all graduate students with at least one course in interpreting research. They have all practiced skills and ideas in and out of school. Yet some of my students doubt the efficacy of having their students practice what will be on the test, even though they have been doing that in my course. To help them, I search for, find, refer to, and tell the story of research evidence to show the efficacy of that principle.

For example, I found a study done by the Navy in which the researchers varied the fit of the practice to the test (Ellis, Wulfeck, & Montague, 1980). In one condition the practice matched the test; in another condition some practice matched the test; and in a third condition no practice matched the test. I explained to my students the details of the study, showed them graphs of the results, and shared with them this quote from the authors' conclusions:

> If the intent of the instruction is to have students remember important pieces of information (as in the present study) then there should be a practice item and a test item for each piece of information. There should not be practice on information that will not be tested and there should not be testing on information that has not been practiced. If there are time and resource constraints so that all the important information cannot be tested, then the course material should be prioritized so that the most crucial information is practiced and tested.
>
> If the intent of the learning program is to have learning transfer to new situations then practice items would not be the same as test items, but both the instructional material and the test should provide an opportunity to practice and perform such transfer. (Ellis et al., 1980, pp. 456–457)

Facts are propositions describing past events, experiences, or states of being. The illustrations for facts are the evidence substantiating the proposition. People show they know facts by recalling and stating the proposition and its supporting evidence.

There are *specific facts,* which need only one referent to be substantiated, and there are more *general facts,* which require several referents. For specific facts, you may use single illustrations supporting the proposition; for general facts, you may use sets of illustrations. For example, here is a specific fact: "Alfred Hitchcock directed the movie *Psycho.*" You need only to show the credits of the movie *Psycho* to substantiate that Hitchcock directed it. However, if you were to say, "Hitchcock directed suspense thrillers," you would have to substantiate that proposition with many referents; you might use the credits showing Hitchcock as the director of many movies that were suspense thrillers.

If you asserted the specific fact, "The United States took part in World War I for only one year," you might present as substantiating examples only newspaper headlines showing the 1917 date of the U.S. entry to the war and the 1918 date of the German surrender. But if you proposed the more general fact, "The United States was reluctant to enter World War I," you might present several examples showing that the United States avoided entry. You might use several quotations from speeches and newspaper headlines to substantiate your claim.

Most often facts are presented in sets and are illustrated that way, too. Figure 5.5 is an illustration of a set of boating terms (facts). A teacher or students may comment on the labeled picture, "The bow and stern are the front and back of a boat. You can remember *bow* as the front of the boat, because you *bow to the front*. The port and starboard are the left and right side of a boat. You can remember that the *port* side is the left side as you face the bow, because it has *four letters, like left*."

Essential Examples Are Clear.   Accurate examples are imperative, but not sufficient. Your examples must also be clear for your students to comprehend and recall. To enhance the clarity of your examples, be sure they have five characteristics.

1. Clear Examples Appeal to Appropriate Senses.   In showing an example, use a medium that will appeal to the same senses that students will use in the real world. If students are to classify birds by sight, then show examples for students to see; use either live examples, physical reproductions, or realistic pictures. If students have obviously observed a certain example of a bird, you could refer to it; but even then, use words that appeal to students' senses so they may visualize it in their mind's eye.

FIGURE 5.5   Illustration of a set of boating terms (facts)

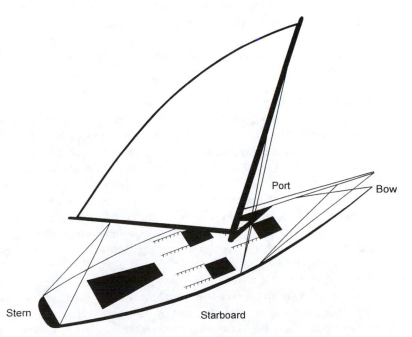

2. Clear Examples Are Brief. Especially early in a unit, use simple brief examples; remove any irrelevant details. Later, when showing examples in all their complexity, adjust the length of the example in proportion to the importance and the complexity of the idea.

3. Clear Examples Use Understandable Language. If the example must be described, use words and symbols understood by students. Scan for possible unknown prerequisites.

4. Clear Examples Accentuate Important Elements. Highlight or have students accentuate elements in the example. Make the elements in the example the "figure" and the case itself the "ground." One approach is to use the most typical and obvious example of a category. For example, for the concept *bird,* use a robin, whose feathers and wings are obvious, rather than a penguin, whose feathers are not apparent and whose wings are more like little flippers.

A second approach is to use pairs of examples and nonexamples to demonstrate that the difference between the example and nonexample is the presence or absence of one attribute. For example, to highlight the defining element of a metaphor—"one thing takes on the characteristic of something else rather than merely resembling it"—you or a student might use this example-nonexample pair:

Example of a metaphor: Bob *is* a bear

Nonexample of a metaphor: Bob *is like* a bear.

5. Clear Examples Relate the Example to the Point. Explicitly show how the elements of the example portray the attributes of the idea. State or have students state each attribute of the idea, then point to each element in the example or note each one orally. Use good transitions from the idea to the example and back to the idea again.

Essential Examples Are Interesting. Even if your examples are accurate and clear, they must also be interesting enough for students to attend to them and be motivated to remember them. First, relate the example to the students' experiences, interests, and aspirations. If you were teaching learning principles to public school teachers, you would use public school cases rather than family cases or training cases. Second, employ some degree of novelty. Include in the example some elements that are unexpected, humorous, or puzzling. Perhaps present your examples in a novel fashion, using gestures and voice variation, or unusual modes such as role play. Third, when you, rather than students, explain examples, use credible realistic examples that have some personal connection to you, the presenter.

Essential Examples Are Generalizable. So that your students will reach full understanding of the idea, and be able to use the examples in the real world, your examples must also be generalizable. Consider following two rules.

1. Use a Range of Examples from Easy to Difficult.   Make the first examples fairly obvious. When teaching students to identify birds, present or have students show a picture of each type of bird on a blank background with its wings and feathers clearly exposed. Later you can point out or ask students to introduce more subtle and complex examples in real situations, such as live birds—sparrows, finches, and nuthatches—with similar gray, brown, and black markings, hidden in fall foliage. Also show examples that may be mistaken for nonexamples, such as penguins, kiwis, and emus.

2. Vary the Types of Examples according to the Range of Cases a Graduate May Encounter in the Real World.   Have students show young and old birds, males and females of each type, from various angles and views, and in varying but appropriate environments.

Given the requirements for creating essential examples, devise and explain your own, or have your students find or create them and then share them with the class. Consider following three steps to produce them:

A. *Specify the idea, noting each important element.*
B. *Produce the basic notion of the examples you will use.*
    1. Edit the examples for accuracy.
        a. Be sure each attribute in the point is matched by the appropriate element in the example.
    2. Edit the examples for clarity. Check for
        a. appeal to the appropriate sense.
        b. brevity.
        c. understandable language.
        d. apparent elements.
    3. Edit the examples for interest. Check for
        a. meaningfulness.
        b. novelty.
        c. credibility.
C. *Adjust the set of examples for generalization and transfer.*
    1. Make the set of examples representative of the range of examples to be encountered in the real world.
    2. Order the set of examples to make it progressively more difficult.

GUIDELINE 2: ORGANIZE ESSENTIAL CONTENT

If you or your students go to the trouble of deriving and specifying essential content, it would seem sensible for you to organize the essentials and then present them in a systematic way. Remember that you can present a draft of a content structure to students and ask them to create their own organization, or you can ask students to organize the essential ideas they have derived. Think first of organizing course content and then of organizing units and lesson content.

Organize Course Content

You can prepare organized materials for the whole course, such as a whole course outline similar to the one we made for the fitness course on p. 84. You could make a visible structure based on an outline, as shown next, or as shown in Figure 5.6. In both illustrations, the course content is organized according to the structure of a research report.

AN OUTLINE AS A VISIBLE COURSE STRUCTURE

A Research Seminar Outline Adapted from a Course by Fred Lopez

   I. Introduction section of research proposal (conceptual view of research)
- A. Identifying a research problem
    1. Why do this piece of research (motivation)?
    2. How does this research relate to professional problems and values?
    3. How does this research problem relate to theory?
- B. Developing hypotheses
    1. How does the research problem relate to theory?
    2. Thinking in terms of moderators and mediators

  II. Methods section of research proposal (procedural view of research)
- A. Designing the procedures for data collection
    1. Using basic research designs in our field
- B. Checking the quality of the method
    1. Checking research for rigor: internal validity
    2. Checking research for relevance: external validity

III. Results section of research proposal (consequential view of research)
- A. Analyzing data using common statistics
- B. Analyzing data using multivariate analysis

IV. Discussion section of research proposal (interpretive view of research)
- A. Interpreting results conceptually
    1. Using theory
    2. Using professional practice
- B. Interpreting results in light of strengths and weaknesses of methodology

Organize Unit and Lesson Content

You can provide organized materials for each unit and lesson in the form of content outlines, overviews, lists, diagrams, charts, task descriptions, checklists, or decision aids.

Research Design Seminar

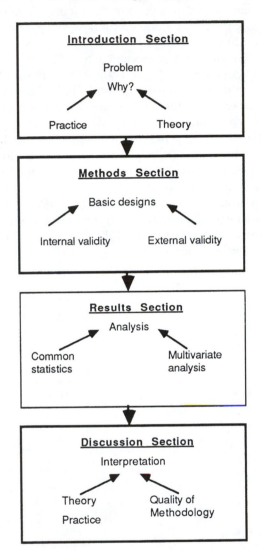

FIGURE 5.6   A chart as a visible course structure

ORGANIZING CONTENT

A young professor asked me to observe his teaching because his students were complaining that he was disorganized and unclear. The hidden message in his invitation seemed to be, "Observe and then pat me on the back and tell me that I'm OK and that my students are wrong." So, I went to his class.

It was a 4-hour session on various helpful types of drugs—chemotherapeutic agents. After 4 hours I came out of the session disoriented. I couldn't tell what was important and what was not. I couldn't follow along. The instructor greeted me hoping for the best. But, I told him, "I think your students have a point. I had little idea of what was important and what was not. I had no sense of structure and organization." I detected a shudder as I put my verbal knife between his ribs. Since I had the knife in, I figured I would twist it a bit. "I think that teachers who really know their subject matter can extract the essentials and put them down on a piece of paper in an organized way." It took the instructor a minute to realize that I had not only wounded him, but I had insulted him to boot, implying that he didn't know his subject matter. Once he realized that, he attempted to leave, muttering under his breath. I said, "Wait a minute. Before you leave, I challenge you. I'll bet you can take the essentials from that 4-hour presentation and put them down on one piece of paper in an organized fashion." He muttered again and left.

Some days later the instructor returned with the essentials of his lesson well organized on one sheet of paper. He had organized all the content in columns starting with the names of eight drug groups (sulfonamides, penicillins, cephalosporins, erythromycins, tetracyclines, chloramphenicol, streptomycin, and miscellaneous), examples of each, its mechanism, whether it is bactericidal or bacteriostatic, its bacterial spectrum, its pharmacokinetics, and finally its toxicity. Here is a small part of his structure.

Group	Examples	Mechanism	Cidal or Static	Bacterial Spectrum	Pharmaco-kinetics	Toxicity
Sulfonamides	Sulfadiazine Sulfamethozole Sulfisoxazole	Intermediary Metabol. Inhibit folic-acid synthesis.	Static	Gram-positive. Some Gram-negative.	Administered orally. Rapid absorption, good distribution, high plasma protein binding, metabolized in the liver. Excreted by the kidney.	Crystalluria, anorexia, nausea, and vomiting. Blood dyscrasias. Allergic reactions.
Penicillins	Penicillin-G Methicillin Ampicillin	Inhibit transpeptidase enzyme. Inhibit cell-wall synthesis.	Cidal	Gram-positive. Some Gram-negative (ampicillin, broad spectrum).	Administered orally (ampicillin) or parenterally (penicillin, methicillin). Good distribution. Secreted by kidney.	Convulsions. High incidence of allergic reactions.

I thought it was so good, I felt I could tease him. "Well, maybe you do know your subject matter after all."

"Yes, it seems I do." He visibly puffed up.

"What are you going to do with this great outline?"

"I don't know."

"What do you mean, you don't know? Give it to your students."

"OK, I'll give the presentation and then hand it out as a summary."

"No, give them the handout first."

"I don't think so."

"Why not?"

"Because they might not come to class!"

"Why?"

"I'm afraid my students would grab the handout and leave."

"Well, let's fool 'em. Let's leave spaces between each category, where students can take notes. After all, these are the absolute essentials. You will be saying a lot more. This way the students will see the benefit of staying and get a notion of the most important ideas and their structure as well." He agreed.

What happened? The next time he gave the presentation, he did not need fancy statistics to see the difference in students' responses about his organization. I interviewed some of his students. "How is this teacher?"

"Easy to take notes from. Clear."

"Why? What makes it so?"

"This. . . ." They pointed to the page of organized essential content.

"What did you learn?"

"I learned many categories of chemotherapeutic agents, examples of each, if they kill bacteria or keep them static. . . ."

Because the structure was so clear and was used continuously in the presentation, the students remembered it and were able to associate specifics with each section. In this way, organized essential content helped students to see the whole picture and the details, helped them follow along, and helped them recall what was presented.

Of course, when students are capable, and when there is time, it is a great learning activity for them to make their own organizers. Even when you make the initial attempt at selecting and organizing the essentials, students can add, delete, and modify as they work with the content.

GUIDELINE 3: PRESENT ESSENTIAL CONTENT IN AN ORGANIZED WAY

From the start of your course, present the essential content in an organized way. You may present the structure directly, or you may have students discuss, revise, and apply the structure; create the structure with you; or create their own structure given the elements of the content.

Present a Course Overview

Use what Charles Reigeluth and Faith Stein (1983) called the *zoom lens* analogy to present the essential content of the whole course. The zoom lens refers to a technique used in many movies: The first scene begins with a wide shot of a city, then the camera zooms in on a neighborhood, then a building, then a window, then through the window to a room filled with the film's characters. Reigeluth suggested that the wide shot of the course be an overview lesson in which you state the framework of the course: its main ideas, how the main ideas are related, and the rationale for dividing the course into units. He also suggested that students apply the broad framework. For example, you could begin a fitness course by describing and illustrating the contents of a complete fitness plan. Note the openness of the teacher to discussing other ways of thinking about the organization.

> This course will give you a complete picture of fitness. You will apply what you learn by creating a total fitness plan for yourself. Let's look at this diagram [Figure 5.7] so you can get a picture of the whole process and the whole course. Tell everyone if you see any other way of looking at the parts of the course and the relationships of the parts of the course based on your experience and way of thinking.
>
> You will learn 1. to create fitness plans and 2. to implement fitness plans. Notice that the key to creating your fitness plan is creating a nutrition plan. There are three other interrelated parts of your plan: 1. increasing and maintaining your strength, 2. your flexibility, and 3. your cardiovascular conditioning. To implement your fitness plans you will have to make early and later plans. In your early plans you will integrate your four separate fitness plans. You will schedule events and select equipment to carry out your plans. Later you will record your progress, adjust the schedules to meet real constraints, and apply principles to maintain your motivation. That is what a total fitness plan includes. Each aspect of the plan represents one unit that you will study. Are there other ways you might think about this content?
>
> Now let's apply this model by looking at some videotapes of people presenting their versions of good fitness plans and then we will discuss if they have the components mentioned in the model.*

Move from One Unit to Another within the Structure

After a unit is completed, you return to the overview and show how the completed unit fits into the big picture and where the next unit fits. Then, zoom in on the next main topic and provide the details. For example, when finished

---

* From Yelon, S., & Reznich, C. (1992). Visible models of course organization. *Performance and Instruction, 31*(6), 10. Reprinted with the permission of the National Society for Performance and Instruction, copyright © 1992.

Fitness Course

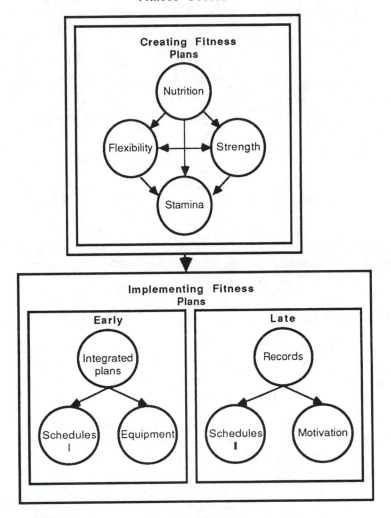

FIGURE 5.7 Visible model of a fitness course

SOURCE: Yelon, S., & Reznich, C. (1992). Visible models of course organization. *Performance and Instruction, 31*(6), 10. Reprinted with the permission of the National Society for Performance and Instruction, copyright © 1992.

with the overview of the fitness course, you might say: "Remember that the key to creating your fitness plan is creating a nutrition plan. Let's take a closer look at what goes into a good nutrition plan." Then you would direct students' attention to the diagram in Figure 5.8. and have them discuss its meaning.

When finished with the nutrition unit, you might say: "So far we have talked about nutrition, which is the basis for all other plans, such as the next topic:

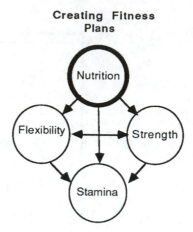

FIGURE 5.8 Diagram focusing on one unit in a course

flexibility. Let's take a closer look at what flexibility planning you should do." Then you would direct students' attention to the diagram in Figure 5.9. and ask them to discuss the connections.

Present Lesson Content in an Organized, Simple Way

Students can get lost in a lesson presentation in spite of well-organized materials. To aid comprehension, present your explanations and demonstrations in an organized, simple, and well-paced manner.

For *organization,* consider following these five rules (Chilcoat, 1989):

1. Provide an overview in each lesson.
2. Present the content in some understandable order.
3. State transitions betweeen points.

FIGURE 5.9 Diagram focusing on the transition between units

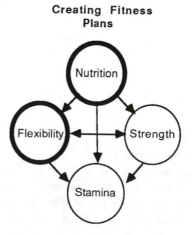

4. State reviews and summaries and label them as such.
5. State the point, give an example, restate the point.

For a *simple presentation,* think about following these ten rules (Brophy & Good, 1986):

1. Reduce the essential knowledge into a simpler form.
    a. Use numbered or bulleted points.
    b. Give ideas names, like the names of the principles.
    c. Organize many steps into groups of steps.
2. Use precise definitions.
3. Choose the best and fewest words to make a point.
4. Use simple sentences.
5. Make few tangential remarks.
6. Avoid audible pauses (e.g., um, uh, you know).
7. De-emphasize unimportant details.
8. Choose examples that embody the idea precisely and most concretely.
9. Provide new information in small doses at a moderate pace.
10. Repeat important ideas (Clark, 1986).

A FINAL WORD

One of the hardest questions about teaching I have ever heard is, "What should I teach?" All too often the answer is, "I will teach whatever is in the textbook." Instead of relying on a textbook, find real-world applications of the subject you teach and then teach the essential ideas, skills, and attitudes that students need when carrying out those real-world tasks. To find the essential content, you must describe the real-world tasks and find within their steps and decisions the embedded skills, concepts, principles, facts, and attitudes. Then, further analyze those subskills, concepts, principles, facts, and attitudes for the ideas embedded within them. Structure those essentials in an organized manner and present them through explanations, discussions, and information-seeking activities. You will find this process of analysis to be not only challenging but also interesting and full of insights and surprises.

ACTIVITIES

The first four activities call for you to list the essential content for varied types of knowledge just as you would if teaching them. The fifth activity asks you to create and evaluate examples, both important teaching skills. Then you have an opportunity to organize course content by creating a visual course model. The next three exercises demonstrate the need to derive essential content regardless of your teaching approach.

1. List an important set of *facts* that you might teach. Name the the set of facts, for example, parts of the digestive system. State how the facts would be organized and describe vivid examples you would use to substantiate them.
2. Identify an important *concept* that you might teach. Define the category of the concept and give a typical example–nonexample pair.
3. Identify an important *principle* that you might teach. Define the principle and give evidence of the relationship of variables.
4. Identify an important *skill* that you might teach. State the ordered, simplified steps of the skill and describe the demonstration.
5. Evaluate *examples:*
   a. Think of a major point students must learn—a key concept or a principle, perhaps. Create an example to illustrate the point. Then check the example: Is it accurate, clear, interesting, and generalizable?
   b. Look in a textbook of any subject matter. Find an example and evaluate it: Is it accurate, clear, interesting, and generalizable?
6. Think of a course you might teach or a large unit of instruction. Begin to create a course *overview* by listing the parts of that subject in any order. Then, make an outline or a diagram to show the relationships among the parts.
7. Is the essential content of a lesson using discussion the same as that of a lesson in which the teacher explains the ideas? Suppose you were going to discuss the factors that cause people to wage war. You have asked your students to read about the topic and come prepared to discuss it. Would you also have to prepare by doing the research, noting the facts and the substantiating evidence yourself, as you probably would if you presented an explanation?
8. What is the essential content of a lesson that focuses on problems, for example, a problem involving fractions where students need to divide four cakes among five people? Do you need facts, concepts, principles, and skills? Which ones? What should students know about each? What should you know about each before teaching this problem-based lesson?
9. Why should a teacher analyze the content in advance if, for example, students are to generate definitions of a concept from examples they have seen, such as a definition of *impressionism?* Why should a teacher analyze the content in advance if, for example, students are themselves to discover the factors promoting good health?
10. Reflection
    a. In a class I am teaching or a class I am taking, what is the essential content?
    b. How can I organize course content?
    c. How is the content organized in a class I am taking?
    d. How can I have students organize the content?
    e. How can I tell students the key points so they can learn and recall them?
    f. What are some examples of ideas that were quite memorable? Why were they memorable?

FURTHER READING

Chilcoat, G. W. (1989). Instructional behaviors for clearer presentations in the classroom. *Instructional Science, 18,* 289–314. (*Note:* This article contains a list of recommendations of what makes an excellent explanation.)

Farnam-Diggory, S. (1994). Paradigms of knowledge and instruction. *Review of Educational Research, 64*(3), 463–477. (*Note:* The author offers a taxonomy of essential content that looks like facts, concepts, principles, skills, and images.)

Gagné, R. M. (1985). *The conditions of learning and theory of instruction.* New York: Holt, Rinehart & Winston. (*Note:* One of Gagné's major premises is to look for essential content.)

Reigeluth. C. M., & Stein, F. S. (1983). The elaboration theory of instruction. In C. M. Reigeluth (Ed.), *Instructional design theories and models: An overview of their current status* (pp. 335–382). Hillsdale, NJ: Lawrence Erlbaum. (*Note:* This chapter outlines a way to organize a course using a zoom lens analogy.)

Yelon, S. L., & Massa, M. (1987). Heuristics for creating examples. *Performance and Instruction Journal, 26*(8), 13–17. (*Note:* Read about what makes a good example.)

Yelon, S., & Reznich, C. (1992). Visible models of course organization. *Performance and Instruction Journal, 31*(8), 7–11. (*Note:* This article makes an argument for making the structure of a course visible to students.)

chapter 6

Learning Aids

OVERVIEW

Create and have students create and use devices that help them learn well, easily, and quickly.

Guideline 1: Select Learning Aids

Guideline 2: Use Learning Aids
        Use an Aid as the Major Teaching Tool
        Use an Aid as a Small but Important Instructional Tool
        Use an Aid as the Sole Means of Instruction

Guideline 3: Anticipate Problems with Learning Aids
        Aids May Make Learning Too Easy for Students
        Students May Not Be Able to Perform without the Aid

When I mention instructional aids to teachers, they often react, "Are you kidding me? Make it easy for my students? I had to suffer through this; let them suffer too!" It is as if making learning more difficult will build a student's character. Will aids make learning too easy? Will students be insulted by a teacher's help? Will students become lazy? Will students be unable to perform without the aid?

First, let's be sure we are talking about the same thing. *Learning aids* are devices or mechanisms designed to make learning more effective, more efficient, and more satisfying. They are not merely media aids or props; rather, they have a specific learning function. Learning aids are mechanisms that simplify and organize complex content and connect new ideas to old ones. They are built to focus attention, ease learning, produce recall, foster transfer, and speed instruction (Clark, 1986; Yelon, 1984; Yelon & Berge, 1987).

Instructional aids come in many formats. An aid may be a small piece of paper, a memorized word, a picture, or a videotape. The following is merely a sample of the array of learning aids that exist:

A *handout* containing a *flow diagram* showing the steps for writing a letter. The diagram has separate branches that specify the steps for business letters and friendly letters. The business branch breaks off further into branches for order forms, billing forms, and letters of complaint.

A *handout* containing a *topic outline and a diagram* portraying information-processing theory. It is to be used in a presentation and is designed to be accompanied by a set of matching transparencies.

A *poster* to be used during demonstration and practice containing a series of *drawings and universal symbols* showing how to operate a power drill.

A *one-page chart* describing the origins, conditions, outcomes, and methods of six teaching approaches to accompany an explanation and discussion.

An *empty one-page chart* with the column titles stating the names of *statistical tests* and row titles indicating characteristics of the tests such as their assumptions. Students must fill in the chart as they study and then discuss each of the tests.

A *pocket-sized, laminated card* that guides a police trainee in deciding when to use a certain degree of force. The learner is led to focus on the degree of danger presented by the other person involved (Desmedt, 1984).

A *pocket-sized, laminated card* that guides a learner through the decisions to make in an emergency situation. The learner answers yes or no to a series of decisions about a victim: Is he or she conscious? Is he or she breathing? The tree ends by prescribing the appropriate first aid.

A *manual of narrative recipes* about how to do word processing. The steps on the left half of the page are broad, and the steps on the right side are detailed. For the broad step, "Select the portion to be cut," the corresponding specific step is, "Select by clicking with a mouse and dragging the shading over the portion desired."

A *laminated checklist* of the qualities to note in a final product. It could contain the standards for checking a mass-manufactured product like a packaged toy; or it could describe the characteristics of a more unique product, such as a plan for the interior of a home produced by a professional.

A *checklist* on a report *assignment sheet* that reminds students of details to keep in mind as they write.

An *excellent example of a final product,* with the desired characteristics clearly labeled. It could be a machined part with its tolerances clearly noted, or it could be an architect's plan with its qualities shown by handwritten notes.

A *verbal mnemonic device,* such as ROY G. BIV to help recall the portions of the color spectrum as we see them: (R) red, (O) orange, (Y) yellow, (G) green, (B) blue, (I) indigo, (V) violet.

A *pictorial mnemonic* containing objects beginning with the same sound as the categories to be recalled. Levin and Levin (1990) used pictures such as an <u>an</u>gel holding a <u>mon</u>key on a leash shooting an <u>ar</u>row in a <u>pan</u> to remind students of the hierarchical categories of plants: <u>an</u>giosperms, <u>mon</u>ocotyledons, <u>ar</u>ales, and <u>pan</u>daneles.

An *audiotape* of the *steps* for cleaning a table in a restaurant. A trainee wearing an earplug listens to the tape, one step at a time, and acts accordingly. When the trainee is able to recall the steps, the tape is abandoned.

A *videotape* of an excellent ski run, with portions shown in slow motion so that the qualities of performance can be noted.

A *model* of a victim needing resuscitation that is linked to a computer which maintains a record of all actions of a rescuer and keeps track of the time.

A *transparency* that places words in a statement strategically so that its attributes are more noticeable. Here is a simple example:

> Instructional aids are
>> devices or
>> mechanisms
>>> designed to make
>> learning
>>> more effective,
>>> more efficient, and
>>> more satisfying.

As you can imagine, you can use aids like this to support an explanation, a discussion, a problem-based lesson, or an independent study. How do you decide among all the possibilities which aid to use for a given circumstance? Consider the purpose of the aid.

GUIDELINE 1: SELECT LEARNING AIDS

There are many ways instructional aids can be used during instruction; however, each aid has its own purpose and should be selected accordingly. During your explanations of ideas, discussions of issues, solving of problems, demonstrations of performance, and observations of student practice, you and your students can use aids to see the structure of your course, to recall a list of ideas or steps, to see the path to take in a task, to focus attention, and to summarize the qualities of an acceptable performance. Figures 6.1, 6.2, and 6.3 are designed to help you choose the right aid for a particular purpose. You and your students can adapt these common instructional aids to fit your learning situation.

FIGURE 6.1   When to use common types of learning aids: Part 1

Type of Aid	Appearance Sketch	When to Use
Flow Diagram	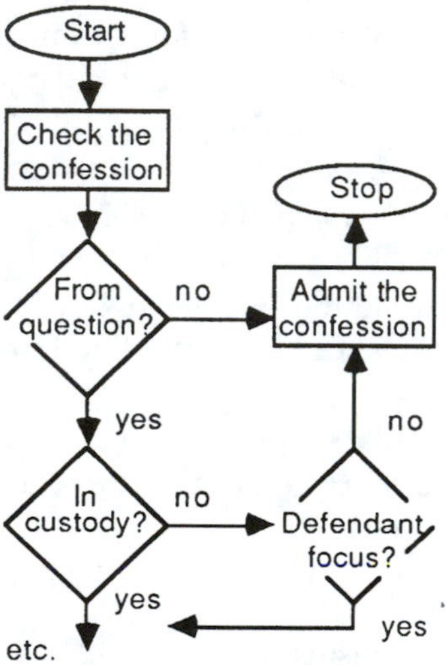	**When task steps branch**
Outline	**Instructional theories** I. Behavioral theories 　A. Programmed instruction 　B. Behavioral approach II. Cognitive theories 　A. Conditions of learning 　B. Component display 　C. Elaboration theory III. Empirically derived 　A. Inquiry teaching	**When ordering clusters of content**
Chart	Characteristics of knowledge types 	Type	Behavior	Criterion	etc.
---	---	---	---
Skill	Do	Checklist	etc.
Concept	Identify	Definition	etc.
Principle	Apply	Definition	etc.
Fact	Recall	Source	etc.		**When comparing subtopics on multiple dimensions**

Type of Aid	Appearance Sketch	When to Use
Drawing	 Bowline knot 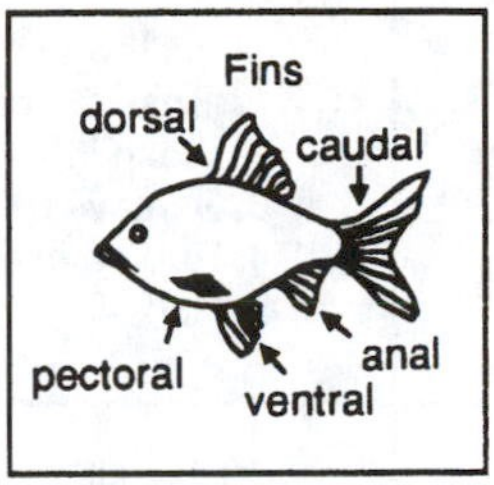 / Fins / dorsal / caudal / pectoral / ventral / anal	When visually simplifying complex stimuli
Mnemonic (verbal and visual)	Huron / Ontario / Michigan / Erie / Superior  — OOMPA! — Objective / Overview / Motivation / Prerequistes / Agenda	When recalling a set of facts
Decision Aid	If noun is... / Then pronoun is... — Masc. Singular / He — Fem. Singular / She — Neuter Singular / It — Plural / They	When requiring different responses from varying situations
Decision Tree	Straightening ear canal / Adult? / no / yes / Child older than infant? / yes / no / Pull ear lobe up / Pull ear lobe down / Brace head Pull ear lobe down	When choosing responses after a series of decisions

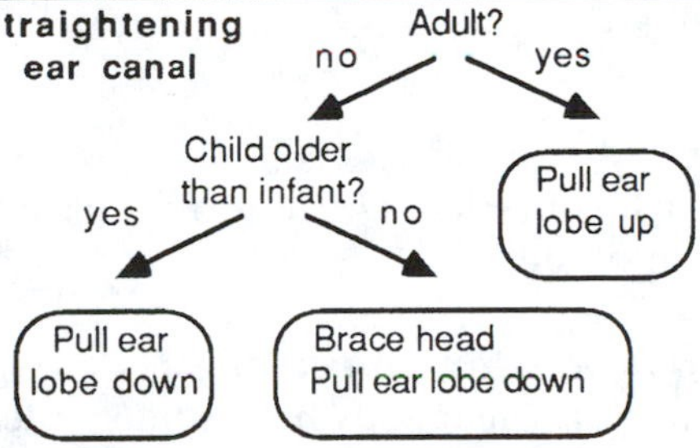

FIGURE 6.2 When to use common types of learning aids: Part 2

Type of Aid	Appearance Sketch	When to Use
Narrative Task Description	Steps to wash and wax a car 1. Rinse the car with warm water 2. Wash the car using a soap-filled sponge 3. Remove road tar with tar cleaner & rag 4. Rub on even thin coat of paste wax 5. Rub off all wax using a chamois cloth	**When verbally explaining a series of steps**
Checklist	Checklist for concept objective ___ 1. New examples & nonexamples given ___ 2. Medium matches real world ___ 3. Calls for identification ___ 4. Stated in behavioral terms ___ 5. Definition used as standard	**When checking criteria in a process or a product**
Annotated Model	**Proper address** Name of recipient → Steve Yelon ← Full street name House number → 459 East 7th Street City followed by comma → Brooklyn, NY ← Official state initials 11218 ↑ Zip code	**When noting criteria for a complex visual product**
Diagram	Loss of self-esteem → Short of breath → Loss of control Shortness of breath cycle Decreased activities ← Depression ← Forced role change	**When relating variables in complex ways**

FIGURE 6.3 When to use common types of learning aids: Part 3

Even though you select an aid to fit a particular purpose, you may need to justify your use of aids.

Seven Good Reasons for Using Learning Aids

1. Functional learning aids help students learn what they need to know.
2. Learning aids save time. In the time you save your students, you may be able to teach more, go into greater detail, or include enough practice to produce mastery. If the aid affords more time, you can teach more people more ideas than you have taught before.
3. Your students are likely to understand explanations, discussions, activities, and readings more quickly and recall them more completely and accurately. By working with a well-structured aid during practice,

students may be better able to recall important information when they work independently in the real world.

4. With a carefully constructed aid, students are more likely to focus on the most important ideas and are more likely to learn those ideas. Not only will students attend to specific portions of the task or the content, but they also may gain insight into the structure of the task and thereby understand it better and be more flexible in its use.

5. The aid carried into the real world may simply serve as a reminder to perform. You can ensure that a task will be performed outside of instruction by making the aid portable and brief.

6. If graduates can take the aid with them into the real world, it may add to their skill and confidence to perform.

7. By using various types of aids for your teaching, you model more than one way of structuring content that students can imitate in their own studies. By using a variety of aids, you may also be able to cater to the particular study preferences of a wide range of students. Once they have been shown how to create and use various types of aids, students may learn and gain confidence to use them independently.

USING AIDS TO SAVE TIME

Some years ago the director of the Center for Electron Optics at Michigan State University, Karen Klomparens, sent me letters to communicate her satisfaction with the use of some learning aids in her lab. She had created checklists of the steps that students must perform when using the electron microscopes. Here is part of what she said:

> Here's a quick update on the checklists for my labs: They're great! We had a lot of success with them this term.
>
> The students like them because they give a *defined* set of criteria needed to use the microscopes unsupervised. My T.A.s [teaching assistants] like them because, for once, they know exactly what skills *I* want the students to have before getting permission to work unsupervised. And, I like them because I can use them to improve the teaching of the course.

In another letter she added,

> We have increased the number of undergraduates, graduate students, life-long education students and technicians trained in the CEO [Center for Electron Optics] from 12-15 per year to 75-80 per year *with* an increase in the quality of the program.

Note in each of the examples in the next section how often learning is made easier and quicker.

GUIDELINE 2: USE LEARNING AIDS

Use a learning aid when you need some help in making an idea clear or when students need some extra help to learn. Use aids when an idea is particularly difficult, when time is short, or when you have many students. Frankly, the only time I wouldn't use a learning aid is when students must learn to make and use their own aids. Remember always to test an aid to see if it truly does make learning easier.

If you build it, use it. Each type of aid will have its own use. The point is to use it. I have seen instructors spend considerable time creating excellent charts and diagrams only to forget to use them during instruction. Trust the aid and use it.

How should you use an aid? Using your creativity, you will probably devise many ways to use aids. Here I offer a few basic approaches for using an aid: as the major teaching tool, as a minor contributor, or as the sole means of instruction.

Use an Aid as the Major Teaching Tool

If you were to use an aid as a major teaching tool, you would focus your students' attention on the aid for most of the lesson. Suppose, for example, that you wanted to use a *task description,* an explicit statement of a task's steps, as a major teaching tool. You would show the steps to students, explaining that the steps represent what students will learn to do. You would focus students' attention on the major steps to give them an overview of the task. As they looked at the task description, you would explain and then demonstrate each step in the description. You would remain open to changes and improvements based on students' suggestions. Then students would use the steps to check their own practice. Finally, you would use the description to check students' test performance. That's using an aid as a major teaching tool!

> ### USING A TASK DESCRIPTION
> ### AS A MAJOR TEACHING TOOL
>
> Once a teacher of veterinary medicine approached me with a problem in the lab she was teaching. The vet students were supposed to extract blood from the jugular vein of a dog and analyze it—a harmless process similar to drawing blood from a human. However, during the lab students were bitten by the dogs; students were hurting the dogs; students were dropping and wasting sterilized equipment; few students collected the sample; fewer still put the sample in the machine; and almost no one had results to interpret. I asked the teacher to make a list of the steps for the task. At our next meeting she returned with a two-page list of the major steps and substeps for the task: gather equipment, restrain the dog, insert the needle, collect the sample, continue collection, and so on. Then we discussed how to teach using the list as an aid.

In the next lab she handed out the steps to all the students. She explained the steps before demonstrating them. Then, step by step, she showed the students the process. Before students went to their stations to perform the task, they committed as many of the steps to memory as they could. Then they got the dogs and proceeded. No one was bitten. No dogs were hurt. Very little equipment was wasted. Each student collected the sample, placed it in the machine, took the readings, and had time to discuss the results. The teacher was satisfied; the students were satisfied; even the dogs were satisfied.

The use of this aid as a major teaching tool showed once again that people are likely to follow explicit instructions. If the instructions are accurate, people following them will perform well.

USING A SIMPLE FLOW DIAGRAM AS A MAJOR TEACHING TOOL

I once knew a judge who taught a seminar to other judges on the topic, admission of confessions by juveniles. After listening to his 2-hour lecture, participating judges would leave shaking their heads and muttering, "What did he say?"

In a judges' teaching seminar the judge attended, the leaders discussed the usefulness of learning aids such as flow diagrams to explain how to perform a branching task. This made sense to him for the task, "how to admit the confession of a juvenile." As part of an exercise, he created a flow diagram that showed two possible outcomes and five interrelated decisions in that process. As you can see in Figure 6.4, a judge assessing a confession by a juvenile could admit the confession or suppress it. After checking the records, the judge would ask if the statement were the result of an interrogation. If it were not, he or she could admit the confession. But if the confession were the result of an interrogation, the judge would have to ask if the defendant were in custody. If that were not true and the focus of investigation were not on the defendant, the judge could admit the confession. And so the flow proceeded.

As the final activity in the judges' teaching seminar, each judge had to teach a lesson. Our judge taught about admission of confessions by juveniles by showing the flow diagram and explaining the decisions. Then he went through a few cases and had each member of his audience make decisions for cases he gave them. Finally, he gave audience members a case as a test, which all were able to pass. And, he did all this in 15 minutes! Recall that ordinarily the judge took 2 hours to teach the topic with moderate success, and now he took only 15 minutes to produce a clearly successful lesson.

Can you imagine the difficulty of attempting to construct this formula for admitting confessions yourself? Use of the aid made the structure of the task clear; it made the important ideas pop out: Students could see that there were two outcomes and five interacting decisions. After using the diagram

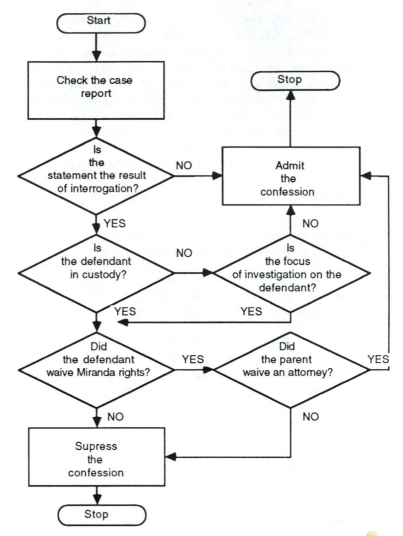

FIGURE 6.4 Flow diagram for determining admissibility of confessions by juveniles

on a few cases, his students relied on the aid less and less because they could recall its structure and contents. The flow diagram certainly saved time, and if used frequently, it could definitely increase the number of people trained. The judges said they were likely to use the flow diagram on the job because it was so compact and easy to use. The flow diagram put the essentials of the task on one page and could be easily placed in a resource book judges use in court. They were convinced by the end of the session that they could use the aid productively.

Use an Aid as a Small but Important Instructional Tool

There are many ways of using aids for a small but important part of your lesson, and there are many types of aids you can use for that purpose. None will necessarilly dominate the lesson, but each will make its own small contribution to learning and will take only a small portion of your students' attention. Consider for a moment a skill you might teach. Relate that skill to the relatively small contributions of the types of aids described next.

Six Aids Making Small Contributions to Teaching a Skill

1. A *flow diagram,* created in collaboration with students, noting all the steps in the skill students must learn to perform
2. A detailed *checklist* used to assess practice, test performance, and real-world behavior
3. A *mnemonic device* that students are assigned to create, which they may use to recall all of the effective techniques associated with each step of a skill
4. A two-column *decision aid* to show which technique to use for what situation
5. A *printed outline* to enable students to recall the lesson after the course is over
6. *Subtitles* inserted during parts of a videotape of an excellent performance, to focus attention each time the performer demonstrates an effective technique (e.g., the effects used by sports broadcasters to highlight a particular performance)

Some aids serve a very specific but important purpose as part of a lesson. For example, an *annotated example* used in part of a lesson can be a powerful aid when used properly to focus on a particular problem. Ask students to discuss the meaning of each annotation.

MAKING A SMALL BUT IMPORTANT CONTRIBUTION USING AN ANNOTATED EXAMPLE

A trainer was having difficulty teaching professional colleagues to write technical legal documents. To resolve the problem, he found a nearly perfect example of a report and perfected it. Next to each portion of the report, he wrote small annotations that explained what made that portion correct. For example, he drew an arrow to dates in the body of the report and wrote in the margin, "Factual evidence presented in chronological order." He put a number next to each annotation proportional to the importance of that report portion in the real world. This way students knew just how critical each piece was and how important each annotation was. When he taught his students how to write that report, he presented the annotated example and pointed out each annotation. He asked his students to review the example in small groups and to explain to the group what each annotation meant. He asked them to discuss what change in the example would make it less than effective. He told his students that it not only was OK to refer to the example frequently as they prepared their reports, it was recommended. As a consequence, student reports were of high quality. When, in spite of everything, a student made an error and inquired about it, the trainer simply showed the student the desired result on the annotated example and asked the student to interpret the annotation. There were no arguments about what was required and what each piece was worth.

To create their own annotated examples, students need to be given criteria, a good example, and instructions to relate the criteria to the parts of the example that follow the standards.

Use an Aid as the Sole Means of Instruction

You can also use aids as the only means of instruction. A common example is the pictures and words at self-service gasoline stations. The symbols deliver all the instruction the learner needs to pump gas. In the world of training, these are known as *job aids*. Aids that make a similar contribution while a person is performing a task are known as *performance aids*. A common example of a performance aid is the message telling you what to do when your copy machine runs out of paper.

USING AN AID AS THE SOLE MEANS OF INSTRUCTION: EXAMPLE 1

One of my former students, Bonnie Mathews, designed and successfully tested a flow diagram for teaching hospital patients to use a videocassette recorder (VCR). The aid combined written instructions and drawings of a VCR into a flow diagram, which accompanied a menu of educational videotapes and the VCR in the parents' room of the hospital. She found that people who had never used a VCR were able to operate the machine with only the use of the aid. Nurses and other hospital staff did not need to assist. She said, "Having self-instructional directions has saved us valuable nursing time." I guess that learning aids can make life easier for instructors, too.

You may decide that some of what you teach can be taught best by the use of an aid. In fact, you may be able to save scarce class time by using aids that teach a portion of the content.

USING AN AID AS THE SOLE MEANS OF INSTRUCTION: EXAMPLE 2

A former student and present colleague, Kathy Doig, a teacher of medical technology, created an outline of a chart for her students (Doig, 1990). She listed blood groups (e.g., ABO and Rh systems) down the side of the chart and created columns calling for the antibody characteristics of the group such as its class, whether it is cold or warm reacting, and its complement required for detection. She wanted her students to learn the basic facts but didn't want to spend valuable class time for that. So, she had them fill in the chart outside of class. She gave the students a bit of credit for completng the chart and handing it in, tested them on it, and required application of the ideas in subsequent classes. This enabled her to use class time to have students learn how to solve problems using the facts, rather than lecturing about the facts.

GUIDELINE 3: ANTICIPATE
PROBLEMS WITH LEARNING AIDS

Instructional aids, like any other solutions to problems, raise new problems of their own. So, be alert for new issues as you use aids.

Aids May Make Learning Too Easy for Students

Solve problems with aids as you encounter them. Some of the first questions people raise are, "Do they make learning too easy?" and "Are they an insult to the intelligence of students?" One teacher I know handles the first question by explaining his intent: "By using this instructional aid, I do not mean to insult your intelligence. I know you could probably create this aid for yourself given the time, but we have a limited amount of time to learn this relatively difficult task. So that we can learn more than we ordinarily might, I will use the aid. If you would rather not take advantage of it, feel free to study without it or to create your own."

Students generally appreciate the help they get. For example, in a session for my doctoral students I show how to read an instructional theory using a narrative task description as a guide. I tell them I know they know how to read and I know they could figure out how to read an instructional theory eventually. But I would rather that they successfully perform this skill as soon as possible. During my explanation and demonstration I ask my students if I should continue or if this is insulting. The consensus is that I should continue.

Students May Not Be Able to Perform without the Aid

Other serious questions about learning aids that people raise are: "Are instructional aids a crutch?" and, "Once students use an aid will they ever be able to perform without it?" To deal with these issues, you might first think about whether or not you want students to use the aid when they perform in the real world. Consider three criteria:

1. Do Performers Need the Aid in the Real World?   People need an aid in the real world for a couple of good reasons. First, for a rarely used skill, people need an aid simply as a reminder. Second, for a very complex or important task, people must use an aid to be sure the performance is successful. Pilots and astronauts always use aids on the job.

2. Will the Use of the Aid in the Real World Interfere with the Effectiveness or the Efficiency of the Performance?   To encourage good performance, we should not provide devices during instruction that will slow performance or counter results in real use.

3. Is It Socially Acceptable for Someone to Use the Aid in the Real World?   We have to be sensitive to the social context of performance. There are occasions when a performer would lose credibility and counter the desired results of the performance by using an aid. For example, a patient might distrust a nurse who had to check a list of steps to do a routine performance. You can use the three criteria for deciding if aids will help or hinder transfer. For example, if a judicial instructor were to use the three criteria, he would consider that the aid for deciding on the admissibility of a confession by a juvenile may be needed in a real situation because of its importance and complexity. The aid is not likely to interfere with performance, and it is socially acceptable to use such an aid in court. An instructor, therefore, might decide to teach judges by having them make rulings using the aid, based on the same information they would get in court.

Suppose you wanted a student to perform without an aid. How would you arrange instruction to make this happen? Sometimes, you have to have students purposefully abandon the aid a little at a time. Sometimes it happens naturally.

PHASING OUT AN AID NATURALLY

Sara Knaggs created a decision tree for use by paramedics to guide their intervention in drug-related crises. Using the decision tree, a paramedic first decided whether the victim was conscious or unconscious, breathing or not breathing. Depending on the answers, he or she acted or moved to another decision. In this case, the decisions led to a diagnosis of the drug crisis and the proper first aid.

The teacher used the aid successfully during instruction but ran into some obstacles afterward. When supervisors saw the aid, they imagined all sorts of abuse. They said, "We can see it now. A paramedic responds to someone who has been found lying on the sidewalk. The paramedic says, 'Get back please,' then consults the aid. 'Let's see. Where are we? Conscious or unconscious? Unconscious. Breathing or not breathing? Hmm, let's see. Not breathing.' By the time the paramedic responds, the patient is likely to be dead."

To check the validity of their concern, the teacher went to talk to the paramedics in the class. She asked one if he remembered the decision aid used in the class.

"Oh yes," he responded. "For a while one of my buddies had it pasted on the inside of the van." He continued, "One person reduced the decision tree on a copy machine and taped it to the back of his clipboard." Just when the teacher thought the critics were right, the paramedic said, "But we don't use it anymore."

She said, "What did you say?"

"I said that we don't use the chart anymore."

"Why not?"

"I can see it in my head."

"What do you mean you can see it in your head?"

"I mean I can see a picture of the chart in my mind. I've used it so many times in training and so many times on the job, that it flashes clearly in my mind when I need it. I can see it in my head."

When students use a well-organized and functional aid several times during practice they are likely to commit the aid to memory.

A FINAL WORD

Why do things the hard way? Why should you and your students struggle unnecessarily? Make learning and teaching easier for you and your students by using learning aids. Use aids when they truly help and are not an impediment to students becoming independent learners. Use what help you can to get students as far as you can and then teach them to create their own aids. A good way to teach students to create their own aids is first to present to them many types of useful aids.

Find the content in your course that is most difficult for students to learn and make an instructional aid today, or think of an assignment that requires students to make an aid. You will not only be teaching students the content, but also showing them a mechanism they can use to teach themselves tough material.

ACTIVITIES

In most of these activities you are asked to create various types of aids and then to think about how you would use them.

1. Think of a mental skill you might teach, such as how to write a paragraph with a good topic sentence and supporting sentences. Draw a flow diagram you might use to teach the skill.
2. Think of a set of facts you might teach, such as the parts of the heart or the parts of a flower. Make a diagram that would make it easy to remember the

parts. Also work with someone else as if you were working with students to make a mnemonic device that consists of a story to help recall the facts.

3. Think of a decision that must be made, such as when to use addition, subtraction, multiplication, or division to solve a story problem. Design an appropriate decision aid or decision tree.

4. Think of a product that students must learn to produce, such as a descriptive report.
   a. Create with someone else, who represents your students, a checklist of criteria to judge the product.
   b. Based on the criteria you devise, make an annotated model of the product.

5. Think of a set of ideas in a course, such as various physics principles. Make a diagram relating all the principles.

6. For each aid you create, state how you would use it in your instruction: as a major teaching tool? a small but important tool? the sole means of instruction?

7. Think of an aid you have used to help yourself learn. What kind was it? How did you use it? How did it help you learn? Once you learned, did you still need the aid? Why or why not?

8. Choose an idea or skill that you think is particulary difficult for students to learn. Refer back to the figures in the chapter to choose an appropriate aid. Sketch out the aid and try it out on a representative student to see if it makes learning easier. Then try it during instruction.

9. How do the other principles you have read about in this text relate to the use of aids? How would you account for meaningfulness and prerequisites in creating aids? How does an aid apply the principles of open communciation and organized essential content?

10. Reflection
    a. What devices can I provide to help students learn?
    b. When can I use flow diagrams, outlines, charts, pictures, decision aids, narrative task descriptions, checklists, annotated models?
    c. For what content do students have the greatest need for an aid?
    d. How should I use the aids?
    e. How can I get students to create their own aids?

FURTHER READING

Armbruster, B., & Anderson, T. (1984). Structures of explanations in history textbooks, or so what if Governer Stanford missed the spike and hit the rail? *Journal of Curriculum Studies, 16,* 181–194. (*Note:* Structural devices are used to help students organize and recall the content.)

Bullock, D. (1982). Guiding job performance with job aids. *Training and Development Journal, 36*(9), 36–42. (*Note:* This early article on job aids contains many lessons for learning aids to be used during instruction.)

Geis, G. L. (1984). Checklisting. *Journal of Instructional Development,* 7(1), 2–9. (*Note:* Read about all types of learning aids that are first and second cousins to checklists.)

Norman, D. (1990). Cognitive artifacts. In J. M. Carroll (Ed.), *Cognitive theory and design in human-computer interaction.* New York: Basic Books. (*Note:* Cognitive artifacts are devices that help people think or learn.)

Scruggs, T. E., & Mastropieri, M. A. (1992, winter). Remembering the forgotten art of memory. *American Educator,* 31-37. (*Note:* The authors describe how clear images and mnemonic techniques aid memory. They also advocate the use of other principles such as meaningfulness and active practice.)

Sokol, M. (1994). Adaptation to difficult designs: Facilitating use of new technology. *Journal of Business and Psychology, 8*(3), 277-296. (*Note:* This is an example of the evolution of learning and job aids to performance aids in the world of work.)

Yelon, S. L. (1984). How to use and create criterion checklists. *Performance and Instruction Journal, 23*(3), 1-4. (*Note:* Just like it says—learn how to make checklists.)

Yelon, S. L., & Berge, Z. L. (1987). Using fancy checklists for efficient feedback. *Performance and Instruction Journal, 26*(4), 14-20. (*Note:* Special forms of checklists are provided to help instructors provide feedback.)

chapter 7

Novelty

OVERVIEW

Vary stimuli to capture and keep students' attention.

Guideline 1: Capture and Maintain Attention
 Vary Your Actions
 Vary Your Program
 Vary Your Techniques
 Teach Creatively
 Use Humor, Suspense, Shock, and Surprise
 Teach Students to Focus Their Attention

Guideline 2: Direct Your Students' Attention
 Use Media to Help Your Students Direct Their Attention to
 the Important Cues
 Stress Important Points

Guideline 3: Provoke Curiosity
 Use Questions
 Use Puzzling Events and Demonstrations

It's difficult for someone to pay attention to a particular topic for a considerable length of time. To hold an audience's attention, some speakers use gimmicks like telling bad jokes or acting silly. Rather than resort to entertainment to grab and keep attention, apply the principle of novelty. The principle of novelty is not about humor and telling jokes; it is not about being a master presenter; it is about helping to arouse, direct, and maintain students' attention.

The *principle of novelty* suggests that to arouse and maintain attention you must vary the instructional stimuli. Produce variation in what students see, hear, and feel as they learn. Your students must attend to ideas and skills if they are to learn them, but students cannot pay strict and exclusive attention to a long explanation, discussion, or activity. Attention wanders; students attend for a while to one thing and then switch to another. When attention is distracted from the message, you have to do something to bring it back. You can do so by periodically changing stimuli—by varying your methods from explanation to discussion, from discussion to simulation, from simulation to reading. When you do explain, you can vary how you say things and what you say; you can move and gesture; and you can vary the media you use. Any change that arouses a student's attention and focuses that attention on the message is appropriate (Berlyne, 1960; Keller, 1983, 1987).

GUIDELINE 1: CAPTURE AND MAINTAIN ATTENTION

You can use novelty to capture and maintain your students' attention by applying six methods:

1. Vary your actions.
2. Vary your program.
3. Vary your techniques.
4. Teach creatively.
5. Use humor, suspense, shock, and surprise.
6. Teach students to focus their attention.

Vary Your Actions

Have you ever wondered what people mean when they refer to a dynamic teacher? The answer turns out to be relatively simple. Dynamic teachers modulate their voices and move. They speak sometimes loudly and sometimes softly, sometimes quickly and sometimes slowly. They gesture, walk around, posture, make faces. Any one of us can be a dynamic teacher and show our enthusiasm by varying our voice and our moves.

Dynamic teachers not only use variation, but they also use it in the right amount and in the proper way. Variation cannot be arbitrary and repetitive; it must be meaningful and patterned. Variation through your movement and voice must be carefully integrated with your message. Your body movement and voice modulation must mean something.

Have you ever encountered a person who moves just to move rather than to connect the movement to the message? One teacher I know paces while he speaks to his class. He paces back and forth regularly and steadily, speaking in a cadence that matches his pace. His pacing is so regular and so steady that within minutes his students are asleep.

Have you ever seen a teacher who unconsciously plays with a piece of chalk while explaining something? This is the person who flips the chalk up and down, up and down; then flips it from hand to hand; and then finally drops it and wonders why the students laugh and applaud. During the explanation the students' attention is directed to the chalk rather than to what is said.

Here is a small example of how variations in voice and movement might be well integrated into a message. Look at Figure 7.1 and try to picture what

FIGURE 7.1   Using voice and movement variation to explain

the teacher is doing and, hear how he sounds as he explains the parts of an objective. In the first picture when the teacher says, "There are four parts to an instructional objective," he says "four" and "objective" a bit more loudly than other words and holds out four fingers to students. He pauses after "parts." He walks left four paces, and in the next picture when he says, "First, there is the behavior, the action, what the person does on the test," he holds up his index finger as he says, "first." He stresses "behavior," "action," and "test" and pauses after saying "action." He picks up a piece of paper as he says "test." Then he takes one step to the right. He says, "Second, there is the condition, the situation in which the test is taken." As he says "second," he holds up two fingers. He emphasizes "condition," "situation," and "test is taken." When he says, "Conditions are what the students are given to work with and what they are restricted from using," he holds up test instructions as he emphasizes "given" and then holds up a text as he emphasizes "restricted."

Get the idea? The gestures, movements, and voice modulations need not be dramatic. They can be subtle moves coordinated with what students should attend to.

Variation in voice and movement is commonly called enthusiasm. To generate your enthusiasm, that is, to be able to do this kind of voice variation and movement without even thinking about it, teach things that interest you. Remember that one of the characteristics of excellent teachers is belief in what they teach. If some topics are not of great interest to you, become interested by finding out why they are important to others. Tell students relevant personal experiences that fit the point you are making. Argue a viewpoint on an issue related to the topic. Then you will naturally vary what you do, what you say, and how you say it. You will change your loudness, tone, or pace to fit the point. If you are angry about an issue, you will raise your voice, speak with intensity, widen your eyes, ball up your fist, clench your teeth. If you are are excited, you will open your stance, increase your pitch, talk quickly, open your mouth, and smile. Don't hide enthusiasm. Once an instructor told me that he was excited about his subject, but his students didn't know that because he didn't show it. Don't keep your enthusiasm for your subject inside. Show it.

What are the payoffs for an enthusiastic presentation? Are students likely to be more satisfied with an enthusiastic presentation than a dull one? Are they likely to learn more?

THE DR. FOX EFFECT

Have you ever heard of the "Dr. Fox effect"? An actor, given the name Dr. Myron Fox, was brought in to talk to a group of educators. He was coached not only to speak with verve and enthusiasm, but also to use double-talk, neologisms, non sequiturs, and contradictory statements. Yet, the audience rated the speaker favorably in spite of relatively meaningless content. So, students may be satisfied by an enthusiastic presentation even when it doesn't make sense (Naftulin, Ware, & Donnely, 1973).

Would students learn more from an enthusiastic presentation? Other researchers tried variations of the Dr. Fox lecture; they crossed the liveliness of the lecture with varying amounts of meaningful content. They found that the greater the substance of the content the more students learned, and the greater the expressiveness the more students learned.

In a review of a number of studies of this sort, Abrami, Leventhal, and Perry (1982) concluded that both satisfaction and achievement are influenced by expressiveness, but satisfaction is affected much more. To produce student satisfaction and achievement, present organized and essential content enthusiastically.

Vary Your Program

You can introduce variation throughout an instructional program by using a varied agenda. Suppose you wanted to apply the principle of novelty to vary the program for your course on interviewing. You could begin the unit by showing a satirical videotape of a terrible interview, follow this with a lively lecture on how to respond to nonverbal cues, a videotaped example of the interviewing procedure, a live demonstration of the procedure, a role play for practice, and a discussion to review the practice. You could ask questions about interviewing, schedule breaks, use voice and movement dynamics to explain and illustrate the interviewing process, vary the amount of information, and change the length of the sessions.

The makers of the the children's TV show "Sesame Street" know how to vary the delivery of a message. The show is based on a magazine format, with scenes interrupted by short advertisement-like segments about letters and numbers. Within and across segments the sounds vary, the lengths vary, the characters vary, the themes vary. There is movement and there is talking. This variation keeps children's attention.

Have you ever watched a child watching "Sesame Street"? Typically a child will be attracted to a segment and watch it intently for a while. Then he or she will become disenchanted; attention wanders. When a child's attention wanders, everything wanders, mind and body. But, on "Sesame Street," as a child wanders from the TV, the scene changes, the sound changes, the characters change, the plot changes—and the child's attention is drawn back. The child's attention wanders and is recaptured over and over. The show's designers understand how to capture and keep the attention of their audience.

Vary Your Techniques

To gain and keep students' attention, vary your instructional procedures. One simple thing to do within a lesson is to break up explanations with examples, demonstrations, practice, and feedback. That's enough variation to keep anyone alert.

Vary your program format across lessons. Sometimes explain the idea to students; sometimes have students discover the concept from examples you provide; sometimes have students discuss the meaning of a study; sometimes run a simulation. Have students work individually and in groups.

Use varied techniques within a lecture. Use a series of short lectures followed by exercises, intersperse short readings or videos in the lecture, and ask students to briefly discuss a point with a partner or write a reaction to an issue during a lecture.

Use group approaches such as a form of the "jigsaw technique" (Aronson, Blaney, Sikes, & Snapp, 1978). First, groups of students study different aspects of a subject such as the American Civil War: political factors, economic factors, social factors, foreign relations, battle strategy, health concerns, personalities. After these groups finish their study, students form new groups composed of at least one person from each original study group. In the new groups, each expert from an original group shares what he or she knows; thus, all students learn what everyone else has learned. My friends and I did this naturally when we would each read a portion of the required readings and then meet, share our notes, and teach one another what we had learned. When we finished, we all had a good grasp of all the ideas we had studied individually.

USING VARIATIONS IN TEACHING TECHNIQUES

An economics professor, Byron Brown, uses variation in his teaching techniques. He writes a weekly newsletter for his students. He responds to questions students have left in his question box. He plays music before class. He experiments with computer projection in class. He gestures and speaks enthusiastically about his topics. He calls students by name in his class of 200. As a consequence, his students call him weird, but as they say, "not scary weird, good weird."

Teach Creatively

Think about unusual ways in which you can teach your ideas. Create memorable experiences for your students. Give them something to talk about after class.

VARIOUS APPROACHES TO CREATIVE TEACHING

In his course on adolescence, Chris Clark has students write stories based on their experiences as teenagers and then find an idea in the human development literature that relates to the story. In class, students read their stories and discuss their relation to the literature. In Jane Vieth's class studying World War II, the students collect stories from veterans and discuss them in class.

A fourth-grade teacher taught her students to think positively in an unusual way (Canfield & Hansen, 1993). One day she and her students listed all the things they couldn't do. For example, a child listed, "I can't do long division with more than three numbers." Then the teacher collected all the papers, put them in a shoe box, and led the class onto the playground. There the children dug a deep hole where they buried the box. The teacher gave an appropriate eulogy about how often they had seen and heard "I can't" but not surviving siblings, "I can" and "I will." In the classroom she hung a paper tombstone that read "I Can't R.I.P." and the date. Later, when students would occasionally try to revive "I can't," the teacher would simply point to the tombstone.

George Ayers, a professor of entomology, is always looking for interesting ways to show how to deal with agricultural pests. To show how grubs move, he blew up a long balloon and explained how these creatures have a muscle they can use to elongate their bodies. He squeezed the center of the balloon to show how the muscle would contract. "But, they also have a muscle that compresses their bodies," he explained, and pressed in the ends of the balloon so students could see how the balloon got fat and short. "Put them both together and the critter can move," he said as he squeezed and compressed the balloon to show the familiar movement of a slug.

Professor Paul Nickel wants his students to be able to detect logical fallacies in people's scientific arguments. After he teaches his students to recognize fallacies, he has them apply the rules to their own papers written earlier in the term and to an article in the tabloid press about how the hole in the ozone layer is making rats crazy. Then, dressed in his pirate hat and eye patch, he becomes Captain Iconoclast and asks his students to watch a film in which a "true believer" espouses biased and illogical scientific views on ecology. As students spot each logical fallacy in the narrator's arguments, they shout the pirate "Yo Ho!" and pop helium-filled balloons. They also write down the fallacies they see and hear. The student who finds the most flaws wins the prized rubber chicken.

My daughter Debbie has never forgotten the day in a college biology class when the teacher explained what makes up a cell. The teacher used a large plastic garbage bag for the cell wall. He said, "The cell contains DNA, the library of the cell," and flung a large biology text into the bag. "And the cell contains cytoplasm," and he hurled in a pitcher of water. In similar fashion he threw in lettuce to represent chlorophyll, tubing for the reticular structure, and a motor for the nucleus. Then he held up the garbage bag, shook it all up and asked, "Is this a cell? No. It has all the ingredients, but it lacks the organization to make all the parts work together."

An article in *Smithsonian* (Wolkomir, 1986) described the teaching of Professor of Physics Jearl Walker at Cleveland State University. To interest his students in molecular adhesion, Professor Walker blew on a spoon and placed it on his forehead. He explained that the spoon stuck to his forehead because the water molecules from his breath on the spoon were attracted to the water molecules on his skin. He proceeded to stick other spoons to his eye sockets and finally stuck a soup ladle to the end of his nose. The students applauded to show their appreciation for this memorable demonstation.

I introduce my instructional design course by talking to various characters whom I recorded on videotape. I play four costumed characters, a nonconformist, a nerd, a business type, and a fraternity member. I introduce the characters and turn on the videoplayer. The characters ask me questions about the course. The nonconformist asks me in a belligerent way what assumptions underlie the course. Then he says he will wait and leans on his elbow. I hit the pause button on the VCR, which freezes his image and makes him appear as if he's waiting. After I explain the assumptions, I hit the pause button again, and he says, "Very interesting, your majesty. OK, now I understand your assumptions, but I have another question. . . ." So goes the introductory session. I find it more fun than a straight explanation of the schedule, requirements, and testing procedures.

Use Humor, Suspense, Shock, and Surprise

Find natural ways to surprise students. Present something unexpected. A college professor of chemistry, Ross Latham, sent me a letter describing, "the best semester beginning I've ever experienced after teaching chemistry for fifteen years." He started his first lecture to 120 freshmen with the opening to Strauss's "Also Sprach Zarathustra" and by exploding hydrogen-filled balloons in a darkened lecture hall. He said it really started things off with a "bang."

Surprise also played a role at a national conference when my training colleague, John Desmedt, and I were ready to present a session on how to train people to handle unexpected events. I introduced John, and John introduced me. As I was starting to speak, a well-dressed man in the third row raised his hand. I was somewhat surprised that someone would interact this soon in the session; I glanced at John, and he nodded for me to call on the fellow. The participant got up and said in a soft voice, "You know, Dr. Yelon, that the content of this handout comes from my brother's work at the University of Southeastern Florida." His voice rose as his speech grew more rapid. "In fact, this handout contains the exact words of my brother's work. So what we have here are stolen ideas and plagiarism." At that point he threw the handout at me and lunged for me. He grabbed my lapels and smacked me up against the accordion room divider. John, an expert in martial arts, was behind him instantly and restrained him in a most persuasive manner. He turned the assailant to the audience and asked him his name and what he was doing there. He stated his name and that he worked for John. Then we made the point that events like this can happen at any time. I bet those participants remember the surprise we cooked up to start our session at the conference.

Once a sixth-grade teacher used humor and suspense well. He told his students that they were having a guest on Friday to help with their biology unit. He said the guest's name was Mr. Insyd. The children pestered him for more information about Mr. Insyd, but he kept mum. Friday he said that Mr. Insyd was in the hall, and that he was kind of sensitive, so he was behind a sheet. The teacher wheeled in a cart. Some students said, "I know who it is!" Then he took off the sheet to reveal a break-apart, life-sized human model. He said, "Let's see what secrets Mr. Insyd holds inside. What do you think is hidden away?" The students talked about Mr. Insyd for a long time.

Always think about the possibility of creating surprises. When doing an experiment, don't telegraph the result. When explaining a study, don't hint at the findings. When providing coming attractions for future classes, leave some suspense. Ask questions. Suggest the obvious or common-sense hypotheses, but leave the results a surprise. Encourage students to follow suit when they are working in groups and when presenting individually.

Some teachers use cartoons, jokes, and humorous stories in their instruction. Some insert their humor into textbooks and materials; some use it in class. You can use *relevant* humor to maximize its inherent surprise. For example, in one strip of the cartoon "Hagar," someone is looking for the Viking Hagar. He is told to look for a fellow with beard and horns. In the last frame, the cartoonist has drawn a goat with beard and horns, a bearded horn player carrying a couple of trumpets, and Hagar the Viking wearing his beard and horned helmet (Browne, 1964). This cartoon or an adaptation of it might be useful in teaching the need for specificity in description. You may be able to find some example of ambiguous language in your domain and create a cartoon after the fashion of the Hagar cartoon. The suspense and the humor of your relevant cartoon will capture attention.

The surprise in a joke or funny story is fine by itself, but you can enhance it even further. If you are telling a story, pause before telling the end and then tell it with expression and force. If you are showing a cartoon that you made, cover the last frame, read the lines up to the last frame, pause, and then reveal the last frame.

Teach Students to Focus Their Attention

Teach students to take responsibility for focusing their attention and keeping on task. Show them the mental skills that help people pay attention and give them practice in using those mental skills, such as:

Monitoring your own attention

Taking periodic breaks

Varying activities as you study

Setting objectives for a portion of work

Keeping in mind the smaller objectives and the larger goals

Asking yourself questions about what is being said

Providing your own practice

Asking yourself for examples of the ideas being studied

Looking for applications of what is studied

GUIDELINE 2: DIRECT YOUR STUDENTS' ATTENTION

It's not sufficient simply to grab and maintain attention to produce learning. Another way to apply novelty is to help your students focus their attention. Have you encountered students who paid attention to an explanation or contributed to a discussion but focused on irrelevancies and missed the key ideas? To learn well, students must attend to the critical portions of a message, for example, the qualities of a skill or the attributes of a concept. Using the principle of novelty, you can help students direct their attention to the most important cues. You may use media or your own comments to direct students' attention.

Use Media to Help Your Students Direct Their Attention to the Important Cues

Use fancy or plain media to help students direct their attention. For example, researchers working on the TV reading show "The Electric Company" wanted to know where children were looking as they watched the show. With a light reflected off a child's pupil, the researchers could trace a child's eye movements on the screen. They found that when children watched a screen showing words and a funny character, their eyes focused on the funny characters' eyes and mouth and did not scan the words. Using this information, the researchers put the actor on the screen for a while and then filled the screen with the word. The word undulated from left to right like a caterpillar as it was said. Subsequent eye movement measures showed that the children focused on the word and moved their eyes over it as it undulated (E. Palmer, personal communication, March 1973; Yelon, 1974, p. 116).

Using a simpler approach, a teacher helped students direct attention to the most important aspects of a long and complex plan. She created a complete example, and to attract attention to the most important aspects of the example, she wrote notes on each page in her own handwriting. She drew arrows from the notes to the spot in the example where the note was illustrated. She and the students reviewed the example in class, emphasizing the notes.

Stress Important Points

I have watched numerous teachers use various strategies to stress important points. Some of the strategies are as follows:

1. Say the idea to be emphasized more loudly.
2. Say it more softly as if telling a secret.

3. Point to it.
4. Put stars next to it.
5. Underline it.
6. Put it on the board.
7. Say that students will see it again.
8. Say it's going to be on the test.
9. Say it's important.
10. Put it in big letters on a transparency.
11. Make a fanfare before saying it.
12. Say to listen carefully.
13. Put it on a poster.
14. Ask students to write down what they think the most important point is.
15. Ask students to discuss what they think the most important point is.
16. Ask students what the title for this unit or lesson should be.
17. Ask students what major problem this unit or lesson may help them solve.
18. Have students create an advertisement for this unit touting its essence.

As a teaching assistant, my daughter Debbie had to present a large amount of technical content to a biology class. She was concerned that students might waste time attempting to write down all the information shown on the overhead, and therefore they might not focus on the most important concepts. Her solution was to key the essential content on the overhead in red and tell her students what she was doing and why.

Another approach is to look a student in the eye to alert him or her to a specific point of particular personal relevance being talked about in a discussion or presentation. For example, if I have a coach in my class, I will make direct eye contact with that person and nod as I mention a particularly good practical idea about teaching a psychomotor skill. If, in a discussion, one student mentions a point that pertains to another student, I might make eye contact with that other student and ask the group who sees any connection.

GUIDELINE 3: PROVOKE CURIOSITY

You can also apply novelty to arouse your students' interest by provoking their curiosity. By challenging students' understanding with questions and puzzles, you can provoke them to ask questions and pursue answers (Berlyne, 1960, 1965).

Use Questions

Asking questions and not answering them right away is an easy way to provoke curiosity. All ideas are answers to questions. Your job is to think of the questions and pose them. You may either answer the questions gradually or let your students find their own answers.

USING QUESTIONS TO GENERATE CURIOSITY

A medical school teacher complained that, after he made an introduction such as, "Today we are going to study the drugs that we use for cancer," his students would fall asleep. Then he realized that his explanations provided answers to questions. He decided that he must ask those questions at the outset of his explanation but not answer them right away.

The next time he explained drugs used for cancer he started by asking, "Is there a cure for cancer? Are there any drugs that we could call a cure? Is the drug cisplatin, used for testicular cancer, a cure? Are there any drugs that do more damage to the cancer than to the host? This is what we will talk about today." He reported that his students were more alert than usual, and when they were asked what they were listening for in the explanation, they said, "The answers to those questions you asked at the start."

Use Puzzling Events and Demonstrations

Puzzles are conditions in the environment that students observe but cannot understand. Puzzles provoke students to ask questions and search out the answers. You can present puzzles and state questions yourself, or you can present a puzzle and let your students raise their own questions.

USING A PUZZLE TO GENERATE STUDENT QUESTIONS

A teacher brought some chicken thigh bones to her sixth-grade classroom. She asked the students to try to bend them, but none could. Then she had them pour a liquid (vinegar) into a container with some of the bones and leave others alone in a glass container. A week later the students took the bones out of the two jars and tried to bend them. Much to their surprise, they were able to bend the ones soaked in vinegar. In class she asked the students to raise questions about what they had observed: "What puzzled you about what you saw? What do you want to know about what you saw?" As an assignment after class, she asked them to use any resources they had to begin to find the answers to their questions.

USING A PUZZLE AND QUESTIONS TO GENERATE STUDENTS' QUESTIONS

In the gym, the science teacher attached a bowling ball to one of the climbing ropes. She moved the ball and the rope as far as she could to the side and held it next to a student's head. She asked the students what would happen if she let go of the ball. They said that it would swing to the other side of the room and then swing back. She asked how far it would swing back. Would it fall short of reaching Ralph's head? Would it come back to the same spot? Or would it continue past and knock his head off? Students made predictions and carried out the experiment. Then the teacher asked students to raise questions about what they observed: "What do you want to know about what happened?"

A PUZZLE COMING FROM A QUESTION
LEADS TO MORE QUESTIONS

Tom asked why the teacher insisted that everyone wash their hands before snacks and lunch. The teacher said that their hands were dirty. Tom turned over his hands and said they looked clean to him. So the teacher asked if they could try an experiment and talk about it later. She asked Tom to wash only one of his hands with soap and hot water. Then he touched his washed hand and his unwashed, but supposedly clean, hand to some sterile media she had placed in flat glass containers. They closed and labeled the containers and put them on a shelf in the classroom over the weekend. She asked the students to talk among themselves and to their families about what they thought they might find in the two containers on Monday. On Monday, when they took the containers off the shelf, they found a few spots of bacteria on the plate made with the washed hand, and extensive colonies of bacteria forming a distinct handprint in the media where the so-called clean hand was placed. Before they looked at samples of the growth under a microscope, the teacher asked students to form questions about what they had seen. Students asked what the spots were, why they grew there, and why there seemed to be a difference in the results.

USING PUZZLING CASES AND HAVING
STUDENTS RAISE QUESTIONS

A teacher provided puzzling experiences and waited for students to raise questions. In one puzzle students wrapped their hands around small empty cans they were using to make soap bubbles and observed that the bubbles got bigger. In another, students watched as the cork popped out of a tube covering a lighted candle.

A medical educator gave students puzzling information regarding patients. For example, she embedded in the lab report of an otherwise healthy patient an incongruous result, a high bilirubin count. The students were to notice any puzzling circumstances, raise questions, and then seek information to explain the incongruity.

A college teacher asked students studying the Harlem Renaissance to read magazines of the time. Students were to find something they wanted to explain further, to raise questions, and to do research to answer the questions.

A teacher frequently posted current newspaper clippings about the unknown sources of scientifically related problems, such as the lack of a good reason for the failure of a spaceship launching. She waited for students to notice the articles and ask questions.

A FINAL WORD

Enjoy your teaching. Have fun with it. Teach what you believe in, and your natural enthusiasm will keep your students' attention and feed your own interest. Use various methods of teaching: Use group discussion, group projects, individual projects, simulations, videotapes, audiotapes, newsletters, videos, songs, poems. Think of creative ways to present ideas, to provide practice, and to test. Think of some topic that you teach and consider the many ways you can introduce variety into that instructional session. Think of a crazy way to present an idea and try it. Have students think of bizarre ways to present new ideas. Add some new wrinkle, no matter how small, to each session you teach. Teaching with this attitude is a pleasure. It will make planning and implementing instruction enjoyable.

ACTIVITIES

Here are some challenging and creative activities. In the first four exercises, you are asked to apply the principle of novelty in various ways. Then you are asked to relate the principle to various teaching styles and to other principles.

1. Think of a particular lesson that you might feel is unexciting.
   a. List five specific ways you can apply novelty to capture and maintain attention.
   b. How might you vary your actions, program, and techniques?
   c. How might you teach creatively? How might you use humor, suspense, shock, and surprise?
2. Think of a particular idea you want to communicate, such as the qualities of a good business letter, the causes of the American Civil War, or the relationship between socioecomic status and political power. Create a visual using novelty to direct your students' attention. Be sure to use the medium to direct your students' attention to the important cues.
3. Think of a major idea you want to teach. Think of that as "the answer." What is the question? Make up one or more questions that you could use to start the segment to provoke curiosity.
4. Think of a principle you might teach, such as how heat and cold affect objects. Plan to create a puzzling demonstration by showing an event or a demonstration that can be explained by the principle.
5. How do various approaches to instruction *build in* novelty? discussion? learning via computer? solving problems? use of projects? discovery of ideas rather than being told?
6. How are essential examples, demonstration, and practice inherently novel? How could you enhance examples using novelty? How could you combine the principles of novelty and meaningfulness and the principles of novelty and learning aids?
7. Reflection
   a. How can I vary teaching and learning events to keep students' attention?
   b. When do I need to vary events to keep students' attention?

c. How can I vary the use of my voice and body?

d. When can I use questions, puzzles, cases, concrete analogies, unexpected events?

e. When can I break up explanations with demonstrations, practice, and feedback?

f. How can I get students to maintain their own attention?

g. How can I use appropriate media to command attention?

h. How can I use activities to keep attention?

FURTHER READING

Aronson, E. Blaney, S., Sikes, J., & Snapp, M. (1978). *The jigsaw classroom.* Beverly Hills, CA: Sage Publications. (*Note:* Learn about a way to vary instruction by an interesting use of collaborative learning.)

Berlyne, D. E. (1965). Motivational problems raised by exploratory and epistemic behavior. In S. Koch (Ed.), *Psychology: A study of a science,* Vol. 5, pp. 284-364. New York: McGraw-Hill. (*Note:* This chapter discusses curiosity.)

Keller, J. M. (1987, October). Strategies for stimulating the motivation to learn. *Performance and Instruction, 26*(8), 1-7. (*Note:* Check the recommendations in the part of the ARCS model that deals with attention.)

Kopp, T. W. (1982, May). Designing the boredom out of instruction. *Performance and Instruction Journal, 21,* 23-27, 32.

Norman, D. (1976). *Memory and attention: An introduction to human information processing* (2nd ed.). New York: Wiley. (*Note:* Read chapter 4, Attention, Effort and Resources, for the psychological basis for novelty.)

Scardamelia, M., & Bereiter, C. (1991). Higher levels of agency for children in knowledge building: A challenge for the design of new knowledge media. *Journal of the Learning Sciences, 1*(1), 37-68.

Tauber, R. T., & Mester, C. S. (1994). *Acting lessons for teachers: Using performance skills in the classroom.* Westport, CT: Greenwood.

Weisberg, M., & Duffin, J. (1995, January/February). Evoking the moral imagination: Using stories to teach ethics and professionalism to nursing, medical and law students. *Change,* 21-27. (*Note:* This article offers a novel approach to teaching attitudes.)

Wlodkowski, R. J. (1991). *Enhancing adult motivation to learn.* San Francisco: Jossey-Bass. (*Note:* Read chapter 3 for a discussion of keeping attention.)

Wolkomir, R. (1986). "Old Jearl" will do anything to stir an interest in physics. *Smithsonian, 17*(7), 112-116. (*Note:* Here is one vivid example of creative teaching.)

Wykoff, W. (1973). The effect of stimulus variation on learning from lecture. *Journal of Experimental Education, 41,* 85-90.

chapter 8

Modeling

OVERVIEW

Demonstrate so students will learn easily and quickly. Provide an enthusiastic, professional appearance for students to imitate.

Guideline 1: Use the Four-Step Approach to Demonstrate Performance
  Tell Students They Will Have to Perform What Is About to Be Demonstrated
  Before Demonstrating, Tell Students What to Observe as They Watch the Demonstration
  Say Each Step and Then Do It
  Ask Students to Commit the Steps to Memory before They Practice

Guideline 2: Use the Four-Step Approach to Demonstrate Thinking Skills
  Tell Students They Will Have to Perform the Mental Skill that Is About to Be Demonstrated
  Before Demonstrating, Tell Students What to Observe as They Watch the Demonstration of the Mental Skill
  Say Each General Mental Step and Then Do It, Saying Aloud How You Are Applying It to a Specific Case
  Ask Students to Commit the Steps to Memory before They Practice

Guideline 3: Use the Four-Step Approach to Demonstrate Attitudes
  Tell Students They Will Have to Show the Attitude as an Integral Part of Performance

Before Demonstrating, Tell Students What to Observe as the
Indicators of the Attitude
Say Each Indicator of the Attitude and Then Do It
Ask Students to Commit the Indicators of the Attitude to
Memory before They Practice

Guideline 4: Demonstrate Your Professional Attitude
Behave Like a Mature, Ethical Professional
Show Concern for Your Subject Matter, Your Students'
Learning, and Your Teaching
Show Enthusiasm for and Enjoyment of Your Work

Your students can learn the most from instruction if, in addition to listening to an explanation of how to perform or discussing the nuances of how to perform, they observe a good demonstration. Some teachers believe that demonstration is easy: Simply show students what to do.

THE WEAKNESS OF AN UNSYSTEMATIC DEMONSTRATION

I asked a group of surgeons two true-false questions to start a workshop on skill teaching. First I said, "True or false: It is easy to teach skills. How many of you think that is true?"

Many hands went up. I looked for the most enthusiatic responders, those who were saying: "Yes, most definitely true."

Second, I said, "True or false: It is easy to teach skills because all you have to do is show students how to perform. How many of you think that is true?"

The room was alive with undulating hands, "Yes, yes, yes!"

I said, "Your responses correspond to a saying in medical education 'See one, do one, teach one.' All you have to do is show people how to do something and they should be able to do it; and once they do it, they are ready to teach it. Let's see if that works."

I took out a 4-foot length of clothesline knotted at each end. I said, as I demonstrated, "Here is a simple skill. Watch as I do it. I hold the rope in the center of the length with my right thumb and forefinger. Now I begin to twirl half the rope counterclockwise.

"After a few twirls, with my left hand, I flip the other half of the rope clockwise. Half of the rope is going one way, and the other half is going in the opposite direction—a most amazing sight. Now that you have seen me do this, you should be able to do it."

I asked one of those who responded most enthusiastically to my true-false questions to come to the front of the room and try. The surgeon came forward and wiggled and twirled the rope to no avail. Others tried and failed.

I said, "If 'see one, do one' worked, we would all be able to perform any skill we had ever observed. We could all hit a home run, deliver a moving speech, and conduct an excellent interview. But learning a skill from a demonstration is not that simple."

A SIMPLE SHOWING OF A SKILL IS UNLIKELY TO BE SUFFICIENT

I asked a group if they knew any martial arts—karate or judo. Only one or two people did. I mentioned all the ways one can strike a blow, using head, feet, knees, elbows, and hands. I said that when most people think of karate, they think of a "chop," a sword hand. I showed a sword hand for an instant and said a bit more. Then I asked each person to make a sword hand. I thought that they should be able to do so because I had just shown them one. What happened? A few had most of the sword hand's features, but all had some error that could result in injury: no tension in their wrists and the backs of their hands, misplaced thumbs, or fingers set apart. What was wrong with my demonstration? Almost everything. Observers were not alerted to pay attention to the demonstration. They were not guided to attend to key features in the demonstration. They were not led to form a clear mental image of the skill. My brief display of the skill lacked what it needed to make it an effective demonstration.

GUIDELINE 1: USE THE FOUR-STEP APPROACH TO DEMONSTRATE PERFORMANCE

Your students are much more likely to learn from a demonstration if they pay attention, if they perceive the important aspects of all the steps, and if they form a mental image of the skill before practice (Bandura, 1977, 1986). To be effective in demonstrating a performance, use a four-step approach to capture attention, focus on key factors in each step, and have students commit the steps to memory (Yelon & Maddocks, 1986):

1. Tell students they will have to perform what is about to be demonstrated.
2. Before demonstrating, tell students what to observe as they watch the demonstration.
3. Say each step and then do it.
4. Ask students to commit the steps to memory before they practice.

Tell Students They Will Have to Perform What Is About to Be Demonstrated

How many times have you gone through an entire demonstration and invited students to perform, only to be met by a blank look and the statement "Oh, I didn't know you wanted me to do it. Could you do it again?" To avoid this frustration, before demonstrating, tell students that they will be performing the task to be shown. Then they will be alerted to pay attention to the demonstration.

> ### USING DEMONSTRATION STEP 1: YOU WILL DO IT
>
> When teaching the sword hand, the karate instructor tells students that in a few minutes he or she will be bringing in some boards that they must break using the sword hand. After that brief announcement, the students are ready to listen and look for what is coming next.

Before Demonstrating, Tell Students What to Observe as They Watch the Demonstration

If students observe a demonstration without knowing what to look for, they are likely to perform inaccurately. Have you ever observed a child watch her favorite sport? You may have seen her watching champion athletes performing at their best. She may have watched one of the best baseball players get up to bat, swing hard, and hit the ball out of the park. When she asked you to throw her a ball so she could hit it, you saw the child shake her arms loose, pull on her shirt and pants, knock dirt off her shoes, and spit into her hands. When you pitched the ball, she took an overhand swing the likes of which she never observed. What happened? Although the child watched excellent performance, she did not know what made it excellent. She imitated irrelevant actions and qualities.

To direct students' attention to the critical aspects of a task, before demonstrating, tell them the steps and qualities to observe in the performance. Then they will know what to pay most attention to during the demonstration.

> ### USING DEMONSTRATION STEP 2: OBSERVE THESE STEPS
>
> Just before showing students how to make a sword hand, the instructor tells them what to look for. With the task description and a sketch of each step on a handout and on a large visual (see Figure 8.1), he says, "When I demonstrate this skill to you, watch for these steps:
>
> 1. With an open hand, pull all fingers together.
> 2. Tuck your thumb in tight to the palm of your hand.
> 3. Arch all your fingers back.
> 4. Pull the first phalanx of each finger forward.
> 5. Check the tension of the tendons in your wrist and the back of your hand."

For ease of recall, you could assign names to the steps, such as "together, tuck, arch, flex," or use a simplified rule or set of rules to sum up the steps, such as "tighten the tendons."

To carry out demonstration step 2 effectively and to explain its essence, you must be consciously aware of the explicit steps and qualities of the task

Step 1- Put all fingers together

Step 2- Tuck thumb back

Step 3- Arch fingers back

Step 4- Pull first phalanx of each finger down

Step 5- Check tension in tendons in wrist and back of hand

FIGURE 8.1 How to form a sword hand

you teach. You must avoid "expertitis," which is characterized by knowing a skill so well and so automatically that you no longer have the words to describe what you do or how you do it.

I first noticed "expertitis" while trying to teach my wife, Fran, how to drive a stick-shift car. On a Sunday we took our car to an empty parking lot. I told her to watch what I do, and I proceeded to drive around the lot shifting from first to second to third gear. I said little and simply showed her how I do the skill. Then I stopped the car and we switched places. Fran sat in the driver's seat, grasped the wheel and the stick, but had little idea of what to do based on my sloppy demonstration. I needed to get back in the driver's seat and do the task again, paying attention to what I did as I shifted gears. I had a severe case of "expertitis," and I needed to do a task description to cure it.

Later I began to notice "expertitis" in others. At times my fine karate instructor had bouts. Once he asked me to leap at my opponent as I punched. After he showed me how, I leaped high into the air as I punched. "No, no. Leap, but keep your feet on the ground." I wondered how I was going to do that. I asked him to do it again and he did. As he leaped, I noticed he kept his feet to the ground. I tried again, but I couldn't do it. I asked him to do it again, this time with his pants rolled up. He did. Then I noticed that he bent his right knee and pushed off with his right foot. That was the key. But he had forgotten to tell me that! With the essence of the skill in mind, I was able to imitate the performance.

I discovered that you need an explicit but lean task description to aid your demonstration and overcome a bout of "expertitis."

Say Each Step and Then Do It

Have you ever watched chefs demonstrating cooking on TV? Sometimes you focus so intently on their physical technique that you miss half the recipe. At other times you are so attentive to the recipe that you miss the technique. You can't efficiently process both the auditory and visual stimuli simultaneously. To help your students follow your demonstration without missing half of it, say what you will do *before* doing it. Then students will focus on the most critical aspects of the task as it unfolds in the demonstration.

USING DEMONSTRATION STEP 3: SAY AND THEN DO

To demonstrate the sword hand, the instructor would say, "First, with an open hand, I pull all my fingers together." The students know just what to look for and where to look. Then the instructor does the step, pulling fingers together. He or she continues in that fashion for each step. For a more complex and speedy task, such as a jumping side kick, the instructor could use videotape to slow or stop the action, so that he or she could intervene to point out its most important aspects before they happen.

Ask Students to Commit the Steps to Memory before They Practice

I have a true–false question for you. True or false: As soon as students see a good demonstration, they should practice. True? No, the answer is false. If people practice right away, they are likely to do the task improperly. Before practicing, students need an accurate and complete mental representation of the skill. They must commit to memory the critical elements of the skill. Then, when practicing, they can match their performance to their mental template of good performance.

USING DEMONSTRATION STEP 4:
COMMIT THE STEPS TO MEMORY

To finish the demonstration of the sword hand, the instructor would ask students to commit the steps to memory. They can either visualize the steps, say them, or write them. For insurance, they could use all of the strategies.

APPLYING DEMONSTRATION STEP 4:
COMMIT THE STEPS TO MEMORY

I was asked to help orient chemistry teaching assistants. I came early for my presentation and sat in the back of the room. An experienced assistant was making his presentation about running laboratories. He said, "One thing you really need as a laboratory assistant is patience. After you demonstrate a procedure, students will come up to you and ask you the same questions over and over again about what you have just shown them. So, be patient!"

As I was listening to his comments, I realized that the teaching assistants were not only living with a problem, but they were turning it into a tradition, passing it from one generation of assistants to the next. After I suggested the first three steps of demonstration, I also suggested that they have the students commit the steps to memory before going to their tables to perform. They could tell the steps to one another, write them down, or close their eyes and visualize them. I said it would save time and reduce those recurring questions.

I had the assistants promise me they would try the four-step procedure, and they did. In the next lab, they asked students to tell one another the steps before returning to their tables to do the experiment. But they really didn't believe me and braced themselves for the onslaught of student questions. None came! The assistants had to wander out into the land of the students to answer questions about what the experiments meant rather than how to do them.

Keep your four-step demonstration *brief.* Emphasize correct performance. Use short sentences, including only essential information about what to do, such as, "First I read. Then I recall the definition. Then I check examples."

Keep your demonstration *observable.* Have your students stand or sit close enough to see and hear. For example, a teacher of nurse practitioners wanted his students to learn how to palpate a thyroid gland. He demonstrated this in front of a typically arranged classroom with rows of seats. Except for those in the first row, almost none of the students were able to see the demonstration clearly. When it was time to check students' practice, the teacher had to repeat his demonstration of the skill to each student. He realized that for students to observe what he was doing, they had to interlace their hands with his to feel what he was doing, and they had to see what he was doing.

Have students observe the demonstration from the *performer's angle*. I once observed a surgeon facing his students, demonstrating one-handed surgical knots. When it came time to practice, the students seemed quite confused. Do you realize what the teacher could have done to make the skill much easier to learn? He could have had his students view what he was doing from over his shoulder. That way they would not have to mentally rotate each move he made.

If you want your students to teach one another by demonstration, then teach them or guide them to use the four-step model. So students will attend to what their peers demonstrate, remind those observing that they are expected to apply what they see. Ask the student demonstrators to state the steps in their method before they present and as they present their demonstration. You could also ask them to review their performance a second time and highlight how they used each step in their method. Then, if students watching a peer's demonstrations elect to use one of the methods, have them commit the steps to memory before practice.

The mnemonic device WASDM (pronounced "waste 'em") can help you to remember the four-step approach:

W   Tell students they **w**ill do this skill in practice (step 1).

A   Tell them to **a**ttend to elements in the skill (step 2).

S   **S**ay each of the steps to the students (step 3).

D   **D**o each of the steps in front of the students (step 3).

M   Ask students to **m**emorize the steps (step 4).

You should be able to use the four-step approach to demonstration in all kinds of teaching settings, for example, in *field training of a performance, in apprenticeships, or in on-the-job training:*

- When you have carefully described the skill
- When you can predict situations calling for the skill
- When you can talk aloud while demonstrating without violating any ethical principles
- When you can demonstrate without interfering with the provision of the product or service you are obliged to provide

USING A FOUR-STEP DEMONSTRATION IN AN APPRENTICESHIP

Imagine a student physician in a clinical setting learning a procedural skill, such as how to excise a skin lesion.

Step 1. Outside the patient's room, the instructor says, "Before we go in to excise Mr. Jones's skin lesion, I want you to know that you will perform this procedure on the fourth patient today who needs it."

Step 2. The instructor continues, "When I excise the lesion I want you to notice how I do these seven steps: First, I palpate. . . ." After the explanation, the instructor says, "OK, let's go in."

Step 3. Inside the room the instructor talks to the patient, "Good morning, Mr. Jones. This is Dr. Y. He will be observing today. As I excise the lesion on your leg, I will tell you what I am doing. Is that all right with you?"

Mr. Jones nods. "Yes. That's fine." Then the instructor starts the demonstration. "OK. First I will palpate the. . . . Now, I will gently insert. . . ."

Step 4. Outside the room after the procedure, the instructor says, "As we are cleaning up, Dr Y., tell me the steps you saw and the most important qualities of each step."

GUIDELINE 2: USE THE FOUR-STEP APPROACH TO DEMONSTRATE THINKING SKILLS

Have you ever seen a teacher show students how to think through a math story problem, or demonstrate how to compose an essay, or show how to comprehend a written passage? Each of these tasks requires mental skill and a systematic demonstration. To demonstrate well and to make each process apparent to novices, a teacher needs an explicit description of the mental process. With the task description of the mental skill, you can use the four-step approach to make the mental steps of an expert problem solver, writer, analyst, or reader visible to students. You can use a variation of the four-step demonstration for mental skills.

1. Tell students they will have to perform the mental skill that is about to be demonstrated.
2. Before demonstrating, tell students what to observe as they watch the demonstration of the mental skill.
3. Say each general mental step and then do it, reporting aloud how you are applying it to the specific case you are working on.
4. Ask students to commit the steps of the mental skill to memory before they practice.

As an overview, consider this example of a four-step *demonstration of a simple mental skill:* how to compute the percentage of calories coming from the fat in packaged foods. Look it over to see how the four steps are adapted to mental skills. Then we will consider each step in more detail.

USING THE FOUR-STEP DEMONSTRATION
OF A SIMPLE MENTAL SKILL

Step 1 (Will Do). "After the demonstration, you will calculate the percentage of calories from fat in a given food product. I will give you the label from a product that lists the calories, the amount of fat in a portion, and the other nutrients."

Step 2 (What to Attend To). "When I demonstrate, I want you to listen and watch for these steps:

a. I find the grams of fat listed in the ingredients.

b. I multiply the grams of fat times 9, the approximate number of calories in 1 gram of fat.

c. I find the total calories per serving listed.

d. I divide the total calories from fat by the total calories per serving.

e. I write the percentage of calories from fat in the product."

Step 3 (Say and Do). "Now watch and listen to the demonstration as I calculate the percentage of calories from fat in this product:

Dry Roasted Peanuts

Serving size 1 oz

Calories 160

Protein 7 g

Carbohydrate 6 g

Fat 14 g

a. I find the grams of fat listed.	In this case I see that the fat content is 14 grams.
b. I multiply the grams of fat by 9.	14 grams × 9 calories per gram = 126 calories from fat.
c. I find the calories per serving listed.	I see that there are 160 calories per serving.
d. I divide the total calories from fat by the total calories.	I divide 126 calories from fat by 160 calories per serving (126 ÷ 160), and that equals 0.7875 (78.75 percent).
e. I write the percentage of calories from fat in the product.	I write 78.75 percent of calories from fat in dry roasted peanuts."

Step 4 (Memorize). "Before you do the example I am handing out, tell a partner the steps for calculating the percentage of calories coming from fat in a product."

Tell Students They Will Have to Perform the Mental Skill that Is About to Be Demonstrated

Tell students you will be showing them an invisible, inaudible process. State that you will be expecting them to use a process like the one you are about to show them, but they should realize that your demonstration of your thinking is only an approximation of what you really do. The point is that they should think. They should use a systematic process to accomplish the task. Show your students the kind of problem or the sort of conditions to which they will have to respond.

Look back at the demonstration of how to calculate the percentage of calories from fat in a given food product. Suppose you were a student listening to step 1. Would you be aware of how the problem would look when it is presented in practice and what you would be required to do?

Before Demonstrating, Tell Students What to Observe as They Watch the Demonstration

Telling students the steps to look for in a demonstration of a mental skill has its difficulties. Here is a challenge: Describe what you do as you identify an example of an apple. What steps do you take? I will bet that specifying those steps is not too easy. We do many mental skills automatically, unaware of the steps we use. To alert students as to what to observe in a demonstration, we must be aware of the steps we use.

Task descriptions of mental skills require significant reflection and testing. It is difficult to be complete and explicit in specifying the steps. It is equally difficult to state the steps in a way that students can understand. Ask yourself:

How do I really do the mental process?

Do I make images in my mind? Do I say things to myself? Do I get feelings?

Do I think the way books say it is done?

Is there more than one effective way to accomplish the process?

Do I approach the process with an understanding of each step, or is it a mindless algorithm?

I suggest that you do the mental task that you want your students to do. You may have to use a very difficult example to slow yourself down enough to be aware of what you are doing. Suppose you wanted students to identify the concept *noun.* Students are given a sentence with one word underlined, such as "The boy put on his coat." You want students to say if the word is a noun or not. Here is how you might derive the general mental skill steps for this task by analyzing one case. Note in the left-hand column how the teacher thinks aloud through the specific steps he or she performs to analyze the case at hand. Then observe in the right-hand column how the teacher states the general steps that could be used for any case.

Specific Step	*General Step*
The first thing I did was to read the instructions. I read "Note which underlined words in these sentences are nouns." I found out	Read the instructions and find out what the task is.

I was to identify the underlined words as nouns or not nouns.

Because I was to identify a noun, I recalled what makes a noun. I recalled that a noun is a word that describes a person, place, or thing. I figured that "things" also meant ideas like "freedom," as well as physical things like a baseball.	If you are to identify an example of a concept, note the name of that concept, and then recall the definition of that concept.
The next thing I did was to read the first sentence to find the word I was to identify. I read, "1. The boy put on his <u>coat</u>." I noted that the word *coat* was my target. Was it a noun? I pictured a coat in my mind.	Inspect the example you are given. Get a picture of the item in your mind.
I checked to see if a coat was a person. No. A place? No. A thing? Yes.	Check the example for the attributes in the definition.
A coat fits one of the requirements: being a thing. That was enough. Person, place, *or* thing. I noted that a coat in that context was a noun.	If the example fits the attributes, label it as an example. If not, label it as a nonexample.

Now the teacher has a rough task description of the mental skill of identification, which he or she can test and refine. The teacher can alert students about what to observe in his or her demonstration of the process of identification.

Tentative Task Description of Identification
1. Note the name of the concept you are to identify and recall its definition.
2. Inspect the example and picture it in your mind.
3. Check the example for each attribute in the definition.
4. If the example has the attributes, label it as an example.

Look back at the demonstration of how to calculate the percentage of calories from fat in a given food product. What were the general steps noted? How were they displayed? Could you have done it another way?

Say Each General Mental Step and Then Do It, Saying Aloud How You Are Applying It to a Specific Case

One big difference between demonstrating mental tasks and demonstrating physical tasks is in the way you carry out step 3. Instead of describing the physical step and then doing it, you state the general mental step from your general task description and then you state how you apply the general step to a specific case. This is the mental skill version of saying the step and then doing it. In the following example, a teacher is describing the way he adapts the saying-and-doing method for solving a division problem: "Suppose we started with this question: Dale wants the same amount of stickers in four boxes. He has 32 stickers. How many stickers go in each box?"

First, I state aloud the first *general mental step*.	I read the whole problem.
Then I do that out loud, *applying the general step to the specific case*.	"Dale has four boxes. . . ."
Next I state the second *general step*.	I reread and sketch out the facts.
Then I *apply the second general step to the specific case*.	"Dale has four boxes." So I sketch ❑ ❑ ❑ ❑
	I say, "32 stickers." And so I sketch ★★★★★★★★★★ ★★★★★★★★★★ ★★★★★★★★★★ ★★

The teacher continues stating each general step and follows with its specific application.

Next is an example of a four-step demonstration for identifying an *example of a concept* (i.e., noun). Note that in step 3 the teacher demonstrates the process of identification by alternating between stating a general step and showing how it is applied to an example in a specific step. Note also that when demonstrating identification of examples of concepts or applying principles to cases, the teacher uses examples or situations in the specific steps that the students have not seen or heard in the explanation, and that students will not see or hear in the practice and the test.

Use the Four-Step Demonstration for Identifying an Example of the Concept

Step 1 (Will Do). "In about 10 minutes, you will be asked to identify nouns as part of an analysis of your writing."

Step 2 (What to Attend To). "When I show you how to identify nouns, watch and listen for the way I follow these three steps. You can use these same steps to identify any concept."

a. Recall the definition.

b. Check each example for each attribute.

c. If an example has the attributes, I label it as an example.

Step 3 (General and Specific Steps, Say and Do).

General Step	Specific Step
a. I recall the definition.	In this case, the definition is: A noun is a word representing a person, place, *or* thing (including ideas such as freedom).

b. I check each example
for each attribute.

In this case, I check each to see if
it represents a person, a place, or a
thing. The first word is *candlestick*.
I check: Is it a person? No. Is it a
place? No. Is it a thing? Yes.

c. If the example has
the appropriate
attributes, I label it
as a member of the
category.

In this case, since a candelstick is a
thing, I label it as a noun.

Step 4 (Memorize). "Before you identify nouns in your writing, tell me
the three steps to identifying a noun and the definition of a
noun."

Here is an example using general and specific steps for the *application of
a principle.*

Use the Four-Step Demonstration for Application of a Principle

Step 1 (Will Do). "As part of you clinical work, you will be writing
predictions and explanations of your clients' behaviors using the
positive reinforcement principle."

Step 2 (What to Attend To). "Watch me use these steps in my
demonstration of how to apply the principle of positive
reinforcement to predict and explain my client's behavior. You can
use these steps for the application of any principle in predicting
and explaining behavior."

a. I study the facts in the case.

b. I recall the principle.

c. I note the independent variable(s) represented in the case.

d. I make an analogy of the case to the principle.

e. I make the prediction and explain it.

Step 3 (General and Specific Steps).

General Step	**Specific Step**
a. I study the facts in the case.	The facts in my case are, "Whenever Jimmy cries, his mom talks to him and feeds him."
b. I recall the principle.	I recall the principle of positive reinforcement: A behavior increases in rate when a valued consequence follows that behavior.

c. I note the independent variable(s) represented in the case.	In this case, the independent variable is the feeding.
d. I make an analogy of the case to the principle.	The principle is: A valued consequence following a behavior produces a behavior increase. In this case, getting fed, a valued consequence, follows the behavior crying. So, the crying will probably increase.
e. I make the prediction and explain it.	I predict that Jimmy will continue to cry because his feeding, a valued consequence, follows his crying behavior.

Step 4 (Memorize). "Write down the general steps to predict and explain and the principle of positive reinforcement."

Can you assign the responsibility of modeling and demonstration to students? Can you assign a learning task to a group and depend on group members to show one another effective mental strategies? Although modeling occurs naturally in student groups when students show one another how to do things, students need guidance in learning complex mental skills. For example, Anne Marie Palinscar and Ann Brown (1984) developed an effective approach to instruction, called "reciprocal teaching," which incorporates a number of principles including teacher and student modeling. Using this approach, a teacher carefully guides students to use specific well-chosen steps to improve their reading comprehension, such as predicting the next portion of a passage. First, the teacher explains and demonstrates by thinking aloud the steps to figure out a passage as he or she reads and interprets. The teacher asks and answers comprehension questions aloud as he or she reads: "What do I think comes next? Because the author mentioned many types of dogs, I think he will tell about some types of dogs next." In subsequent passages, the teacher begins to ask these questions of students: "What do you predict the author will mention next?" In this way, he or she begins to conduct a dialogue with students. Then students take turns being the "teacher" as the instructor coaches them in the process of interpreting new passages. They think aloud and ask themselves and others the comprehension fostering questions.

In a similar fashion, Whimbey and Lockhead (1982) teach reading comprehension, analogical reasoning, and mathematical problem solving by showing transcripts of the thinking of good problem solvers. After demonstration, they place students in small groups to think aloud as they practice problem solving, thereby continuing the modeling while practicing. In this way you can teach any type of thinking skills and problem solving by teacher demonstration and careful guidance of student modeling (Rosenshine & Meister, 1994).

Ask Students to Commit the Steps
to Memory before They Practice

Before students put into practice the mental skill that has been demonstrated, they should be able to recall the steps. Telling another person how they might proceed is an excellent check to see if they have a clear idea of what they are to do. Of course, their knowledge of the skill will sharpen as they practice and get feedback.

GUIDELINE 3: USE THE FOUR-STEP
APPROACH TO DEMONSTRATE ATTITUDES

Modeling is a powerful tool for learning. When we see credible, impressive people behave with precision and confidence, we want to act as they do. This is most apparent by the way young people are influenced by behavior they see on TV. When I worked for a year at Children's Television Workshop, I saw letters to the makers of "Sesame Street" about children imitating either the chef who falls down the stairs after announcing "Ten ice cream sodas" or the character who paints numbers on chair seats and the heads of bald men (E. Palmer, personal communication, March 1973). There are often stories in the newspaper about people imitating crimes they have seen on TV. I remember a newspaper article about children on the playground packaging grass and sugar and pretending to sell drugs. But there are positive models, too. There are stories of children imitating the way they saw someone on an emergency show dial 911 or use the Heimlich maneuver. I also remember one encouraging story about the character Fonzie from the TV series "Happy Days." The Fonz took out a library card in one episode. For the next three months, the American Library Association reported a 500-percent increase in new library cards for children ages 9 to 14.

Can we, as teachers, influence students' attitudes, too? Can we apply the principle of modeling in a systematic way to influence students' choices? Consider using the four-step approach to demonstration for the purpose of teaching attitudes.

1. Tell students they will have to show the attitude as an integral part of performance.
2. Before demonstrating, tell students what to observe as the indicators of the attitude as they watch the demonstration.
3. Say each indicator of the attitude and then do it.
4. Ask students to commit the indicators of the attitude to memory before they practice.

Tell Students They Will Have to Show the
Attitude as an Integral Part of Performance

Most attitudes are an integral part of a performance. It is not that we just want students to shoot a foul shot, operate a machine, or make a sale—we want them to do it with a certain attitude. We want students to be confident as they approach the foul line and shoot, to be concerned for safety as they operate the machine, and to put the customer first as they negotiate a sale. Because people demonstrate an attitude as part of a skilled performance, before you demonstrate, emphasize the attitudinal standard of the skill. So, a medical instructor might say to students as the first step in a demonstration: "After the demonstration I want you to excise a skin lesion according to the steps, but I also expect you to do so showing concern for the patient."

Before Demonstrating, Tell Students What to Observe as the Indicators of the Attitude

Part of your challenge in teaching attitudes is specifying that attitude. How do you know that a physician cares about patients? How do you know that an athlete plays with confidence? In the same way that you specify any standard, you have to be able to tell your students what you will look for as overt indicators of attitude.

Study the expression of an attitude. Think of performers who show the attitude and those who do not. What does the successful performer do that makes him or her different from the unsuccessful one? Does the concerned physician sit down and talk slowly and calmly with patients? Does the unconcerned physician keep one hand on the doorknob and talk quickly and curtly? Does the concerned physician keep eye contact with the patient when explaining treatment clearly and verifying patient understanding? Does the unconcerned physician write notes while briefly mumbling an explanation and then leave? Does the confident athlete shoot the foul shot with little hesitation, distraction, and extraneous behavior? Does the unconfident athlete hesitate, look around, and make extraneous comments and movements?

Once you have your definition of a proper attitude, include that defintion in the task description and tell students that is what they should note during the demonstration. The medical instructor might say, "I want you to observe that as I excise the skin lesion, I show that I am concerned about the patient and I am thinking about the patient's welfare. For example, when informing the patient, I will sit down, make eye contact with the patient, and explain slowly and carefully what will happen. I will ask the patient for questions or ask the patient to tell me what he thinks is going to happen. As I proceed with the excision, I will inform the patient of what is happening. I will also check the patient's degree of comfort throughout and give him encouragement by saying how much time is left. Note that I will again sit down, make eye contact, and explain slowly and carefully what he should do at home."

Say Each Indicator of the Attitude and Then Do It

Just as you would in demonstrating any skilled performance, state what you will do to show the attitude and then do it. Before entering the examination room or in the room, if ethical, the medical instructor might tell the medical student, "I am now about to inform the patient about what will happen as I excise the skin lesion.

Watch how I show that I am concerned about the patient and I am thinking about the patient's welfare. I will sit down, make eye contact with the patient, and explain slowly and carefully what will happen. I will also ask the patient for questions or to tell me what he thinks is going to happen and if he is worried about anything."

Then the medical instructor sits down, faces the patient, and says, "Mr. Anderson, to make sure you are most comfortable, I would like to explain what will happen as we go. Is that all right? OK. First I will numb the area. . . . Before we proceed, do you have any questions or concerns about what will happen?"

Ask Students to Commit the Indicators of the Attitude to Memory before They Practice

Ask your students to tell you specifically what the standards are for their performance, including the attitudes they are to display. The medical instructor doing the demonstration might say, "OK. You have the basic steps clear for excising a skin lesion. Before I let you try one yourself, tell me how you will act in regard to the patient as you prepare, carry out, and follow up on the procedure." The medical student might answer, "I will be careful to treat the patient with concern." The instructor might then ask, "How exactly could you do that? What should I look for in your behavior?" The student might reply, "Watch how I take my time with the patient before the procedure by sitting down and maintaining eye contact as I explain the procedure carefully and explicitly. You can watch for the way I check comprehension by asking questions or by asking the patient to tell me the gist of what I said. . . ."

GUIDELINE 4: DEMONSTRATE YOUR PROFESSIONAL ATTITUDE

The modeling principle also applies to you, the instructor, as a model of attitudes. Should you act as a model of an ethical person? a professional? a mature adult? a confident problem solver? The answer is a resounding yes! Throughout all contacts with students, the modeling principle implies that you behave ethically, enthusiastically, and professionally (Bandura, 1977).

Types of Interrelated Attitudes to Consider Modeling
1. Behave like a mature, ethical professional.
2. Show concern for your subject matter, your students' learning, and your teaching.
3. Show enthusiasm for and enjoyment of your work.

Behave Like a Mature, Ethical Professional

Model the professional attitudes you expect from your students now and in the world outside of instruction. Some teachers lose their credibility by preaching one way and behaving in another. I observed a physician who would speak frequently about being unbiased in dealing with patients. One day he walked up to the door of an examining room with his students, took the chart for a new patient off the door, and said aloud, "Oh no, another one of these fat freeloaders." His students may have listened to his lectures about bias, but his behavior negated any influence his teaching may have had. The sad thing is that some students may imitate his behavior, rather than follow his rules.

When modeling professional behavior, share your personal and professional experiences and your emotions. In relevant contexts, recount stories of your own experience with a difficult ethical problem, what you thought, and how you felt.

Show Concern for Your Subject Matter, Your Students' Learning, and Your Teaching

As an instructor, you have some responsibility to teach more than knowledge and skill. You should be aware of the attitudes about your subject that you wish to engender in your students and act accordingly. For example, by being prepared and by making it apparent that you are prepared, you communciate your concern about your subject, students, and teaching.

MODELING ATTITUDES TOWARD THE SUBJECT

Professor Ron Dorr wants his students to love thinking and writing. For years, he has assigned a reading about Abraham Lincoln and asked his students to write an interpretive essay. Each time Professor Dorr makes the assignment, he, too, writes a new interpretation.

When he comes to class he bubbles over about a new wrinkle he has found. He reads his essay in class with verve. He describes how he got the idea so that his students can see "a mind at work."

When a student presents an idea Dorr has not heard before, his eyes go wide, his mouth opens, he hits his forehead with his palm and exclaims, "Did you hear that! Did you hear what Jan said? I never thought of that! She said that the author was trying to say. . . ."

Dorr's students say that, given his enthusiasm for the subject, the least they can do is to show their interest by trying hard and being prepared.

Show Enthusiasm for and Enjoyment of Your Work

Do you enjoy your work as a teacher or trainer? Your enthusiasm is shown by relevant animation and voice modulation. The attitude of enthusiasm is compelling.

Must instructors be demonstrative and outgoing? Must all of us be highly animated and expressive? I think not. Enthusiasm is relative. The changes in our demeanor need not be extreme, nor do we have to be unusually demonstrative to show students how much we care about what we teach. To generate your enthusiasm in your own way, teach what you believe and refer to your experience. For example, one professor would usually speak quietly and make small controlled gestures when he lectured. Something changed when he traveled to help scientists gather and interpret data received from probes sent far into space. When he returned to class, he behaved differently as he told his students about this work. He spoke just a little more loudly and made bigger gestures. Later, when evaluating his course, the professor asked his students what they liked best and why. They said they really enjoyed his lectures after his trip because he was so excited!

A FINAL WORD

When you apply modeling well, you automatically benefit from other principles such as open communication and active practice because you are clearly communicating what is to be practiced. For example, if the task you demonstrate is related to student interests, you get a bonus by applying meaningfulness. In addition, because demonstrations vary depending on the type of knowledge, you can't avoid applying essential knowledge. Furthermore, you automatically apply novelty because you are varying what students sense. Considering all of these added payoffs, modeling is definitely worth applying.

Don't just tell students how to perform. If you want students to perform, *show* them how. Have other students show them how. And if you want students to perform well, show them how to do that. Be explicit. Show students step by step exactly what makes an excellent performance. Demonstrate the kind of person you want your graduates to be in the real world. You can have a profound effect on your students' performance by applying the principle of modeling.

ACTIVITIES

In these activities you have a chance to try the four-step demonstration method on physical and mental skills and attitudes. You are asked to vary what you do while staying true to the purposes of each of the four steps. One exercise is to help you figure out how all the other principles connect to modeling.

1. Think of a *physical skill* that you might teach, such as how to perform a computer function like printing, or how to shoot a foul shot. State the steps of the skill. Then, plan to conduct a demonstration by following the four steps. Jot down what you might say or do for each step.
2. How could you perform each demonstration step in a slightly different way and still be effective? Consider that the purpose of the first step is to capture a learner's attention. The second and third steps are to direct attention, and the fourth step is to help learners form a mental template of the skill to use in practice. Staying in line with these purposes, vary the steps you said you would take in activity 1.
3. Decide on a *mental skill* that you might teach, such as how to solve a problem, how to study a chapter, how to write an essay, how to compare and

contrast several ideas, how to analyze a design, how to evaluate an article. State the steps you would take mentally. Then, note what you might say or do for each step of a four-step demonstration. How does your plan differ from the physical skill plan?

4. Consider an *attitude* that you might teach, such as showing confidence, pride, or caring as it pertains to a skill. First state exactly what you would look for as indicators of that attitude. Then plan a demonstration using the four steps. Note how this plan differs from the other two.

5. List five ways that you could model a professional attitude for your students. How would you show an attitude of a mature and ethical professional, concern for your subject matter, interest in your students' learning and your teaching, or enthusiasm for and enjoyment of your work?

6. How would you teach your students to demonstrate to one another when working together on projects? How could you use the four steps to show them the four steps?

7. How could you combine modeling and demonstration with meaningfulness? with open communication? with aids and novelty? with essential content? with practice?

8. Reflection
   a. How can I show students how to recall, think, act, and solve problems?
   b. How can I best demonstrate what students must do so they are ready to practice?
   c. What mental skills should I demonstrate to students?
   d. How can I ensure that students attend to the crucial parts of demonstrations?
   e. How can I increase the likelihood that students will remember what is shown?
   f. How can I act as a model of the behavior and the attitude that I expect students to show?

FURTHER READING

Bandura, A. (Ed.) (1977). *Social learning theory.* Englewood Cliffs, NJ: Prentice-Hall. (*Note:* Bandura's work serves as the foundation for most recommendations about modeling.)

Bettencourt, E., Gillete, M., Gall, M., & Hull, R. (1983). Effects of teacher enthusiasm on students on-task behavior and achievement. *American Educational Research Journal, 20,* 435–450. (*Note:* Sincere teacher enthusiasm creates positive student attitudes.)

Collins, A., Brown, J. S., & Newman, S. E. (1989). Cognitive apprenticeship: Teaching the craft of reading, writing and mathematics. In L. B. Resnick (Ed.), *Knowing, learning, and instruction: Essays in honor of Robert Glaser* (pp. 453–494). Hillsdale, NJ: Lawrence Erlbaum.

Diener, D., & Dweck, C. (1978). An analysis of learned helplessness: Continuous changes in performance, strategy and achievement cognitions folowing failure. *Journal of Personality and Social Psychology, 62,* 217–222. (*Note:* This article demonstrates what to do when things go wrong when teaching people to think clearly.)

Gredler, M. E. (1992). *Learning and instruction: Theory into practice.* New York: Macmillan. (*Note:* Chapter 11 discusses Albert Bandura's social cognition theory.)

Palinscar, A.S., & Brown, A. L. (1984) Reciprocal teaching of comprehension fostering and comprehension monitoring activities. *Cognition and Instruction, 2,* 117–175. (*Note:* This effective teaching approach for a mental skill, reading comprehension, uses modeling by having the teacher and the students demonstrate by thinking aloud. Also see Rosenshine & Meister, 1994, for a review.)

Rosenshine, B., & Meister, C. (1994) Reciprocal teaching: A review of the research. *Review of Educational Research, 64,* 479–530.

Schon, D. A. (1987). *Educating the reflective practitioner.* San Francisco: Jossey-Bass. (*Note:* How to get the most out of demonstration. Read most carefully the section on the dialogue between coach and student.)

Whimbey, A., & Lockhead, J. (1982). *Problem solving and comprehension* (3rd ed.). Philadelphia: Franklin Press. (*Note:* This book calls for students to model thinking aloud for one another as they practice problem solving.)

Yelon, S. L., & Maddocks, M. (1986). Complete demonstration. *Performance and Instruction Journal, 25*(1), 3–9. (*Note:* Read about the basis for the four-step approach to demonstration.)

chapter 9

Active Appropriate Practice

OVERVIEW

Be sure each student practices what is required on tests and in the real world to ensure learning, retention, and transfer.

Guideline 1: Provide Active Individual Practice
            Provide Individual Active Practice in Every Instructional
                Setting
            Maximize Individual Active Practice

Guideline 2: Provide Appropriate Realistic Practice
            Design Practice Conditions and Behaviors so They Function
                Realistically
            Design Practice to Match the Test to the Type of Knowledge
            Require Reporting of Mental Skill Practice
            Decide Systematically if Practice Should Be In or Out of the
                Instructional Setting

Guideline 3: Fine-Tune Practice
            Provide Challenging Practice
            Promote Automaticity
            Encourage Flexibility
            Vary Practice
            Provide Independent Practice
            Clearly Specify and Guide Practice
            Distribute Practice
            Provide Advanced Practice
            Motivate Students to Practice

Proper practice, central to effective instruction, produces competence. All of the other principles prepare students for it. To be sure your students learn a desired skill, design into your instruction active practice of the skills required in the real world (Gagné, 1985; Gagné & Driscoll, 1988; Gropper, 1983; Schon, 1987; Yelon & Berge, 1992).

However, not all student activity is practice. What is practice? Think of practice as "action testing." When you ask your students to practice, you do so to see if their performance meets certain standards. When students reach the standards, you move to another skill. If students do not reach the standards, then you guide them to refine their performance and try again. You continue practice as part of the assessment process until each student is prepared for the test and for performance in the real world.

Why *active* practice? There are at least three good reasons.

1. When students use information, they are more likely to learn and recall. How many times has the following scenario happened to you? You listened to a presentation and comprehended what was being said. As the speaker explained, you nodded as you followed the argument. But then a friend approached you just a few minutes after the presentation and asked, "What did you learn from the presentation? What were the five main points?" You thought back but could not remember the five main points. What happened? You couldn't remember the points because you never used the information. This principle calls for active practice, active application of information. When students use information, it is more likely to be acquired and recalled.

2. If students are active, they will recall the activity and associate that with the learning. Have you ever heard a parent ask a young child, "What did you learn in school today?" You probably know the typical answers: "Nothing," or "I don't know." Wise teachers provide active practice for their students and remind them of what they did during the day. Then when the students get home, they recall the activity and associate that with what they learned.

ACTIVE PRACTICE PROMOTES RECALL

Once I gave a short college course to 300 people for the extension service at Michigan State University. The course was about child psychology and concentrated on discipline. In one segment, I talked about rules. After explaining the standards for good rules, I assigned an activity:

1. Find a partner.
2. Each of the partners think of your home and your child, and state a rule.
3. Listen to your partner's rule and review it using four standards.

The 300 students participated with gusto. They each set a rule and advised their partners. I had to struggle to get them to continue with the next part of the program.

In a follow-up evaluation, participants were asked what they liked most in the course, what they remembered best, and what they had used. The answer to all three questions was what they had applied—setting rules.

3. The activity will give you at least suggestive evidence that your students are learning. Teachers often ask how they can tell that they are doing a good job teaching and that their students are learning. Have you ever finished teaching a class wondering how well you did? On some days you may feel that you did very well; on others you may feel that things went poorly. To support or deny your intuitions, you need some evidence. There is a simple way to get evidence that your students are learning if you allow them the opportunity to perform. Require active practice to give you evidence that your students are learning and that you are doing your job well.

ACTIVE PRACTICE REVEALS LEARNING PROGRESS

The researchers at Children's Television Workshop did not know if the children watching "Sesame Street" were learning as the TV series progressed. Researchers could tell whether children were paying attention by seeing if they were looking at the screeen, but they had no idea whether most children were acquiring the ideas put forth (E. Palmer, personal communication, March, 1973). Researchers could tell from the behavior of some children that they were learning. The letter "A" would appear on the screen, and the child would yell "A." In those cases the researchers had a good idea that something was happening. But other children would sit very still staring at the screen. If they were thinking about the content, no one could tell. Perhaps you have seen similar students in some of your classes.

To find out what these children were doing, the researchers used the "stop-tape" technique. The researchers would stop the videotape and ask the child what was happening (Yelon, 1974, p. 141). The child would come alive and tell about all sorts of events he or she saw—how Big Bird came down the street looking for Snuffleupagus, and so on. The researchers then had some idea of what students were learning from the show. Without stopping and asking, they would have had no idea what the children were thinking and learning. That is a convincing argument for using active practice. You must stop to find out what students are learning by having them respond overtly.

GUIDELINE 1: PROVIDE ACTIVE INDIVIDUAL PRACTICE

There are two strategies to consider in applying active practice: Integrate active practice into every instructional setting, and be sure that every individual has the opportunity to practice.

Provide Individual Active Practice in Every Instructional Setting

Ask *each individual* to respond in the way expected in the objective, or in a way that will lead to that final performance. How can you provide active practice for each individual? Is it possible to use active practice in all settings?

> *Three Settings for the Use of Individual Practice*
> 1. Use individual practice in a tutorial.
> 2. Use individual practice in field settings.
> 3. Use individual practice in small or large groups.

Use Individual Practice in a Tutorial.   You may think that it would be easy to provide individual active practice in a tutorial. Yet many tutors and many mediated tutorial materials dominate the instructional session by talking and demonstrating rather than allowing the student to perform. As a rule of thumb, consider allowing a student to perform at least half the time during a tutorial.

Use Individual Practice in Field Settings.   Sometimes, in field settings when students work one-to-one with a mentor, mentors are reluctant to let the apprentices perform. The mentors with whom I have spoken feel that their apprentices are likely to make dangerous and costly mistakes. When you are afraid to allow students to perform in the field because they do not have the prerequisites, the experience, or the confidence they need, you can use a shaping approach to give students active practice and increase your confidence in your students.

Help students practice in the field by gradually approximating full participation. First, require students to use *active observation* in a number of ways. For example, you could ask your students to

1. answer questions,
2. solve puzzles,
3. resolve problems after they observe,
4. present a critique and give feedback to a performer step by step, quality by quality, using a checklist,
5. create a checklist after observing a procedure, or
6. find a simpler way to perform or a variation of a procedure.

Second, ask students to perform under *guided conditions*. You could ask your students to do a part of the task or the whole task, preferably the whole task, under the most basic conditions, with relatively attentive verbal and physical assistance and supervision. Third, and finally, have students do an *independent performance*. You could have the student do the whole task under ordinary conditions, for any type of case, with realistic assistance and normal supervision.

Use Individual Practice in Small or Large Classroom Groups.

For small or large groups there are several strategies for active practice.

Use a programmed lecture with all group sizes. Begin by explaining an idea, such as the concept *behavioral terms*. Give the definition: "words that denote observable action." Follow with some examples and nonexamples, such as "to write an explanation of inertia," versus "to understand inertia." Then ask your students questions to see if they have learned the concept. You may pose the question in several ways.

Put these five phrases on the overhead projector:

1. Knowing computer basics
2. Appreciating the power of a computer
3. Discovering how a computer works
4. Printing a document using a computer
5. Thinking clearly about technology

Ask your students to answer individually which of the phrases uses unambiguous behavioral terms and to state aloud why he or she thinks so. Read the question aloud to pace students' thinking, then give them time to answer silently. Ask who chose answer number 1. If anyone did, ask why. Proceed through all the choices and then give your opinion of the choice that fits the definition best.

Another strategy is to provide a handout with questions about which of several phrases is stated in unambiguous behavioral terms. Ask the students to answer the questions individually. When they are done, tell them to turn to one other person to check and justify their answers. Then ask students what they chose as the best choice for each question and why. Confirm their answers.

Another form of active practice would be to provide a certain amount of time for students to work in pairs. Each student must contribute at least five phrases in behavioral terms, then each partner must check the other's contributions. If you have time when they finish, have pairs of students trade phrases and check their work.

To help students recall an idea, ask them to paraphrase it aloud to a partner, or to write it and then exchange it with a partner. As individuals, they summarize several ideas and compare them. If you want students to apply ideas, ask them to write applications or draw diagrams, describe metaphors, make predictions, or create examples.

At times you might have students make choral responses for basic facts. After explaining the differences between goals and objectives, I ask my students whenever those topics come up, "A goal refers to what?" They all answer, "Real-world performance." I add, "And an objective refers to what?" They all answer, "The test." That simple basic association becomes second nature to the students.

Given more time, have your students do more extensive assignments in class such as analyze an essay or a project. Sometimes they can begin in class and get confirmation from peers so as to work with confidence outside of class.

As a prelude to active practice by all students, consider tutoring one student in front of others. By viewing one student, your students will gain a great deal of procedural information that they can put to use in their own practice. In a similar fashion you could have a discussion with a small group selected from a much larger class. Some call this technique the "fishbowl" because everyone is looking at the group as if they were in a fishbowl.

Maximize Individual Active Practice

As a rule of thumb, use at least half the instructional time for active student practice. Toward that end, consider an experiment with what we might call a "virtually silent lesson," that is, a silent lesson on the part of the teacher. Can you construct a lesson in which the students do all or most of the thinking and talking and still learn what you want them to? Many teachers think so, and many students love the process. I will bet that you have the fondest memories of the "projects" you undertook in school or training programs. To maximize individual active practice, you may use problem solving or well-designed exercises.

Use Well-Designed Problems instead of Lecture.   Some teachers maximize the amount of active practice and minimize telling through the use of problem solving. They design or take advantage of problem situations and ask students to formulate questions, collect and analyze the data, and draw conclusions.

> ### MAXIMIZING STUDENT ACTIVE PRACTICE THROUGH PROBLEM SOLVING
>
> Imagine a class in which students are given problems to solve within their prerequisites with little or no preliminary explanation, for example: "We want to go on a class trip, but we must raise enough money for a class trip." The students work alone or in groups to find the information they need to solve the problem, such as (a) the likely destinations, (b) cost of transportation to destinations, (c) times available for the trip, (d) how much money would have to be raised, (e) sources of funding, and (f) how much to earn each month to meet the desired total. They find and test various solutions. They consult with the teacher, but they do not listen to formal lectures on how to solve each problem. Individuals and groups present their solutions and listen to others present theirs. Students and teacher respond to the solutions and decide on one to implement. Students decide on responsibilities and proceed.

This is a wonderful way to teach, but it doesn't just happen. To implement maximum active practice, you will need the proper conditions.

1. Well-Designed Problems.   Design problems to represent real-world conditions, but do not completely formulate them for the students. Students learn many skills and ideas by defining problems as well as solving them. For example, the teacher assigning the class trip did not spell out all the subproblems and the steps for students to take. Although not all skills and ideas to be learned this way are predictable, the problem can be designed to result in the learning students need. Suppose that the teacher suggesting the trip wanted students to learn to write letters inquiring about services and costs. In that case, the teacher might want to structure a part of the problem to require correpondence.

2. Students with Adequate Subject Knowledge.   Your students will need enough subject matter knowledge to make progress and to avoid unnecessary frustration, but they do not necessarily need ideal prerequisites. They can learn information needed to solve the problem just as they would in the real world.

3. Students with Research Skill.   Your students must be capable of doing the type of research needed to solve the problem.

4. Students Who Can Work Cooperatively.   Your students must be capable of working cooperatively in a group.

As you can see, as part of implementation, you may need some careful preassessment of knowledge and some purposeful training in research and group process skills.

Use Carefully Structured and Guided Exercises instead of Lecture.
Some teachers maximize individual practice by carefully structuring and guiding exercises that individual students or pairs of students could accomplish with the prerequisites they have. The exercise could be a *simulation.*

USING A SIMULATION TO MAXIMIZE ACTIVE PRACTICE

Police trainers wanted to train detectives to handle a hostage-taking. The training began in a room that was made to be the command post for the detectives assigned to the case. After a very brief introduction the detectives were shown a videotaped news report that described the hostage-taking. A person playing their superior assigned them the case and provided them with the available information. The room was equipped with a fax and a phone, walkie-talkies, and other communication devices. The detectives had to proceed based on the information given. They could do whatever they thought was necessary: collect more information, possibly contact the hostage-takers, assign officers. They could also consult with experts to learn what they might do and what consequences their actions may have. Time was ticking away and things were happening every minute. When the case was finished, the detectives had a discussion summarizing their actions, the consequences, and what principles they derived from the experience. I don't think they will ever forget it.

The exercise could be an *application of skill steps* that students have seen demonstrated.

MAXIMIZING ACTIVE PRACTICE BY APPLICATION OF A SKILL

A medical educator conducted a workshop for physicians on how to teach psychomotor skills. During the morning of the workshop the physicians briefly heard of a way to teach skills and saw a demonstration lesson. For the rest of the morning, for a simple skill such as how to take a blood pressure, they stated an objective, wrote the steps for the skill they would teach, and planned their lessons. In the afternoon they were assigned real students to whom they had to teach the skill they had planned. In groups of four physicians and one student, each physician taught the student. After each lesson, the medical student, the medical educator, and the physicians evaluated and discussed what they had observed. When all the lessons had been taught, the whole group assembled and listed ideas they had discovered about the teaching of skills. About 75 percent of the workshop was active individual practice.

The exercise could be simply *reading and answering questions* or it could be a complex *project* carried on outside of a classroom and evaluated and discussed by peers in the classroom.

MAXIMIZING ACTIVE PRACTICE BY A VARIETY OF IN-CLASS AND OUT-OF-CLASS EXERCISES

I conducted a doctoral seminar for which I did not explain the content—instructional theories. Rather, I showed the students how to read an instructional theory and how to extract its essentials to make a checklist and an application. Students read the next theory at home and responded to guiding questions about the essential ideas of the theory. They wrote out their answers and brought them to class, where in pairs they reviewed each other's answers. I circulated and listened to their conversations. I monitored the way they worked together and gave advice on how to proceed more harmoniously or more efficiently. I also brought to the attention of the whole group any content difficulties, ambiguities, or conflicts. Then at home, using their basic knowledge of the theory, students created an observational checklist and an application, which they brought to the next class. In pairs they reviewed the checklists and applications. When the review was completed, the whole group contributed ideas to a cumulative chart describing all the characteristics of the theory, such as its origins, outcomes, taxonomic classifications, and techniques, and comparing the theory to others studied. We varied the kind of student activity, from written checklists and applications to activities such as an oral presentation of a theory and its application, a summary of the theory in graphic form, and creating a theory of your own.

GUIDELINE 2: PROVIDE APPROPRIATE REALISTIC PRACTICE

Why appropriate practice? Why is it necessary to ask students to perform the same behavior, under the same conditions, and up to the same standards as required in the final exam and in the real world? Let me give you an example that will make the reason clear to you. Consider the extremely dangerous, possibly deadly, real-world situations in which police officers are mortally wounded. Suppose that officers are typically shot by an assailant who is 10 feet away or closer. The deadly incident takes only a couple of seconds, yet the assailant fires at least three shots. About half of the time there is more than one assailant, and the lighting is low. Suppose that shootings resulting in police fatalities occur during felony arrests and robbery-in-progress calls, and also during "routine" responses such as domestic disturbances and traffic stops.

Given those real-world conditions, how would inappropriate or insufficient practice look? Should we have officers stand in a well-lighted firing range, with a single target 30 feet away, and ask them to aim and fire when ready? Do they face any danger? Is the lighting low? Is there more than one target? Is the officer likely to have to fire after moving quickly? Is anyone likely to be shooting at the officer? Is a potential assailant close by? Is the officer given the opportunity to decide if he or she should state a warning, draw a weapon, take cover, and fire?

The answer to all of these questions is probably no. Basic firearms practice on a firing range is definitely necessary preliminary practice, but as you can imagine, it is not sufficient, final, realistic practice to prepare an officer for the real world. It is less than appropriate as final practice. It doesn't match real-world demands in ways that affect performance.

Imagine instead two scenarios that more closely match the real-world conditions and behaviors. Two police trainees are equipped with practice batons and handguns that fire paint balls. They walk up four flight of stairs and proceed down a darkened hallway. They arrive at the apartment they were told to call on because of a loud argument. They hear several voices shouting obscenities. They begin to knock on the door and announce themselves. As they knock, they hear two quick shots. After a few seconds someone opens the apartment door, and they see a wounded man on the floor next to a card table. Someone shouts, "They went into the bedroom. Watch out. They have guns!" There are several people moving through the rooms.

Equipped as in the first scenario, two police trainees are driving a police car around a simulated city at night. As they pass a street corner, they notice at the jewelry store one man backing out holding a pistol and a plastic bag. Along with several bystanders, they also see a second man holding a pistol and a plastic bag who sees them. He takes cover in an adjacent doorway. The trainees notice a car double-parked near the store with a woman sitting at the wheel yelling at the men to get in the car.

In the two scenarios do the police trainees face any danger? Is the lighting low? Is there more than one target? Are the officers likely to have to fire after moving quickly? Is anyone likely to be shooting at them? Is a potential assailant close by? Are the officers given the opportunity to decide if they should state a warning, draw their weapons, take cover, and fire?

The answer to all the questions is probably yes. This situation more closely matches real-world conditions. The behaviors required in this practice would also match more closely what is required in the real world. Granted, it is a simulation, and the officers know they will not be shot to death, but it still comes fairly close to reality. Officers would have to talk, move, and decide what to do. The standards would match the real-world standards. The officers would have to respond according to the law as they would in the real world. If they must fire their weapons, and if the assailants fire theirs, the paint balls would show who or what was hit. This is a more appropriate, realistic practice.

The idea of appropriate, realistic practice is to match the conditions, behaviors, and standards required of graduates in the real world. To do so effectively, follow four rules:

1. Design practice conditions and behaviors so they function realistically.
2. Design practice to match the test to the type of knowledge.
3. Require reporting of mental skill practice.
4. Decide systematically if practice should be in or out of the instructional setting.

Design Practice Conditions and Behaviors so They Function Realistically

What does the police example have to do with you? Everything. Based on what your students must do in the real world and on the final exam, design and provide practice that is a high-fidelity simulation of those conditions, behaviors, and standards. If, because of resources or because of danger, you must compromise the reality of the conditions and behaviors, design the conditions and behaviors that you do use so they function as they would in the real world. In the example, the store the assailants come out of need not be a real storefront, but it must function to reveal the assailants gradually as they back out, and to hide them should they reenter it. The officers' weapon need not be the one they use on the street, but it must function similarly in ways that affect performance, such as the way it feels, the way it aims, and the way it fires.

To assess the appropriateness of the elements of a realistic practice simulation, ask six questions about its elements:

1. What practice conditions would affect performance?
2. Will the given practice conditions affect performance here, as they would affect performance in the real world?
3. What are the most critical aspects of the performance?
4. Will a student be able to demonstrate the most critical aspects of the performance in the practice?
5. What are the essential components of the performance standards?
6. Will the practice allow observers to note the essential components of the performance standards?

Design Practice to Match the Test to the Type of Knowledge

I am about to tell you a rule so simple that I am continually amazed when people do not follow it. The rule is: Have the practice for any type of knowledge match the test.

Perhaps for *skills* the rule is more obvious to people. You test students by asking them to perform the skill and so, for practice, you ask students to perform the skill. You practice for a piano recital by playing the piano.

Suppose that you test your students' knowledge of *facts* by asking them to write down the facts from memory. The rule means that to practice, you should ask your students to recall those same facts in the same way. Both the test and the practice require spelling the 100 spelling demons.

Suppose, also, that you test your students' knowledge of *concepts* by asking them to identify previously unseen examples. The rule implies that, to practice, you should ask your students to identify previously unseen examples. Both the test and the practice present "new" examples and nonexamples of mammals and require students to recognize the mammals.

Suppose further that you test your students' knowledge of *principles* by asking them to apply the principles to previously unseen cases. Surprise! The rule specifies that, to practice, you should ask your students to apply the principles to previously unseen cases. The test provides new cases about movement of objects and asks the students to explain them using designated principles of physics.

Table 9.1 shows the consistent relationship between practice and tests for skills, facts, concepts, and principles.

Require Reporting of Mental Skill Practice

What if you must provide appropriate practice of a mental skill? To assess mental skills, you have to be able to observe a student's hidden mental process. How? A powerful yet simple approach is to have students work in pairs and think aloud

TABLE 9.1 Tests and practices for types of knowledge

	Test	Practice
Skills	Perform the skill Example: Here are data. Set up the spreadsheet and insert the data. (New data used)	Perform the skill Example: Here are data. Set up the spreadsheet and insert the data. (New data used)
Facts	Recall the idea. Example: List the ten principles.	Recall the idea. Example: List the ten principles.
Concepts	Identify "new" examples. Example: Which of these examples is a complete objective? (New examples given)	Identify "new" examples. Example: Which of these examples is a complete objective? (New examples given)
Principles	Apply the principle to a "new" case. Example: For these situations, predict if motivation is likely according to the principle of meaningfulness. (New situations given)	Apply the principle to a "new" case. Example: For these situations, predict if motivation is likely according to the principle of meaningfulness. (New situations given)

to their partners about how they are answering a question or solving a problem (Bloom & Broder, 1950).

When thinking aloud during a performance interferes with the task, have students explain what they were thinking after practice. If it is possible, create observable evidence to help support the students' recollection of what they were thinking (e.g., ask students to keep a written record of their thoughts as they progress). A medical instructor asks students to jot notes of their questions and the patient's answers as they take a patient's history. You may also consider using videotape playback to help students recall the decisions they made. The tape may also help provide evidence of the logical flow of the interaction.

If you don't ask students to think aloud, you have little basis to advise about improvement and you may be prone to misinterpret a student's difficulty. The story to illustrate this point is adapted from a classic example described by William Burton (1952, p. 139). Imagine a student who writes only the answer to story problems. He does not show any of his work. Some answers are exactly correct, but some are so far from any mathematically correct answers that you cannot diagnose the student's misconceptions. When you ask the student how he gets his answers he says, "I read the problems very carefully." You inquire further, "Yes, but how do you read them?" He says, "It goes like this. When I see many numbers in the problem, I add. When I see only two numbers, I subtract. But, when I see two numbers and one is much bigger than the other,

I know that it's a tough problem. I divide them and check if they come out even, and if they don't, I multiply." Not exactly what you thought, right?

Decide Systematically if Practice Should Be In or Out of the Instructional Setting

There are three questions that you can ask to decide where practice should take place.

1. Is the Practice about a Difficult and Important Topic?   Don't use valuable time in class or out of class for practice of anything less than a difficult and important topic. Once you have chosen a topic deserving practice, decide if you want to provide the practice in or out of class. Ask question 2 about practice in class.

2. Does Practice in Class Check Students' Progress or Their Preparation for Outside Practice?   The two main purposes of practice in class are to assess student learning and to prepare students for independent work. If you wish to achieve either of these purposes, divide the topic into logical segments and then state and evaluate questions or exercises to insert at the end of each segment.

- Will the knowledge asked for by the questions contribute to test performance, outside practice, or study?
- Will the questions assess students' comprehension as I proceed in class?
- Can I present the questions so that each individual gets a chance to respond?

Ask question 3 about practice out of class.

3. Is Practice Out of Class Used When Time Is Not Otherwise Available and When Students Are Ready for It?   The two main reasons for practice out of class are the shortage of time available for practice in class, and the readiness of students to practice on their own. If the practice is too time-consuming to be worth class time and if students are adequately prepared for practice, have them practice out of class. Choose an activity that reflects test performance or that will produce learning that contributes directly to test performance. Give students the questions, problems, or formats to use as practice or to serve as models to create their own practice. Check the implementation (Yelon, 1991):

- Will each individual get a chance to practice outside of class?
- Is the practice out of class the same performance as required on the "test" and for real-world performance?

- If students are to do this outside practice to be ready for the next class, do I have a way to hold students accountable?

GUIDELINE 3: FINE-TUNE PRACTICE

You will find that providing practice can be a complex process. You may have to attend to several variables to be sure your practice is most effective. Consider these rules to fine-tune your practice.

Provide Challenging Practice

Practice must be challenging and lead to high standards. Have your students go beyond previous levels of competency in each practice set (Keller, 1987). For example, a challenging sequence is having students recognize a good objective, then edit an objective, then write one, then write one quickly.

Promote Automaticity

Practice must lead to automaticity where high levels of accuracy or speed are required or when the task is used infrequently by the trainee. For example, some degree of automaticity is required for cardiopulmonary resuscitation. Require students to perform a skill repeatedly until it can be done without thinking (Salisbury, Jacobs, & Dempsey, 1987). Remember learning to dance? First you had to follow the steps: left, right, together. Then, you had to talk to your partner, so that you had to follow the steps without thinking about them. That's practicing to promote automaticity.

Encourage Flexibility

Practice must lead to flexible performance. Have students practice identifying situations in which the skills are appropriate, and give permission to students to produce variations of performance according to a principle (Yelon & Desmedt, 1988; Yelon, Desmedt, & Williamson, 1988). John Desmedt, a police trainer, demonstrated a step-by-step approach for grabbing a struggling person's wrist so as to gain control and move the person. After trainees had practiced the steps on relatively sedate subjects, he instructed the subjects to move a bit more and gave the trainees permission to vary the steps to accommodate the change in conditions.

Vary Practice

Provide enough variety in style and content of practice to keep students alert and interested in practicing (Keller, 1987).

Provide Independent Practice

Give students time to practice on their own. Provide the materials and the instructions to follow and the checklist to use to assess their own performance.

Clearly Specify and Guide Practice

Here are several hints for preparing and guiding practice:

1. Give brief and precise instructions for practice, including the performance qualities desired.
2. Be sure students are able and willing to practice.
3. Inform students why they are to practice, what to practice, how to practice, and when possible, what to observe that indicates that their performance is adequate.
4. Attend to students' practices and prompt them through a successful practice.

Distribute Practice

Distribute practice to promote retention and to reduce fatigue and error. Simply schedule practice of skills in short sessions over time, just like practicing piano a little every day (Sage, 1984; Schmidt, 1982).

Provide Advanced Practice

Practice must proceed from basic to advanced. Schedule practice of skills to go beyond mere attainment to produce fluency, speed, and automaticity, and encourage students to provide their own feedback as they would on the job. Require advanced practice using many, varied, and progressively more difficult experiences.

Motivate Students to Practice

Practice must be motivating. To maintain the energy and motivation to pursue practice and to resist the pressure to stop practicing, tell students three things. First, tell why trainees must practice the same task several times. Tell them why they must rehearse a speech four times: "Our brains are limited in how much information we can work on at once. That's why you and I have to practice a speech over and over again to get it right. You can't attend to and remember all the parts of your speech and all your moves, gestures, and voice intonations at once. You have to practice repeatedly to focus your attention gradually on each part of your speech and to put it gradually together to remember the whole thing."

Second, tell students about the nature of automaticity. Say, for example, "I want you to be able to do your task automatically. When I say automatically I mean you will be able to give your speech with all the gestures and moves without paying much attention to what you are doing. It will be like walking. Most of the time you walk automatically. You don't pay attention to each step. You can do other things while you walk. To be able to pay less attention to your speech making, you have to learn which cues you can ignore while making your speech (Sage, 1984). You have to find and pay attention only to the most important cues, like transitions between important sections of your talk. I will help you by pointing out the cues you should attend to and those to ignore."

Third, explain the connection between practice and students' immediate and long-range goals. You might say, "By being able to make good speeches, you will be able to influence people and have your ideas adopted."

Teach Mental Practice

Practice must include mental exercise when resources are unavailable or when students are tired. When actual practice is inconvenient or inappropriate, teach students to visualize performing correctly (Sage, 1984; Schmidt, 1982). Most world-class athletes, such as speed skaters, downhill skiers, golfers, basketball players, martial artists, and distance runners, now use visualization to practice at any time in any environment. They commonly imagine a very comfortable place to put themselves at ease and then go through all of the steps of the skill they must perform. Often they will associate a verbal trigger or a sequence of words with the action so they can cue the sequence in their minds in a flash.

Use Checklists to Monitor Practice and Save Time

Although it is difficult to be able to check the practice of every student, it is absolutely necessary in practice for important tasks. You can save time by creating checklists and teaching students to check their own work or to check a partner's work. By the time students show their work to you, it is likely to have few errors. Also, by using the checklist as a memory and reporting device, you will save time in analyzing students' work.

Have Students Take Responsibility for Practice

At first, take the responsibility for and control of practice. Gradually turn over control to students so they may learn to plan and carry out their own real-world practice. Therefore, one goal of your instruction should be that your students learn how to provide their own practice. A final exam should require students to prepare themselves to perform in a real or realistic setting, to monitor their own performance, and to plan ways to improve their performance for their next real-world encounter. For example, your final exam might require students to prepare to give a particular speech other than the types they have done so far, to give that speech, and to think aloud about the way they will prepare for the next speech.

Seven Ideas to Teach Students about Practice

1. How to practice; for example, they must rehearse a speech aloud at least four times before a graded performance.
2. What criteria to apply to their performance; for example, the checklist to be used to grade the final speech.
3. What makes a practice; for example, a whole repetition of the speech.
4. How to determine when to stop practicing; for example, when there are no hesitations and transitions are smooth.
5. How to maintain motivation and curb anxiety throughout practice; for example, concentrate on the message when speaking.
6. How to allow oneself to take risks and to explore possibilities; for example, try to introduce at least one new item, such as a story, in each new speech.
7. How to create safe simulations (Schon, 1987, p. 37); for example, find others who are willing to act as an audience for you.

In summary, you must ask three important questions to design your practice to make it the most effective active and appropriate practice:

1. Will each individual get a chance to practice?
2. Is the practice the same performance as required on the "test" and the real world performance?
3. Have you fine-tuned your practice to increase its effectiveness?

GUIDELINE 4: USE STUDENT LEARNING ACTIVITIES PURPOSEFULLY

A word of caution: Student activity is not necessarily practice. Be sure that practice is the application of ideas and skills and that other activities are carried out appropriately for their purpose and are not misrepresented as practice. There are two strategies for using practice and other learning activities purposefully:

1. Select purposefully from five types of student learning activities.
2. Implement student learning activities thoughtfully.

Select Purposefully from Five Types of Student Learning Activities

Practice is just one of five types of student activities. All five are important. Students learn something from each type of activity. Use the five student activities at various times to create more learner-centered instruction:

1. Motivation activities
2. Orientation activities

3. Information activities
4. Application activities (practice)
5. Evaluation activities

Note that any of these activities can be performed by individuals or groups of students. When should you have groups of students carry out learning activities? Have groups work together when group social skills are a teaching goal, when students may gain from one another's modeling of physical and thinking skills, when social support is needed for motivation, when division of labor will be efficient, when a change of teaching style is needed, and when guidance is adequate to ensure that all students are fulfilling their responsibilty. In addition, have groups work on application activities when a team skill is being taught.

To understand where each type of student activity fits into instruction and what is and what is not practice, let's look at each type.

Motivation Activities.   The purpose of a motivation activity is to create enough interest in learning that a student has the drive to sustain the effort required to learn. Motivation activities create curiosity by raising unanswered questions and puzzles. They reveal to students the connection between what is to be learned and their past experiences, their present interests and their future aspirations. Motivation activities also show students the likely payoffs for reaching the objectives and applying the learning in the real world. Motivation activities have served their purpose if your students express and demonstrate their willingness to continue to work to learn. Your students state where, when, and why the task is done; they state personal reasons for learning and using the task; and they show enthusiasm for learning and using the task. Suppose there was a need to train supervisors to perform tasks such as stating expectations to staff, giving feedback to staff members, supporting staff, and interpreting mission statements. Here are some examples of motivation activities for supervisory training:

1. Ask students to list the advantages afforded by an approach to supervision.
2. Have students interview supervisors to find the biggest problems on the job.
3. Have students review job descriptions to extract the most important tasks required of a supervisor.
4. Have students ask successful supervisors for the most important skills that they should learn and for reasons to learn those skills.

Orientation Activities.   The term *orientation* refers to knowing one's location in space and time. The word is used in the same way that hikers refer to orienteering, using a map and compass to find out where they are in relation to their destination. When students successfully complete an orientation activity, they know where they are in the subject matter, where the course or segment fits in the curriculum, what they know now as their starting point, where they are going, and what tentative path might get them there. In pursuing an orientation activity, students secure information and make plans that enable them to find their way. They learn to state how the task appears when it is done completely and accurately, the general makeup of the task, where it fits into a broader context, how present knowledge relates to the task, which present knowledge will be used in this task, and the instructional schedule for learning the task.

Here are some examples of orientation activities for supervisory training:

1. Have students check their own knowledge and skill on a self-adminstered and self-scored assessment device.
2. Ask students to set their own individual objectives specifying the particular supervision knowledge and skill they desire.
3. Have students choose from a list of resources those activities they would like to engage in to reach their objectives.
4. Plan a calendar of events leading to the attainment of the objectives.
5. Draw a diagram showing where students' knowledge and skill are at the moment, where they are going, and in so doing, show how the field looks to them.

Information Activities.   As the term implies, an *information activity* helps students acquire and recall ideas. By participating in an activity, students can commit information to memory, figure out the definition of the concept, discover the relationships among factors in a principle, or observe and note the steps and standards of a mental or physical skill. Each idea students acquire leads them closer to the instructional objective. When students have successfully completed an information activity, they can express their understanding of the idea. They can state the derived facts or definition, write about them, or draw a diagram illustrating their relationship. They learn to state from memory the basic ideas to be applied in the task, such as a concept's definition and its prime examples, a set of facts in an organized structure, a principle's definition and its substantiating evidence, and the steps, standards, and timing of a skill.

Here are some examples of information activities for supervisory training:

1. Ask students to observe and extract the steps performed in a videotape of an excellent supervisor performing a task such as providing feedback to a staff member.
2. Have students read and synthesize the basic principles for the procedures that experts prescribe for a task such as giving feedback.
3. Without having been told how to do so, have students plan what to say to a real staff member who needs feedback to improve.

Application Activities.   Once students acquire an idea and can recall it, they can participate in an application activity. *This is what I refer to as practice.* In an application activity, students use acquired ideas. For example, your students may organize and synthesize learned facts to support an argument; they may analyze new cases to identify examples based on a known concept, or they may predict the results of an action based on an acquired principle.

You can create an application activity calling for students to perform with simplicity at a basic level, or to perform with fluency and automaticity at an advanced level. Your beginning students may practice performing a mental or physical skill. Your avanced students may integrate knowledge and skill to complete a complex project.

Vary the condition, length, and scope of the practice situations in an application activity as real conditions demand and as student preparedness permits. When an application activity has met its purpose, your students are able to demonstrate the use of the ideas they learned in realistic conditions. They can identify examples among nonexamples of *concepts,* use *facts* as needed to support thought and action, predict or explain events according to *principles,* and perform *skills* accurately at the right time.

Here are some examples of application activities for supervisory training:

1. Have students try their skill at a supervision task such as giving feedback to a staff member.
2. Have students evaluate the performance of others, using the criteria they have derived.
3. Have students explain the task to a novice.

Evaluation Activities.   When any instructional element or activity is completed, students may pause to reflect on the event and its meaning (Schon, 1987). They may consider not only what happened and how it happened, but also the qualities of the event and its ramifications. In the process of reflection and evaluation, students may derive their own criteria or apply standards given to them. Based on their evaluation, students may decide to redo an activity. Alternatively, they may decide to remotivate themselves when their energy is lagging, reorient themselves when their progress is unclear, refine their information when their information is incomplete or distorted, or reapply their skills when their skills are inadequate. Students may also think about the way they proceeded and how they might proceed in a similar activity.

When an evaluation activity is successful, students have a sense of how well they have done, what to do immediately, and what to do the next time they are engaged in a similar student activity. They can state their strengths and weaknesses and the actions they need to take to improve the accuracy and completeness of their recall of basic ideas, of their application of ideas, and of their process of learning. They also can state with confidence what they can do in the real world.

Here are some examples of evaluation activities for supervisory training:

1. Review a videotape of a feedback session with a staff member and criticize it.
2. Think of your own supervision ideas and skills in need of reconstruction or reapplication.
3. Think of ways the activities to learn about supervision could be improved.
4. List supervisory skills you feel confident using.

Implement Student Learning Activities Thoughtfully

Once you have made a purposeful selection of an activity, you must plan to carry it out well (Brophy & Alleman, 1991). Here are seven rules to follow to implement student learning activities:

1. Use a well-designed and tested activity.
2. Use an activity when it has substantial advantages.
3. Use an activity only when you know you can carry it out.
4. Inform students about the purpose and nature of the activity.
5. Justify the activity.
6. Evaluate the activity.
7. Connect activities.

Use a Well-Designed and Tested Activity. Use a student activity when it is properly designed and tested to achieve a substantial immediate result that will contribute to an important objective. As an illustration, use a tested motivation activity that provides a credible and convincing simulation of a potentially hazardous performance.

Use an Activity When It Has Substantial Advantages. Because student activities may cost you more in time and resources than segments that you dominate, be sure the student activity has significant advantages. For example, be sure a motivation activity has a stronger impact than a pep talk. Pare the activity down to its essentials and design it to serve more than one purpose if possible.

Use an Activity Only When You Know You Can Carry It Out. Use an activity when you and your students are willing and able to participate. Your students must have the skill and knowledge to follow the activity's instructions. Use the activity when you have enough help to plan, manage, and evaluate it. Be sure you have the needed equipment and the time to conduct the activity properly and to integrate it with other aspects of your instruction.

Inform Students about the Purpose and Nature of the Activity. Inform your students of the specific function of an activity. Students who are about to participate in an activity have certain expectations. For example, some of your students may be used to application activities. If instead you ask these students to discover ideas, you may violate their expectations. Your students may also assume that they are to duplicate the performance you demonstrated and that they previously practiced. They may be surprised when they discover you have assigned an activity that involves transfer to varying conditions. To be most clear, say what they are to do and give written instructions to refer to as they practice.

Justify the Activity.   Justify the activity to your students. Your students may expect you to dominate the instruction. They may believe that student activities are merely time fillers, gimmicks, or a break for you, the instructor. At the start of instruction, provide your strongest reasons for choosing student activities, such as the likelihood of serving the instructional purpose best and the worth of the activity considering the result.

Evaluate the Activity.   Assess your students' immediate accomplishments. As part of your routine use of student activities, check that the purpose of the activity has been accomplished. Ask:

- What interest do students have now?
- How well oriented are students now?
- What ideas have the students acquired?
- How well were the students able to apply what was learned?
- How aware are the students of how well they have done and what to do under similar circumstances?

Connect Activities.   Make transitions between instructional segments. Plan to move carefully from each explanation you give to each student activity and back again.

A FINAL WORD

If you were to ask me for the most powerful of all the principles, I would say active appropriate practice. It is a straightforward idea that is often ignored. If you want to be able to help students perform well in the real world, have students practice what they must do on the test, and have the test reflect real-world conditions, behaviors, and criteria—this is where you can make profound changes in your teaching. You will be greatly rewarded when you find that your students can perform as they should inside and outside of the instructional setting.

ACTIVITIES

Here is some active appropriate practice applying the principle of active appropriate practice to various types of knowledge and applying the five kinds of learner activities. In the first four activities you will note how practice is a critical part of continuous assessment in the teaching of concepts, principles, skills, and facts.

1. Describe the conditions and the behaviors of a test you think students should take to show they have mastered a *concept* so well that they are ready to perform in the real world.
   a. Be sure the examples in the conditions are ones students have not seen during any other part of instruction. Be sure the behaviors call for identification.
   b. Describe the practice students must have to be prepared to do the test. Describe the practice conditions and the practice behaviors. Do the conditions match the test? Are you using different examples than you used during other portions of instruction? Does the behavior match the test?
   c. For the practice that you just described, state how you will be sure each student will get practice. State whether you will have students do this during your instructional session or outside of that session, and why you made that decision.
   d. Describe how you might fine-tune this practice. Consider each rule and if and how you should apply it here.
2. Describe a test for a *principle*.
   a. Be sure the cases in the conditions are ones students have not seen during any other part of instruction. Be sure the behaviors call for application.
   b. Describe the practice. Do the conditions match the test? Are you using different cases than you used during other portions of instruction? Does the behavior match the test?
   c. State how you will be sure each student will practice and whether students will do this in class or outside.
   d. Describe how you might fine-tune this practice.
3. Describe a test for a *skill*.
   a. Be sure the conditons represent the variations of conditons in the real world and the behaviors call for performance of the skill.
   b. Describe the practice. Do the conditions and behavior match the test?
   c. State how you will be sure each student will practice and whether students will do this in class or outside.
   d. Describe how you might fine-tune this practice.
4. Describe a test for a *fact*.
   a. Make sure students must recall, without aids, as required in the real world.
   b. Describe the practice and check for matching conditions and behavior.
   c. State how you will be sure each student practices and whether students will practice in class or outside.
   d. Describe how you might fine-tune this practice.
5. Think of a particular idea or skill you would like to teach. State the full range of activities you might have students do throughout the lesson or unit. Describe an activity for motivation, orientation, information, application, and evaluation.

6. Think of an activity to teach a particular topic. How could you use discussion in the activity?

7. How could you ensure meaningful practice? How does the principle of prerequisites relate to practice? How might you apply novelty and learning aids to practice? How does modeling relate to practice? What part of open communication relates to practice?

8. Reflection
   a. How can I provide practice in recalling, thinking, and solving problems?
   b. How can I provide practice so students will learn and transfer their learning?
   c. How can I be sure that each student gets the opportunity to practice?
   d. How can I have each student practice, even in larger classes?
   e. How can I have students practice inside and outside of class?
   f. Can I use a programmed explanation with recognition or true-false questions, or with students working in pairs?
   g. Can I tutor a student in front of other students in a lecture?
   h. How can I ensure that students get the most realistic practice?
   i. How can I provide advanced practice?

FURTHER READING

Brophy, J., & Alleman, J. (1991). Activities as instructional tools: A framework for analysis and evaluation. *Educational Researcher, 20*(4), 9-23. (*Note:* A comprehensive and practical article about the use of learner activities.)

Croft, D. J. (1990). *The teacher's activity handbook* (5th ed.). Boston: Houghton Mifflin. (*Note:* Consider what sorts of activities are described. Are they all practice?)

Eitington, J. E. (1989). *The winning trainer* (2nd ed.). Houston: Gulf Publishing. (*Note:* Many alternative forms of instruction are presented in the form of student activity. What sort of activities are they?)

Lave, J., & Wenger, J. (1991). *Situated learning: Legitimate peripheral participation.* New York: Cambridge University Press.

Newmann, F. M., & Wehlage, G. (1990). Five standards of authentic instruction. *Educational Leadership, 50*(7), 8-12. (*Note:* Hypotheses are made about activities that engage students.)

Schon, D. A. (1987). *Educating the reflective practitioner.* San Francisco: Jossey-Bass. (*Note:* How to help students get the most out of practice.)

Taylor, C. (1992). *The ethics of authenticity.* Cambridge, MA: Harvard University Press.

Yelon, S. L. (1992). An algorithm for incorporating practice in and around a lecture. *Performance and Instruction, 31*(9), 22-26. (*Note:* One way to decide where to provide practice.)

Yelon, S. L., & Berge, Z. L. (1992). Practice centered training. *Performance and Instruction, 31*(8), 8-12. (*Note:* An approach to instruction dominated by practice.)

chapter 10

Pleasant Conditions and Consequences

OVERVIEW

Make learning pleasant in order to produce enjoyment of subject matter. Make sure students are rewarded for learning and studying, to foster persistence, confidence, and self-esteem.

Guideline 1: Associate Pleasant Conditions with Learning
　　　　　　 Provide Pleasant Conditions before Instruction
　　　　　　 Provide Pleasant Conditions during Instruction

Guideline 2: Provide Pleasant Consequences
　　　　　　 Teach Tasks with Valued Natural Consequences
　　　　　　 Use Feedback and Praise as Rewards for Subskills
　　　　　　 Use a Systematic Approach to Reward Desired Behavior
　　　　　　 Respond to Undesired Behavior Responsibly
　　　　　　 Prevent Undesired Behavior by Anticipating Conditions,
　　　　　　　　 Behaviors, and Their Consequences

To understand pleasant conditions, think about the opposite. I'll bet that you can recall some subject that you have disliked, maybe even hated, since elementary, junior high, or high school. Why is that? How did you learn to hate that subject? Can you recall the situation that originated your dislike for the subject? Students usually learn to hate a subject by associating that subject with something or someone that made them feel terrible. For example, many people mention being humiliated, embarrassed, frustrated, or made to feel dumb during or after a test.

HOW TO CREATE TEST ANXIETY BY VIOLATING
PLEASANT LEARNING CONDITIONS

Here is a question about your feelings: "True or False: I enjoy taking tests." Some people say that their answer depends on the subject. Very few say, "True, I love taking tests—give me a test, please." Most people say, "False, I feel a bit nervous and queasy taking tests." Unfortunately, some people say they are *extremely* anxious about tests. They are the ones whose palms sweat, who hyperventilate, and who can't remember a thing on tests. How do they get that way? How do teachers create a test-anxious student?

Picture a young child in school. Let's pick a subject, a basic subject. Math would be good. The teacher starts the session by saying to the class, "Today class, we are going to have a special test, T - E - S - T. It is very important that you do well."

Then the teacher hands out the tests. As the children start working, the teacher picks out the target child for the day, the child to be ruined. The teacher walks over to that student and says, "May I see your paper please?"

What's the kid going to do? Refuse? The child says, "Here," and hands the teacher the paper.

The teacher looks at the paper, shakes his or her head, and clicks, "tsk, tsk, tsk." Then the teacher returns the paper, saying, "Finish anyway."

Feeling that his or her ego has been squashed, the child is paralyzed for some time. As soon as the child recovers, the teacher says, "OK, time is up, pass your papers in, please."

When grading the papers, the teacher varies the old song, "Accentuate the positive, eliminate the negative." Instead, he or she eliminates the positive and accentuates the negative. The teacher notes everything that is wrong and does not mention anything that is right. The teacher uses red ink, an emotional color, and says things like, "When will you learn?" "What will your mother say?" and "Why can't you be like your big brother?"

Once finished with this commentary, the teacher returns the paper to the little victim. The child looks at the front and back and even the edges of the test paper to see if the teacher said anything good. The next time the teacher announces an exam, you can see the child's palms begin to sweat. The child is hooked—test-anxious.

If you want to create a student who is anxious about a subject and, perhaps, about learning in general, if you want a student to avoid anything to do with that subject, then punish the student when he or she is learning that subject. See to it that the student fails to learn or perform by making the tasks too vague and too difficult. Don't tell the student the objectives, ignore the prerequisites, don't explain clearly, don't provide practice; then, when the student does poorly, make sure he or she is embarrassed, humiliated, and ridiculed. If you ultimately want the student to drop out of the instructional program, punish in this fashion repeatedly.

Sometimes well-meaning teachers are not aware of the way they contribute to unpleasant conditions.

ASSOCIATING UNPLEASANT FEELINGS WITH A SUBJECT

My first-grade teacher was walking around the classroom as we were doing our math worksheets. When she came to my desk and looked over my shoulder, she said, "Oh Stephen! Let me have your paper, please." She looked at the paper and turned to me, "Stephen, how much is seven plus five? Get up and tell the class what you put down." I got up and muttered, "Thirteen." Then she turned to the class. "Class, how much is seven plus five?" The class answered, "Twelve!" I was so embarrassed I crawled under my desk and wouldn't come out until recess when everyone left the room. Since then I have always had uncomfortable feelings about numbers.

Once I observed a training program in which retired professionals were being trained as facilities inspectors. From 8 AM until noon, the instructors would read and explain rules that must be followed by facilities. Few examples were given. The instructors provided lunch in the same room and then continued explaining rules from 1 PM to 5 PM. If time permitted and the instructors remembered, they provided a 10-minute break in the morning and another in the afternoon. Instructors assigned reading for the evening.

This schedule continued for two weeks. At the end of the first week, instructors called in those participants they noticed nodding off during the training sessions. In some cases the participants were dismissed from the program on the rationale that if they couldn't take the stress of the training, they couldn't take the stress of the people pressuring them when they were acting as inspectors.

I wonder if the trainees who lasted will always associate the subject of facilities inspection with feelings of boredom and anxiety. I also wonder if the trainers realized that handling the stress of boredom in training is quite different from handling the stress of dealing with the real-world pressure of people who want a good facility rating.

Students do not need to be pressured, humiliated, or embarrassed to encourage them to work hard; students need to feel respected and safe. If they feel psychologically unsafe, they may have to concentrate on defending themselves instead of learning.

GUIDELINE 1: ASSOCIATE PLEASANT CONDITIONS WITH LEARNING

It's fun to learn. I love it! I want my students to love learning, too. I want them particularly to love to learn the subject I teach—instructional design. I feel this way about instructional design because I learned the topic from people I liked, who treated me with respect, who encouraged me, and who made the learning a pleasure. Sometimes they guided me, sometimes they gave me the tools to learn on my own. But they always showed that my learning was important to them. Of course, the learning was hard. But even the hard work became a pleasure because it was connected to what I remember as good times.

Your students, too, can enjoy learning under similar benign, nonthreatening conditions and associate their joy in learning with your subject. Thereafter, they will respond to your subject with the positive feelings they got from insight, interest, and accomplishment. The message seems clear: Associate conditions that produce positive feelings with desired performance (Keller, 1983, 1987).

What does that mean: "conditions that produce positive feelings"? Does it mean serving milk and cookies, or giving students pats on the head? No, but it does mean being respectful and compassionate, considering the feelings of your students, so they have a chance to learn to love your subject and to love the process of learning itself as much as you do. However, you never know what will be considered positive or pleasant. You may arrange a situation that you think is pleasant but the student feels is not. To create a pleasant and informal environment for a faculty workshop, I played music as participants were arriving. I noticed one participant growing more and more agitated as he sat and waited. Finally he addressed me and said, "I wish you would shut off that music. Music is for listening, not for background. If you don't shut it off, I will leave!" Although my intention had been to create a relaxed environment, I had created a tense situation for at least one participant.

Consider two phases for providing pleasant conditions:

1. Provide pleasant conditions before instruction.
2. Provide pleasant conditions during instruction.

Provide Pleasant Conditions before Instruction

Associate pleasant conditions from the time of your first encounter with your students. Before instruction starts, consider meeting with potential students and spending time in friendly interviews talking about real-world performance and about student experiences, interests, and aspirations. When planning the course, consult with potential students about their preferences of pace, sequence, topics, degree of detail, and level of mastery of the course (Clark, 1986). Allow them to pursue their personal preferences in what to study, how to study, when to study, and what projects to pursue. For example, when possible, let those students who enjoy working with others do so.

Provide Pleasant Conditions during Instruction

Here are two strategies for providing pleasant conditions during instruction:

Make Learning Psychologically Safe. Attend to students' psychological comfort by enhancing their self-image and building a relaxing atmosphere conducive to learning.

First, say and do things that show you respect them and support their studies:

- I know this is tough, but I also know you can do it.
- You can always come to me when you need help.
- Any question is a good question.
- The only stupid question is the one not asked.
- I'm glad you're in this class.
- If you want extra help, just call.
- I would like to know how you arrived at that [incorrect] solution. Why did you make the decision to go in that direction?
- Take me as far as you can in the problem until you run into a roadblock.
- You are a responsible person. First do these two and. . . .
- I was thinking about your question the other day and. . . .

Second, *do not* say things that will make students feel they are unworthy or stupid:

- I don't think you can do this, but try it anyway.
- You are one of those whom I don't think will make it.
- How could you have gotten that answer?
- Weren't you paying attention?
- Oh boy! We have to go back to the start.
- Why do you bother coming here?
- Will you do this if I assign it?
- You know that you will have to work to get this done.
- This problem is only for the intelligent.

Harsh statements are easy to make. Long ago I saw a cartoon by artist Phil Frank that showed a student lying in the aisle of an auditorium and the teacher standing in front of the class holding a smoking pistol. The teacher was saying something like, "Any other questions?" All too often teachers wound students with verbal bullets, implying that their comments or questions are stupid. What do you think would be the reaction of the other students watching that exchange?

Beware of the consequences of thoughtless statements. An instructor conducting a judicial seminar asked the participants why judges have the power to put someone in jail for contempt without due process. A participating judge gave an answer, which the instructor promptly and strongly refuted, implying that the person responding was not only ignorant but also inadequate as a judge. The judge who stated the opinion was mortified. The other participants were shocked. When the instructor asked another question, no one would answer.

Beware of comments that encourage sexism or racism. For years a psychology teacher would use a cartoon to illustrate the idea of positive reinforcement. The cartoon showed a male student working at a desk. Within his view was a woman in a negligé. Two psychologists stood nearby, and one was saying to the other something like, "Our new incentive method gets students through these units in record time." For years some students would laugh at the cartoon and the teacher thought he was making the point in a clever way. Then students who were uncomfortable and insulted by that cartoon started to speak up. They told the teacher they felt the cartoon alienated women. The cartoon implied that the woman was merely a reward for the male student. Students told the teacher that by using this cartoon he was demonstrating agreement with those implications. This hurt their feelings, and those hurt feelings were associated with this class. At first the teacher was shocked and surprised by these remarks; then he rationalized his approach. Finally he realized the effect such a cartoon might have. He became more discriminating in his choice of examples. When in doubt, he tested the examples to assess their possibility of offending.

I learned another lesson in subtle sexism when one of my students pointed out that in my published course notes most of the teachers who were examples of good teachers were men and the satirical negative examples of teachers were women. I was completely unaware of this situation. A count of my examples confirmed the student's comment, and now in my examples I consciously balance the number of male and female teachers, both inept and effective.

Third, say and do things that make the environment relaxed:

- Use naturally occurring humor about yourself or the subject.
- Before and after class, find out what your students have been doing.
- Keep to business but don't be unnecessarily rigid about times and protocol.
- Greet students by their names.
- Be explicit about what is required on tests and projects.
- Assure students that the practice you assign will help them perform well on tests and projects.
- Be explicit and timely with feedback.

Fourth, *do not* make statements that make students anxious:

- This test is extremely difficult.
- If you had trouble with the homework, this test is going to be a killer.
- Only one-third of you should pass this exam.
- I may not be able to get the assignment feedback to you before the exam.

There are things you can consider doing in your classes and workshops to ensure a positive association with what is learned. Many of these actions are also applications of other instructional principles. Think about how these actions may enhance a student's self-esteem. Think about which would build a relaxing atmosphere conducive to learning.

- Arrive early to the session and greet each student by name.
- Before the session discuss events and assignments for the class.
- Conduct "talk sessions" or group office hours when students may ask and answer questions and meet other students.
- Use natural humor and stories based on experience in the course of an explanation.
- Use variation such as voice modulation and frequent relevant activities.
- Provide practice that is clearly preparation for the "test."
- Provide clear feedback as quickly as possible.
- Provide personal comments in addition to praise and feedback.
- Recognize and interact with students in informal situations, such as a lunch in a cafeteria or a brunch for the class at your home.
- Demonstrate in words and actions your thinking about the class from the students' perspective and your wish to have them learn:

"This is a hard topic. So, I have made this little diagram. . . ."

"I have been thinking about the best way to make this clear, and I thought of this analogy. . . ."

"So that you will be ready to learn today's concept, I want to make sure you recall what we discussed last week."

"I want first to give you an overview of the main steps. But don't worry, we'll look at all the details in just a few moments."

"Because this next topic is complex, and because I talk and diagram quickly, I have put the essential ideas and the diagram on this handout, which matches the projections."

"I know you are concerned about the test. I promise that the test problems will be similar to the real-world problems we will do in class. How will they be different? They will have slightly different conditions and factors. When we work the problems in class today, I will show you how to vary the conditions and factors so you will be prepared for anything that comes along."

Make the Learning Environment Physically Comfortable.   Physical conditions, like psychological conditions, are important for motivating students. Maintain a pleasing atmosphere by attending to the appearance, the location, the safety, and the level of comfort in the learning environment. By doing so, you send a message to your students that you care about their learning enough to attend to all the factors that may have some influence.

Strive for a pleasant physical environment in your classes and workshops to ensure a positive association with what is learned:

- Make the temperature comfortable.
- Keep the air circulating, especially in a small, enclosed meeting room.
- Provide bright lighting.
- Clean the room and structure it for the purpose.
- Play music the students like before and after class.
- Provide adequate seating and space for work.
- Provide a visual setting that is neutral by clearing the wall of postings from other sessions and by posting diagrams and slogans that are critical to the class objectives as well as attractive.
- Begin and end on time.
- Provide frequent short breaks that begin and end as scheduled.
- Attend to any cues of physical discomfort as the session proceeds, such as people shedding their clothes or bundling up, or cocking their heads to hear.

When students finish a course, they should feel good about the subject. At the very least they should feel neutral about it. Keep in mind the poster one of my colleagues had on his office door: "Things that are surrounded by unpleasantness are seldom surrounded by people."

GUIDELINE 2: PROVIDE PLEASANT CONSEQUENCES

Pleasant consequences also have a powerful influence on performance. In general, students will repeat behaviors that produce satisfying results (Chance, 1992; Keller, 1987; Skinner, 1968).

Five Applications of Pleasant Consequences
1. Teach tasks with valued natural consequences.
2. Use feedback and praise as rewards for subskills.
3. Use a systematic approach to reward desired behavior.
4. Respond to undesired behavior responsibly.
5. Prevent undesired behavior by anticipating conditions, behaviors, and their consequences.

Teach Tasks with Valued Natural Consequences

Results may be naturally forthcoming from a performance. For example, an edible cake is a natural consequence of proper cooking. Results may also be artificially provided. For example, a certificate is an artificial reward for demonstrating cooking skills. Many tasks have natural consequences. Consider the natural consequences of each of these tasks:

- Buy the best-quality product so that it performs the way you want.
- Repair a machine so that it works.
- Shoot the ball so that it goes through the basket.
- Operate a computer so that it creates the report you want.
- Read the mystery story and get the solution.
- Read the instruction manual and operate the computer.
- Analyze the situation so that you find the factors affecting your progress.
- Interview people so that you find out how they see a problem.
- Take the picture so that you get a clear image with good depth of field.
- Buy and sell stocks so that you make a profit.
- Write a report so that you convince someone to act.
- Present an idea so that people understand it and want to apply it.

One of the best ways to apply the principle of pleasant consequences is to teach tasks having natural consequences that are valued by students. To do so, consider following four steps:

1. Know what your students value.
2. Inform students of the consequences of the task.
3. Sequence a series of naturally rewarding events.
4. Reward subskills done well that are not naturally rewarding.

Know What Your Students Value.   Teaching a task valued by students implies that you know what your students value. What consequences do students desire? Most people want to

- explore new things.
- gain new knowledge.
- improve their present skill and knowledge.
- control what happens to them.
- be independent.
- have free time to do what they want.
- feel competent and know that they have done well.
- be well thought of and recognized for their accomplishments.

But there are extensive individual differences among students as to what they want, how much they want it, and the opportunities they have to get it. Some students value working with others, some love to create products, some enjoy directing others. To account for those differences, assess the rewards your students desire in the same way and at the same time that you assess students' experiences, interests, and aspirations.

Inform Students of the Consequences of the Task.   When you discover what rewards students seek, you may also find that students don't yet know enough about the task at hand to make a connection between it and the things they value. For example, you may have a student who wants to be efficient but who doesn't know enough about setting and naming format styles on the computer to know that this will save time. In cases like these, you must teach students about the positive consequences of proper performance: "If you learn to set format styles, you will save even more time than you save now by ordinary word processing. Let me show you how."

Sequence a Series of Naturally Rewarding Events.   Once your students understand that, if they learn the task to be taught, they will be able to attain the consequences they desire, you may implement a plan based on a series of naturally rewarding events.

1. Begin by planning to teach students a real performance that will produce the consequences they value.
2. Then make sure that the explanation of instructional content, the demonstration, the practice, and the test match the real-world performance.

By applying these two steps, a sequence of naturally rewarding events follows:

- By working hard to learn the essential content, the student gets the natural consequence of understanding the demonstration of the desired performance and being able to do the practice.
- By practicing well, the student gets the natural consequence of doing well on the test.
- By working hard and doing well on the test, the student gets the natural consequence of skillfully and confidently performing as he or she should in the real world.
- By performing well and confidently in the real world, the student gets the real-world natural consequence, the desired result of the performance.

SEQUENCES OF NATURALLY REWARDING EVENTS

In teaching physicians how to teach procedural skills, a medical educator has them first write an objective about the medical procedural skill they would like to teach.

If done well, they are able to create a focused task description for the skill.

If that is done well, they can create the explanation, demonstration, and practice.

If the parts of their plan are done well, they can put together a whole lesson.

If the lesson plan is done well, they can successfully and easily teach the real students brought in during the afternoon.

If they carry out their plan well and the students learn well, they have a template they can easily use back on the job.

If they have created a good mental template, they can use the skill-teaching approach on the job.

If they use the approach on the job, their students learn easily and well and they tell the teacher about it—and the teacher feels pretty good, too!

I was sitting in a coffee shop when a familiar looking woman noticed me and approached me. She said, "Dr. Yelon, I was in your class 7½ years ago. I am now teaching first grade. I wanted to thank you because I have used what I learned in your class in my teaching, and I wanted you to know it works." What a neat reward for me! The real-world performance I taught her was producing the natural consequences that she valued.

Reward Subskills Done Well that Are Not Naturally Rewarding. When you write a persuasive business letter clearly and forcefully, you stand a good chance of getting some fulfilling natural consequences. The response may tell you that your client agrees with you and will do what you say. But you may find, when teaching a complex valued task like writing a business letter, that you have to teach many subskills, such as formatting the page or applying rules of logic, that do not by themselves yield those results. Clients do not stand in the classroom and remark over the letter format or point out how clever you are in applying a logical rule.

You may also find that the real-world application of a whole task might be delayed until the student has become fully competent and certified or until the situation for application presents itself. Think of all the anatomy, physiology, and biochemistry, all the theories, tests, and procedures that a student physician has to learn before doing a full history and physical exam. Each of the separate ideas and procedures cannot produce the valued results of the whole physical exam.

In those cases, do three things. First, point out that subskills and contributing ideas are part of the whole task and eventually lead to the natural rewards forthcoming from applying the whole task in the real situation. For example, formatting a letter is part of writing a client, which leads to client agreement. Basic anatomy is part of a physical exam, which leads to accurate diagnosis.

Second, provide informational rewards, such as feedback, for work that would lead to acceptable real-world performance or would be acceptable in the real world: "That's a neat letter format, which will only enhance your credible professional image and will not distract from your persuasive message"; "You show excellent knowledge of anatomy, which will help you be most accurate in looking for certain cues as you do a physical exam."

Third, praise the student: "Good work, John. Way to go!" Praise has the power to produce motivation to carry on a task (Cameron & Pierce, 1994).

Use Feedback and Praise as Rewards for Subskills

How should you provide feedback and praise for subskills? Consider these rules.

Use a Reward Sandwich.   When giving feedback, sandwich what students must do to improve between the qualities they must maintain. Note in Figure 10.1 how the feedback points out the contribution of the student's effort to the real-world natural consequence.

Refer to the Consequences of Inadequate Performance.   When commenting on an inadequate performance, refer only to the performance and its consequences; and refrain from commenting on a student's personality. Instead of saying to a manager trainee, "You are being arrogant," you might say, "You interrupted team members three times and did not post what they said. What are the consequences of leading a meeting in that way?"

Use Self-Assessment.   When using checklists for feedback, let students first check their own performance on skills or written reports. This self-assessment may give them a sense of control and add to the rewarding consequences of the task.

FIGURE 10.1   Using a reward sandwich

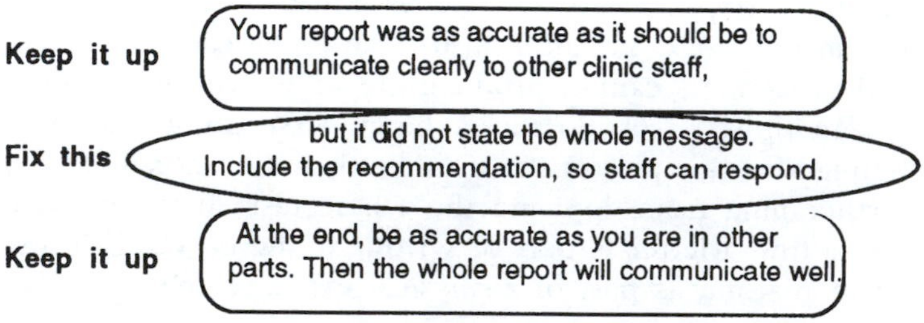

Keep it up   Your report was as accurate as it should be to communicate clearly to other clinic staff,

Fix this   but it did not state the whole message. Include the recommendation, so staff can respond.

Keep it up   At the end, be as accurate as you are in other parts. Then the whole report will communicate well.

Vary Styles of Praise.   You can express praise in many ways. You could comment directly to the student: "Good, acccurate, complete, and professional report." You could comment to others with the student listening: "Bob's report had several professional qualities. . . ." You could give a handshake, give a pat on the back, applaud, provide a certificate, give the grade the student earned, or post the student's work. Blanchard and Johnson (1981) in *The One Minute Manager* suggest saying how good the behavior makes you feel and then pausing to allow the person being praised to "feel" how good you feel.

From the vast array of possible methods you must find the type of praise your students appreciate. A reward is not always what it appears to be. Rewards may mean different things to different students at different times. There was a student in an elementary school who loved math. One day the class had to skip math because of an assembly. Near the end of the day the student reminded her teacher in a whisper to include the math lessson before the end of the day. The teacher thanked the student aloud for reminding him to give the math lesson and praised her for her love of math. The rest of the students groaned. The student swore and left the room. The teacher couldn't understand what happened.

When you find praise that is appreciated, use only enough to increase the rate of behavior. Overdoing praise can become annoying and possibly embarrassing to the student. Discontinue the use of these rewards as the task produces its own natural consequences.

Sometimes, for a given performance, you have to search carefully for something to praise. Mike, a boy whose lifestyle was a cross between calamity and catastrophe, was the last driver of the go-cart for the day. All the other boys had taken their turns getting pushed down the steepest hill in the camp. Now it was Mike's turn. His counselor helped with the helmet, strapped on the number, started the stopwatch, and pushed Mike down the hill. Like a magnet, the large utility pole attracted Mike and his go-cart. Mike crashed the car into the pole head on, wrapping the axle around the base. While the boys on his team were jeering, the counselor, Bill Moy, was trying to think of something positive to say. Finally he said, "Mike, that was the most spectacular crash of the day." Mike replied, "Oh, Bill, sometimes you make me feel so good."

Use Intermittent Praise and Shaping.   After a student starts to perform as he or she should, you need not praise the student for every good performance. You can praise every few good responses. Intermittent reinforcement is quite powerful. You may even increase the standards and "shape" the behavior by rewarding successively better performances (Skinner, 1968). For example, at first the students in a teacher education program were able to get praise for each good lesson plan. Then students were praised for about every three acceptable plans. During the first semester students would be praised for a simple lesson plan that included a few errors. By the second semester they could get praise only for an error-free, simple lesson plan; however, they could be praised for a more complex plan with a few errors. By the third semester students would be praised only if a complex lesson plan was error-free.

Use a Systematic Approach to Reward Desired Behavior

Make a Plan. How do you plan to increase the rate of a particular behavior? Consider following these six steps:

1. Decide on the desired behavior.
2. Reduce complex behaviors to simpler subskills.
3. Cue the desired behavior.
4. Arrange conditions so the desired behavior can occur.
5. Observe the students.
6. Provide rewards contingent on the desired behavior.

USING THE SIX STEPS TO INCREASE DESIRED BEHAVIOR

1. **Specify behavior.** Fred Lopez wanted his students to conduct a discussion about psychological issues.
2. **Reduce complex behaviors.** Fred knew that even though his students anticipated a valued reward for conducting a discussion, they still might not participate. Why? The task was too much and too hard. He knew that they would not conduct the discussion if they expected that they could not be successful. To ensure that his students would perform and get rewarded, he decided to teach the task in increments that were not too hard to attempt. He anticipated that his students could successfully perform a reasonable portion of the whole task, such as making good contributions to the discussion. Then they would be told that their responsible efforts produced worthy results. He believed that this feeling of responsibility for learning a portion of the task would give his students the confidence to continue to learn and perform the whole task.
3. **Cue behavior.** Fred told his students what he wanted them to do and demonstrated how a good contribution should sound.
4. **Arrange conditions.** Fred assigned a reading the students could comprehend given their prerequisites. He gave the students the open discussion questions based on the readings along with the assignment. He had them talk among themselves for a few minutes about the discussion questions before the start of the formal discussion.
5. **Observe behavior.** Fred observed to ensure that students were contributing the way they should.
6. **Reward behavior.** When Fred saw and heard his students make appropriate statements, he said something like, "Thanks for that relevant contribution. So your opinion is. . . ." When the session was almost done, he said, "The contributions today were on the

mark. That's the kind of discussion in which professionals would learn from one another. Keep it up."

Respond to Undesired Behavior Responsibly

What if your students act in a way you would like to change? For example, students

- don't keep up with their studies.
- don't come to sessions.
- talk about irrelevancies during presentations and group work.
- pack up before the session is done.
- don't cooperate in project groups.

Consider a thoughtful approach based on consequences. There are two general steps for dealing with undesired behavior:

1. Decide whether to intervene.
2. Deal with undesired behavior, considering its consequences.

Decide Whether to Intervene.   Before taking any action, consider whether the behavior is

1. your responsibility. (Is it your job to affect this aspect of the individual's or groups' learning?)
2. within your control. (Can you influence the situation and the consequences desired by students?)
3. worth bothering with. (Does it significantly affect the course's results?)

If the answer to any of those questions is no, then ignore the behavior. For students who don't keep up with their studies, you may decide that they need to monitor themselves. Rewarding them for keeping up with their studies is not your responsibility. Furthermore, you may feel that the situation outside of class is not within your control although the consequences for keeping up with their work may be. Depending on how far students are falling behind, you may decide that it is not worth bothering.

If the answer to all of the three questions is yes, then you should do something about the behavior. You may think that you should monitor students' cooperation within learning groups because it is part of your job and, therefore, your responsibility. You might reason that the lack of cooperation of one student may affect the learning of several other students. You might think that because the behavior takes place primarily in class, you can control the situation and some of its consequences. You might believe that if students continue this behavior, it will significantly affect their major project and thereby affect their performance in the course. Under these conditions it may be time for you to act.

Deal with Undesired Behavior, Considering Its Consequences.   To work on a problem, ask and answer six questions about the behavior and its consequences. Note that this is merely one way of looking at the behavior and its consequences.

What Is the Situation and the Behavior?   It is important to be most clear and state the behavior in observable terms. Consider this situation. When students are working in groups of five on their research project, Gary, in group 2, talks almost the whole work time, insists that his research idea is the only one to work on, and characterizes everyone else's ideas as "silly," "simple-minded," "impractical," and "not good enough for a serious research project." When it is time for the group to come to consensus, Gary will not agree on any but his own ideas.

Why Is the Behavior Happening in This Situation?   State hypotheses as to the possible consequences for the student. Confirm these hypotheses by talking to the student and the rest of the group. What is the student gaining by this behavior? I speculate that the student may be gaining attention, controlling others, and maintaining his self-image as the "authority."

What are the effects of this behavior? I think that the other students are afraid they are not going to get this project done. They are likely to want Gary out of their group. They are likely to be frustrated and angry. They are likely to be insulted by Gary's remarks. They are likely to come to me and ask me for some help (and they do).

What message is the student sending by exhibiting the behavior? I think the student may be saying, "I am the boss; I know more than you. I don't trust this whole group. I am the only one who can do this project to my standards. I want to be sure I get an excellent grade, and if I am to do that, I must have absolute control of this project."

What Is the Desired Behavior?   I want the student to learn to present his ideas to a group and allow others to present their ideas, evaluate all the ideas based on the criteria suggested by the group, and agree to implement the idea that is most advantageous according to the criteria.

What Consequence Will Naturally Follow the Desired Behavior?   If Gary does the desired behavior, he will not get as much attention, will have less control, and will be less likely to be seen as the authority in the group. He may think he will not get as good a grade as he would have working by himself. The group will choose a project they are all satisfied with based on adequate criteria, and they will move ahead.

What Consequences Might You Provide to Foster the Desired Behavior?   If I think the natural consequences are not adequate to produce cooperation, I will state that part of the project grade is based on my observation of the quality of the group dynamics as well as peer ratings of each group member's teamwork. I may need to praise Gary for work well done in the group and for his cooperation. I may also need to indicate that the project chosen by his group has a good chance of getting an excellent grade and being a useful and professional research project.

How Can You Cue the Student to What Is Required and What Consequences Will Follow?   I may start by asking Gary about the progress of his group, what is causing that degree of progress, and what should be done to foster progress. I may tell Gary my observations and suggestions directly if they do not flow from questions I pose. I might say,

"Your group is not making adequate progress. I think your behavior is a factor in slowing the progress. I observed that you talked almost the whole work time. You insisted on your research idea as the only one to work on. You characterized others' ideas as 'silly' and 'simple-minded' and dismissed other ideas as 'impractical' and 'not good enough for a serious research project,' and you did not agree on any but your idea. [I may ask why he acted that way to assess my hypotheses about consequences.]

"Your teammates seem frustrated and afraid they will not do well. I believe you want to do well. Is that right? So, here is the approach I suggest. Next session, present your ideas to the group, but leave time to let others present their ideas, evaluate all the ideas based on the criteria suggested by my checklist and the group's standards, and agree to implement the idea that is most advantageous according to those criteria. Do you agree with that approach? Do you want to role-play any part of the approach?

"As a result you will get closer to a good professional product and thereby a good grade. In fact, this approach should definitely help toward that end because I will be looking at cooperative behavior as part of the project grade. I think you will still be influential and you will be more likely to get a good grade compared with working by yourself. Working this way, you and your group will choose a project you are all satisfied with. If you are all satisfied, everyone will be willing to move ahead and will get more work done later because of the commitment to the project. I will check with you after the next session to see how things went."

Prevent Undesired Behavior by Anticipating Conditions, Behaviors, and Their Consequences

Don't wait until there is a problem. Anticipate and prevent problems. For example, ask yourself: How could I prevent the problem of silent students? I want students to respond to discussion questions, but they just sit there.

Consider two steps to preventing undesired behavior by anticipating conditions, behaviors, and their consequences. First, consider the common reasons and consequences for that behavior under the usual conditions. Ask yourself: What possible reasons might there be for this student's behavior? What consequences might students expect for their behavior under these circumstances? Second, create ways to prevent undesired behavior by changing the influencing conditions or consequences.

Hypothesize Common Reasons and Consequences for the Undesired Behavior. Suppose you would like to prevent the problem of students not responding in a discussion. You would first ask for the reasons why students may not respond to a discussion. Here are eight hypotheses:

1. They have nothing to say because they are not prepared. "I will look dumb because I don't know what to say."
2. They fear people will evaluate their answer. "I'm afraid that the teacher or classmates will criticize me and I will be embarrassed."
3. They feel that their answer is common and unimportant, or off the track and strange. "I will appear simple or weird."
4. They feel that others in the group have the responsibility and they are not expected to respond. "If I keep quiet, someone else will answer. Nothing will happen to me if I don't say anything."
5. They don't understand the question because it has been poorly phrased. "I will give an unrelated answer, and people will think I'm dumb."
6. They don't have enough time to think about and form an answer. "I will give an answer that is not thoughtful, and people will think I'm silly or crazy."
7. They have already heard their answer mentioned. "People will think I'm not trying to think by merely imitating someone else."
8. They don't care. "I gain nothing by answering or responding. In fact, I use my energy and get punished for it."

Create Preventive Countermeasures for Each Reason. After deriving and checking plausible reasons for the undesired behavior, consider preventive countermeasures for each one. Here are conditions that may eliminate reasons given for students being silent. These countermeasures turn out to be good general tips for *asking questions and conducting discussions.*

1. Give students the problem or question they are to answer before they begin preparing to respond. Give enough classroom preparation and adequate time to read, either outside or inside of class, and to understand the preparatory material. Remind students of a common or similar experience they have had as a basis for their comments.

2. Defer evaluation until you have everyone's ideas mentioned and posted. Thank people for their contributions, rather than saying "That's good." If you praise all contributions, the praise means nothing. When you praise only a few, you discourage some contributors because they feel their idea is not as good as the one you praised. Allow counterarguments by participants to the ideas already mentioned; do not allow characterizations of the ideas or of the people stating the ideas.

3. State that all comments are acceptable. You want to see the range from simple and usual to far out and uncommon.

4. State that everyone is expected to respond, even if just to second another's response and explain why they agree.

5. Post a precisely stated open question, one whose answer must yield more than a yes or no or a one- or a two-word answer. Ask students to give their response and explain how they thought of it.

6. Give students a chance to formulate their answers. For example, you could simply wait 15 to 20 seconds. You could have each student write down his or her response and then try it out on a partner before reporting to a larger group. They may then report as individuals, or in a safer way, as partners.

7. When an answer is given, ask for others who had similar responses and ask them to elaborate or explain why they chose the same answer.

8. Before starting a discussion, explain or ask how the topic relates to the students and also explain why a discussion with full participation is needed to be able to accomplish the objective.

USING EIGHT PREVENTIVE MEASURES TO AVOID SILENT STUDENTS

A trainer of special education teachers asked her students to be able to take a stand on a new law that calls for certain students with special needs to be placed in regular classrooms. She said they must be able to give reasons for their stand at a simulated public hearing. To make the issue concrete, they were given a detailed scenario of a particular child with cerebral palsy who is possibly eligible for the program. Each student was assigned a role such as a special education teacher, a classroom teacher, a parent of the child, a child, or another parent.

The students were assigned some research articles on the subject and the law in their state. The teacher said all would be expected to express their opinions in the forum. She explained that in the future, as special ed teachers, each of them would be called on in the real world to think about this issue and other similar ones, for which they will have to express their opinions to parents, other teachers, and administrators. They would also be implementing this law and must be prepared for the various attitudes they would encounter. Having a discussion like this would encourage them to think and express themselves as they would in the real world.

When students entered class 2 days later, they saw the question posted on a large piece of paper at the front of the room: "Why are you for or against Public Law 123?" The teacher moderater explained, "Everyone will have a chance to be heard. At first, all ideas are welcome and will be posted on the board. After all have had their say, people may respond with counter-arguments to what is posted. At no time will verbal attacks on individuals be tolerated. Please address the ideas."

Before the students were to respond aloud, the moderator asked all concerned to take 2 minutes to jot down or review what they had written as responses to the question and then share those ideas with a person nearby. Then each person responded, comments were posted, and others who agreed were polled and asked to elaborate or explain their interpretation.

You could apply the eight preventive measures in a simpler way for getting students to answer simpler, more convergent questions. Consider posing the question and making it visible on a screen: "Which of these is the best example of a meaningful attention-getter?" If it is a multiple-choice question, read the question and the choices aloud. Then ask students to make their choice without saying it aloud: "Is the best example of a meaningful attention-getter a, b, c, or d?" Sometimes ask students to tell the person next to them their choice and explain why they made that choice. Then poll the class: "How many said a?" Then, "Why did you choose a?" Finally, explain what you think was the best answer and why. For questions that involve producing an answer, post the question, ask students to write their answer, have them discuss it in pairs, and then ask for open responses.

A FINAL WORD

Who wants to learn in grim and uncomfortable surroundings? Who wants to work hard to learn and go unrewarded? Not me and, I will bet, not most of your students. Students want to learn in pleasant settings; they want to learn tasks that will result in natural payoffs; and they want to get recognition for hard work and fine performance. Arrange your instruction so they can get what they want.

Pleasant conditions and consequences, together with the application of meaningfulness and novelty, form a potent combination of principles working in your favor to motivate your students to learn and use what they have learned. Even prerequisites, open communication, and active practice can contribute to pleasant conditions when students feel comfortable in using what they know, in knowing where they are going, and in practicing what they will be required to do.

Pleasant consequences of behavior may mean more than you think possible at the moment. I recently received a letter from a student who was an advisee many years ago. She is now a manager of a large agency. She wrote that there was something I said to her about the quality of her performance when she was a student that kept her going for years afterward. She was writing to thank me for praising and encouraging her at that time. The strange thing is that I have no recollection of saying those things, but I do thank her for reminding me about the profound effects of praise.

ACTIVITIES

Use these activities to plan for and carry out application of pleasant conditions and consequences. The first three activities apply pleasant conditions and the rest apply pleasant consequences.

1. What are five aspects of instruction that may be seen as pleasant or positive by students in a class you know? Think of physical and psychological factors and what the teacher and students say and do, as well as what is in the instructional environment. If you can't think of five positive aspects that exist now, add things that may be seen as positive.
2. Think of five aspects of that instruction that students may see as unpleasant and negative. Next to each one, list a way to either eliminate or change the aspect in a positive way.
3. How does the application of each of the other principles relate to pleasant conditions?
4. In one column, list five important ideas and skills that you might teach. In a second column, list the natural consequence of knowing and using the idea or performing the skill properly. If you can't think of a natural consequence, think of the larger skill to which it contributes and its consequences.
5. Think of a task that you might teach. When a student does that task well in practice or in a test performance, what are at least three different ways that you can praise that student? Think of varying means of comunication as well as varying statements. Then add a statement that specifies some part of the performance that needs improvement. Follow with a repeat of the praise to "finish the sandwich."
6. Think of some undesired student behavior that you have observed. If that student were in your class, would it be your responsibility to act? If so, plan your approach to changing that behavior using the six steps noted in the chapter.
7. Think of a recurring undesired student behavior that you have seen, such as students not responding in a discussion or students being late to class. List the likely reasons for the behavior in one column and list preventive measures in a second column. Think of conditions and consequences.
8. Reflection
   a. How can I make learning satisfying so students will keep learning and using what is learned?
   b. How can I reward students who do learn? How can I use a reward sandwich?

FURTHER READING

Ames, C. (1992). Classrooms: Goals, structures and student motivation. *Journal of Educational Psychology, 84*(3), 261–271.

Ames, C., & Ames, R. (Eds.). (1985). *Research on motivation in education: Vol. 2. The classroom milieu.* Orlando, FL: Academic Press.

Bacon, E. H. (1989, November). Guidelines for implementing a classroom reward system. *Academic Therapy, 25,* 183–192.

Blanchard, K., & Johnson, S. (1981). *The one minute manager.* New York: Berkeley Books. (*Note:* The essence of the book is use of positive reinforcement.)

Cameron, J., & Pierce, W. D. (1994). Reinforcement, reward, and intrinsic motivation: A meta analysis. *Review of Educational Research, 64*(3), 363–424. (*Note:* This review of research shows that rewards and praise generally encourage intrinsic motivation and discourage intrinsic motivation only in a very particular circumstance.)

Chance, P. (1992, November). The rewards of learning. *Phi Delta Kappan,* 200–207. (*Note:* Good arguments about rewards producing motivation.)

Eccles, J. S., Wigfield, A., Midgley, C., & Reuman, D. (1993). Negative effects of traditional middle schools on students' motivation. *Elementary School Journal, 93*(5), 553–574.

Good, T. L., & Brophy, J. (1995). *Contemporary educational psychology.* White Plains, NY: Longman. (*Note:* Read chapter 15, "Helping Students to Value Learning," especially pp. 409–417.)

Keller, J. M. (1983). Motivational design of instruction. In C. M. Reigeluth (Ed.), *Instructional design theories and models: An overview of their current status* (pp. 383–436). Hillsdale, NJ: Lawrence Erlbaum. (*Note:* Check the underlying principles and research for the ideas of pleasant conditions and consequences.)

Keller, J. M. (1987, October). Strategies for stimulating the motivation to learn. *Performance and Instruction Journal, 26*(8), 1–7. (*Note:* Check the "S" part of the ARCS model.)

Maehr, M. L., & Midgley, C. (1991). Enhancing student motivation: A schoolwide approach. *Educational Psychologist, 26*(3-4), 399–427.

Malone, T., & Lepper, M. (1987). Making learning fun: A taxonomy of intrinsic motivation for learning. In R. Snow & M. Farr (Eds.), *Aptitude, learning and instruction: Vol. 3. Cognitive and affective process analysis.* Hillsdale, NJ: Lawrence Erlbaum.

McDaniel, T. R. (1987, May). Practicing positive reinforcement. *The Clearing House,* 389–392. (*Note:* Ten techniques for the use of pleasant consequences.)

Meece, J. L., & Holt, K. (1993). A pattern analysis of students' achievement goals. *Journal of Educational Psychology, 85,* 582–590.

Skinner, B. F. (1968). *The technology of teaching.* Englewood Cliffs, NJ: Prentice-Hall. (*Note:* Skinner, the father of behaviorism, talks about the application of reinforcement to teaching.)

Skinner, E. A., & Belmon, M. J. (1993). Motivation in the classroom: Reciprocal effects of teacher behavior and student engagement across the school year. *Journal of Educational Psychology, 85,* 571–581.

Stipek, D. J. (1993). *Motivation to learn: From theory to practice* (2nd ed.). Englewood Cliffs, NJ: Prentice-Hall.

Wlodkowski, R. J. (1991). *Enhancing adult motivation to learn.* San Francisco: Jossey-Bass. (*Note:* Read chapters 7 and 8 for strategies for using pleasant consequences with adults.)

chapter 11

Consistency

OVERVIEW

To produce learning and transfer, design instruction so that all elements are consistent with achieving a productive real-world performance goal.

Guideline 1: Create Consistent Instructional Elements
        Relate the Real-World Performance Goal to the Terminal
           Objective
        Relate the Content to the Objective
        Relate the Instructional Methods to the Objective
        Relate the Tests to All Other Components
        Beware of Inconsistencies

Guideline 2: Create Consistency between Instruction and the
   Real World
        Promote Transfer beyond the Instructional Setting
        Use the MASS Model to Promote Transfer

Do you ever wonder how experienced teachers and trainers can quickly design a coherent, adequate, and effective unit of instruction? I believe that experienced teachers use "the secret" of instructional design in course development and revision. That is, they coordinate instructional elements into a consistent system so students are more likely to learn and use what they have learned.

GUIDELINE 1: CREATE CONSISTENT INSTRUCTIONAL ELEMENTS

Most teachers discover the secret or they extract the secret from instructional writings such as curriculum and instruction articles (Cohen, 1987; Neidermeier & Yelon, 1981; Yelon & Berge, 1988). The secret, an accepted premise based on the writings of Ralph Tyler (1950), is that *adequate instruction is integrated and consistent.* Integration and consistency mean that all parts of instruction fit together, as shown in Figure 11.1.

Five Rules about Instructional Consistency
1. Relate the real-world performance goal to the terminal objective.
2. Relate the content to the objective.
3. Relate the instructional methods to the objective.
4. Relate the tests to all other components.
5. Beware of inconsistencies.

Relate the Real-World Performance Goal to the Terminal Objective

Notice in Figure 11.1 that real-world performance and terminal objectives are directly related. This means that, to be consistent, your instructional objectives (i.e., the competencies to be learned and shown by your students at the end of

FIGURE 11.1 The secret of instructional design: All instructional elements are integrated and consistent

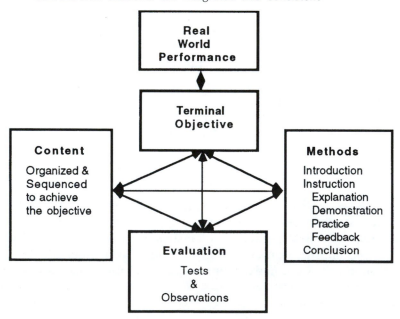

instruction) should represent a needed real-world performance. Consider real-world performances in all contexts, such as work, recreation, family, or community contexts. To be worth the instructional effort, your real-world performance goal should be relatively important and complex.

Let's consider one goal, one real-world competence for a responsible citizen in a democracy or one real-world skill for a contributing worker in a productive organization:

"Express a personal point of view in written form."

How might your students eventually express their personal viewpoint in written form in the real world? They might write a letter to an editor, a TV show producer, or a friend; they might write a memo to a supervisor at work; or they might send a note of complaint or praise to a business. One possible instructional objective for your unit in a writing course might be,

"Given a choice of topics, such as a purchase, a TV show, or a news item, students will write a letter expressing an opinion. The opinion must be clearly stated and well supported by logic and fact."

The objective matches the real-world performance. Part of the design is now complete; your real-world performance goal and the instructional objective are consistent.

Relate the Content to the Objective

Notice also in Figure 11.1 that content is connected directly to the objective, the test, and the method. These links mean that to be consistent, you should use appropriate methods to teach the knowledge necessary for your students to reach the objective and to pass the test. Derive the content by describing the steps of the task and by analyzing each step for embedded ideas and subskills.

The content of your unit on writing should be the knowledge and skill needed to express a well-supported opinion in writing:

1. Your students should learn to apply *rules,* such as, "Support each assertion with facts that logically lead to your opinion."
2. Your students should also learn to recognize examples of *concepts,* such as "opinion, logical relationship, and supporting *facts.*"
3. Finally, your students should learn to perform *skills,* such as "making transitions between a main point and a supporting point."

More of the design is now complete; your content, instructional objective, and real-world performance goal are consistent.

Relate the Instructional Methods to the Objective

In Figure 11.1, methods are linked to the objective, the content, and the test. To be consistent, your instructional methods must include

> a way to *introduce* students to do the performance specified in the objective,
>
> a way for students to get the information about the essential content required (*explanation*),
>
> a way to view a *demonstration* of how to apply the ideas and do the performance,
>
> an opportunity to *practice* the behavior specified in the objective,
>
> *feedback* regarding student progress toward achieving the objective, and
>
> a *conclusion* regarding student accomplishment.

Start the unit on writing with an *introduction* consistent with the other elements:

1. Ask students for reasons why they need to learn to express their opinions in writing.
2. Tell students they will learn to express their opinions in writing.
3. Explain that the main idea of the unit is to support an opinion with logic and facts.
4. Relate this unit to previous work on letter writing, and reveal that in the unit there will be information about how to state an opinion, a demonstration, and practice.

Continue either by explaining the steps or by having the students derive the steps and standards by analyzing good and poor opinion letters. Then demonstrate how to express an opinion in writing. Then require students to practice writing an opinion letter. Give feedback and further practice as needed and conclude the unit with a summary, discussion of its relation to other units, more motivation, a restatement of the objective, and a test.

Now even more of the design is complete; your method, content, objective, and real-world performance are consistent.

Relate the Tests to All Other Components

Tests, shown at the bottom of Figure 11.1, are connected with objectives, content, and methods. For your evaluation to be consistent, your tests must measure the attainment of the competencies described in your objectives and the ideas and skills you taught. The test may be a written exam or a demonstration of a skill.

The final evaluation in your unit on writing must assess the students' ability to write a letter expressing an opinion that is clearly stated and well supported by logic and fact, or in line with the standards the students derived.

All the elements of the design are now complete and consistent: your evaluation, method, content, objective, and real-world performance.

To produce student competency, all the elements of an instructional system must be consistent.

1. The instructional objective must match the real-world performance goal.
2. The evaluation must test the objective.
3. The content must be essential to the objective.
4. The method must teach the essential content via motivation, explanation, demonstration, and practice.

The following is an example of a consistent plan for a whole course where students have choices in what they study, and where a variety of methods are used.

A CONSISTENT INSTRUCTIONAL PLAN: EXAMPLE 1

In a health course, students decided that they wanted to learn how to plan and follow a fitness program according to the American Heart Association Guidelines as part of their daily activity at home and at work. The instructional objective written by the students with the aid of the teacher was that, at the end of the fitness course, given their own circumstances such as daily activities, age, and weight, students would write a total fitness plan, including

1. a diet plan for nutrition,
2. an exercise plan for flexibility, strength, and cardiovascular conditioning, and
3. a written record of their compliance for a month, according to the fitnesss guidelines of the American Heart Association.

The content of the fitness course negotiated by teacher and students included five major units:

1. Nutrition
2. Flexibility
3. Strength
4. Cardiovascular conditioning
5. Record keeping

Each unit contained many concepts, principles, and skills needed to produce each part of a fitness plan.

The method for each unit of the fitness course was based on a variation of the "jigsaw technique" (see p. 154), where a group of students was responsible for researching and teaching each unit (Aronson et al., 1978). The typical approach consisted of the following:

1. An introduction researched and presented by a group of students stating why that part of the fitness plan is needed
2. A short explanation divided between the responsible student group and the teacher, showing students the main ideas they needed; a learning aid made by the group, consisting of definitions and examples of the standards by which to judge that portion of the fitness plan; and a group activity, in which students had to annotate a good example with the standards provided
3. A demonstration of how to create and follow that portion of the plan
4. A practice session in which all students made that portion of the plan
5. Feedback from peers and the teacher about the quality of the plans

The test was a final project, which asked students to consider their own circumstances and write a total fitness plan including (a) a diet plan for nutrition; (b) an exercise plan for flexibility, strength, and cardiovascular conditioning; and (c) a written record of their compliance for one month according to the fitness guidelines of the American Heart Association.

You can use the consistency principle for any goal, mental skill, physical skill, or attitude. You can use it for creative problem solving or routine use of formulas. You can apply it to create courses, units, and lessons. You can use it for lectures or discussions, teacher-centered instruction or student-centered instruction. You can guide students to create their own consistent self-study unit.

For example, here is a plan for a unit on creative problem solving using student-centered group discussion and cooperative learning as the primary methods. Notice how all the elements are consistent.

A CONSISTENT INSTRUCTIONAL PLAN: EXAMPLE 2

For a unit on creative problem solving, instructors wanted graduates to solve open-ended problems with relatively original solutions according to five principles of creativity. The instructional objective was: Given an open-ended problem, such as creating a better study environment, individual students or groups of students will demonstrate a problem-solving process and produce a solution in some visible medium. The process must follow five creative problem-solving principles:

1. Deferring evaluation
2. Forcing relationships
3. Reframing
4. Decomposing and rebuiding
5. Stretching

Also, the solution must be relatively original and measurably reduce the concern raised.

The content of the unit included seven small lessons:

1. Deferring evaluation
2. Forcing relationships
3. Reframing
4. Decomposing and rebuiding
5. Stretching
6. Integrating the principles
7. Assessing solutions

Here is the method used in the first lesson about assessing solutions:

1. An introductory discussion about what constitutes an open-ended problem, and a brainstorming session listing open-ended problems they had encountered
2. A brief discussion to define the criteria "relatively original" and "measurable" as they might apply to solutions
3. A demonstration by students showing how to evaluate a solution using the criteria
4. A two-phase practice segment in which individual students evaluate given solutions, and then groups of students follow the same procedure
5. Feedback sessions in which students check their practice.

Here is the method used in the next five lessons:

1. A brief explanation of each principle by the teacher so that an introductory discussion could follow in which students could brainstorm where, when, and how that principle would be useful
2. A discussion to derive various specific applications or techniques that follow the principle
3. A demonstration by students showing how to use the techniques derived

4. A two-phase practice segment, in which individual students apply the principle to an open-ended problem, and then groups of students apply it
5. Feedback sessions in which students criticize the process and the solution

Here is the method used in the last lesson:

1. A brief explanation by the teacher of the importance of an integrated approach using all the principles and the standards learned
2. A discussion to derive various combinations of approaches integrating the procedures into a whole strategy
3. A demonstration made by students of one strategy
4. A two-phase practice segment in which individual students apply the whole strategy to an open-ended problem, and then groups of students use the whole strategy as well
5. Feedback sessions in which students criticize the whole process and the solution

The two-part test asked individuals and groups to solve open-ended problems using the principles. Their solutions were evaluated according to the derived standards in the unit.

When planning, you can enter at any point in the diagram (Figure 11.1). Although the usual approach is to start with goals and objectives, you can begin thinking about an instructional system with the content or the test, for example. But by the time you finish, all pieces need to be consistent. Consider also that when revising your instructional plans, if you change one part, you must change the rest.

Beware of Inconsistencies

If all the elements of an instructional system are consistent—as they appear to be in the unit on writing, the fitness course, and the creative problem-solving course—students are likely to learn from the content and method, perform competently on the test, achieve the objective, and perform well in the real world. If, however, any of the instructional elements are inconsistent, there is a chance that your students will not be able to perform adequately in the real world. The greater the inconsistencies among methods, contents, objectives, tests, and real-world performances, the greater the likelihood of failure.

Many inconsistencies are possible, and each one has its own effect. For example, if the real-world performance and the objective are inconsistent, the rest of the instruction is inconsistent and misdirected. Specifically, if the desired real-world performance is "expressing an opinion in writing," and the objective and test are about "choosing an opinion from several statements given," students are unlikely to master the much more complex expressive performance required in the world outside of school. If the test is inconsistent with all other elements, students may complain about test fairness: "Why are you teaching and practicing one thing and testing another?" If the content or the methods are inconsistent with the rest of the elements, students may complain about missing content or lack of practice: "Nobody ever told us how to do that. We never had a chance to try that."

But, if the elements of instruction are consistent, students are more likely to perform well at the end of instruction and in the real world. Students are likely to praise instruction: "I was able to learn easily because everything fit together and led to the same result: to express opinions in writing." Considering the useful consequences of the notion of consistency of instructional elements, this is one idea that should not be kept secret.

GUIDELINE 2: CREATE CONSISTENCY BETWEEN INSTRUCTION AND THE REAL WORLD

At the apex of Figure 11.1 is the real-world performance goal. Your main purpose for creating a consistent instructional system is to motivate and enable your students to *transfer* what they have learned. You want your students to transform what they have learned and apply it in the real world. Here are two strategies for creating consistency between instruction and the real world:

1. Promote transfer beyond the instructional setting.
2. Use the MASS model to promote transfer.

Promote Transfer beyond the Instructional Setting

Your instruction alone will not produce transfer. To get your students to apply what they have learned, you must promote transfer both in and out of the classroom. Just because your students have learned something and can perform on a test does not mean that they will ever use it outside of the learning setting. If you are bent on seeing the fruits of your teaching, you must actively pursue transfer.

Think of your own performance as a student in and out of school and training programs. Can you recall something you learned but never used? Why was that? Was it in part because you didn't care enough to bother? Perhaps it was because the situation never came up or because you never noticed that the situation was right to use what you knew. Maybe it was because you really didn't remember how to do what was needed. Or maybe it was because you were discouraged by those around you or you were constrained by the lack of supplies or equipment.

On the other hand, can you recall something you learned in instruction and have used many times? Why was that? I wonder if it was a product of your caring enough to apply what you learned, your ability to recognize its application to a situation when it came up, your memory of how to do what was needed, and the encouragement by those around you (Alderman 1988; Beaudin, 1987; Yelon, 1992). Based on these hypotheses, consider some rules to promote transfer.

Use the MASS Model to Promote Transfer

To produce transfer, follow four rules using the applications of principles we have already considered:

1. *Motivate* students to learn and use what they have learned.
2. Make students *aware* of when to use the new skills and ideas, especially when they have a wide choice of responses.
3. Enable students to master and apply the *skills* to be used.
4. Promote psychological and physical *support* in the real-world context in which the knowledge is to be used.

You can remember the four rules using the mnemonic MASS:

M   Motivation
A   Awareness
S   Skill
S   Support

Motivate Students to Learn and Use What They Have Learned.   Before, during, and after instruction, inspire students to use certain skills and ideas to reach real-world goals. You can provide most of this inspiration by honestly assuring them of the real, high-priority need to use what you will teach them. Show that the pressure in the real world to perform in a new way exceeds the pressure to maintain the status quo. Demonstrate that the skill will be effective and make a significant difference, and convince students that they can employ the skill. Show them that they need to learn these new ways to think and act because their present performance will not lead to the real-world goals.

MOTIVATING STUDENTS TO LEARN AND USE SKILLS

Police recruits know that they will have to control aggressive people on the job, but they often think they can do that using their present skill and strength. At the start of training, trainers require recruits to arrest aggressive subjects in realistic simulations. The recruits discover a gap between what they thought they could do and what they actually can do. The dissonance is great enough to motivate recruits to learn new procedures. To add to this motivation, trainers show recruits how powerful they can become using the procedures they will learn and eventually apply in the real world. Trainers also describe the success of past students in using these skills.

Make Students Aware of When to Use the New Skills and Ideas, Especially When They Have a Wide Choice of Responses. During instruction show your students how and when others have applied the ideas they are to learn. Teach your students to distinguish when, where, and why to use the ideas and skills taught. Use aids that show students how to choose the right approach for varying situations.

MAKING STUDENTS AWARE OF WHEN TO USE WHICH SKILL

New police officers must learn to use the right procedure at the right time. When should they simply use their presence and voice? When should they use restraining procedures? When should they strike with an impact weapon? When should they use lethal force? Using lethal force at the wrong time could result in the death of an innocent citizen. Merely using presence and voice, when lethal force is required, could result in an officer's death. For these reasons police trainers created an aid to show when to use each procedure (Desmedt, 1984). Trainees are taught using the aid. They learn to distinguish among categories of situations and then to make the most appropriate choice of procedure.

Enable Students to Master and Apply the Skills to Be Used. Use on-the-job training or high-fidelity simulations to produce mastery. Give students plenty of practice in applying principles and modifying procedures so they are prepared for the variations in the real world. Let your students know in a number of ways that you intend for them to apply what they have learned. State real-world objectives, provide realistic practices, have students practice choosing procedures and modifying them to fit varying real-world conditions, and give reliable and realistic tests. If possible, coordinate your instruction with actual workplace operations. For example, you could ask students to write real instructions, memos, or letters for their work as an activity in the course.

So your students can remember ideas they need, teach them memory strategies such as how to use mnemonics, how to engage in frequent spaced practice, and how to practice to automaticity. So they can apply the ideas to the real world, teach them adaptation strategies such as troubleshooting, applying principles, thinking analogically, and solving problems creatively.

HELPING STUDENTS MASTER AND APPLY SKILLS

Police recruits must adapt skills learned in training to each real-world situation. After explaining and demonstrating the basic steps to move an uncooperative person, trainers add the mnemonic "roll the ball," which is based on a principle of physics regarding initiating rotational momentum

(Yelon et al., 1988). Recruits move from simple, unrealistic practice where an uncooperative subject does not react, to complex, realistic practice where the subject's behavior is unpredictable. Trainers require recruits to practice changing basic steps to fit the situation.

Promote Psychological and Physical Support in the Real-World Context in Which the Knowledge Is to Be Used.   Before instruction begins, ensure that the performance the students will learn will meet an important need. State to students that the performance will fill a real need that will aid them in achieving personal and organizational goals.

When you are teaching people to perform in a specific work environment, coordinate the instruction with other interventions such as job aids, task redesign, and incentives. Coordinate with authorities in that work environment so they encourage new ways of performing and so they relate the job to what was taught. Encourage supervisors of students at work to model what was taught, to use the course's terminology, and to give students time and opportunity to use and perfect what they have learned. Be sure that supervisors provide the physical support: the space, the equipment, the materials, and the other staff to enable students to use their new expertise.

During instruction show psychological support by telling students the extent to which new behavior will be supported in the real world. Teach students how to engender their own support; teach them to encourage one another when applying their learning in the real world. Have students write plans where they anticipate and overcome obstacles to proper performance, and have them role-play situations in which they must resist the temptation to resort to old behaviors.

After instruction, provide your graduates with job aids, reminders, and new materials (e.g., after a writing class, provide a writing checklist). When possible, provide coaching and practice sessions.

PROMOTING PSYCHOLOGICAL AND PHYSICAL SUPPORT

Police trainers use the same weapons, materials, and forms in training as are supplied on the job. The trainers conduct workshops for the recruits' job associates, teaching them the same procedures as the recruits have learned. They encourage associates to remind and motivate new officers to use their new skills in appropriate situations. In addition, trainers provide a newsletter that includes job aids and brief refresher sessions for new officers.

A FINAL WORD

Now you know the "secret" of instructional design! Coordinate the real-world performance goal with your test, objective, instructional method, and content. It is an elegant idea; simple, yet powerful. When you apply this secret you will be amazed at how organized you are and how well your students will learn.

Have in mind the real-world performance goal when you employ the principle of consistency. Always be thinking of transfer as you plan to teach. But, if you seriously wish to produce transfer, you cannot rely on instruction alone. You will have to use other interventions before and after instruction, such as job aids, rule changes, organizational development, incentive systems, and simple reminders. To produce excellent real-world performance, you must think in terms of a whole performance system.

ACTIVITIES

I suggest doing the first creative activity many times for many topics and using many types of instructional approaches, by yourself and with other people. If you do, you will be better able to create consistent instructional plans in an efficient and versatile way. The analytic mental skill involved in the second activity can help make you a perceptive consultant. Try it. The third activity is good preparation for maximizing the likelihood that your students will use in the real world what they learn in class.

1. Practice using the "secret of instructional design" to plan your instruction.
   a. Think of a real-world performance goal.
   b. Think of how you might test whether or not someone is able to do the real-world performance.
   c. Describe the test in the form of an objective.
   d. Think of the ideas and skills that a person should know to perform well on the test.
   e. State what students would practice, what demonstrations they would see, and what information they would receive in order to do well on the test.
2. Choose a class that you have taken recently. Practice using the "secret of instructional design" to analyze that instruction. Check each aspect of an instructional segment for consistency with the other aspects: what content is explained or what information students seek, what students are shown as a demonstration, what students practice, what the test comprises, what objective students are given or derive, what real-world performance students are preparing for.
3. How is each instructional principle embedded in the principle of consistency? Return to Figure 11.1 and point out where and when in that diagram you would apply each principle.
4. Practice planning to use the MASS model to promote transfer in your teaching.
   a. Think of a particular unit of instruction.
   b. How can you *motivate* students to learn and use what they have learned?
   c. What can you say and do to make students *aware* of when to use the new learning?
   d. What can you do to enable students to master and flexibly apply the *skills* to be used?
   e. What can you do to promote psychological and physical *support* in the real-world context in which the knowledge is to be used?

5. Reflection
   a. How can I adjust the consistency of my objectives, test, practice, content, and explanation so students will learn and use what they have learned?
   b. How can I increase the likelihood that students will use what they learn?

FURTHER READING

Alderman, F. L. (1988, April). *A guide to implementing effective transfer of training strategies.* Paper presented at the 1988 National Society for Performance and Instruction Annual Conference, Denver, CO. (*Note:* This paper and the article by Beaudin, 1987, have practical suggestions for trainers to produce transfer.)

Baldwin, T., & Ford, J. (1988). Transfer of training: A review and directions for future research. *Personnel Psychology, 41*(1), 63-105.

Beaudin, B. P. (1987). Enhancing the transfer of job related learning from the learning environment to the workplace. *Performance and Instruction Journal, 26*(9/10), 19-21.

Broad, M. L., & Newstrom, J. W. (1992). *Transfer of training.* Reading, MA: Addison-Wesley.

Cohen, S. A. (1987, November). Instructional alignment: Searching for a magic bullet. *Educational Researcher, 16*(8), 16-20. (*Note:* A discussion of the need for consistency in instruction.)

Cormier, S., & Hagman, J. (Eds.). (1987). *Transfer of learning: Contemporary research and application.* San Diego, CA: Harcort Brace Jovanovich.

Foxon, M. (1993). A process approach to the transfer of training, Part 1: The impact of motivation and supervisor support on transfer maintenance. *Australian Journal of Educational Technology, 9*(2), 130-143.

Guberman, S. R., & Greenfield, P. M. (1991). Learning and transfer in everyday cognition. *Cognitive Development, 6,* 233-260.

Larkin, J. H. (1989). What kind of knowledge transfers? In L. P. Resnick (Ed.), *Knowing, learning and instruction: Essays in honor of Robert Glaser* (pp. 283-305). Hillsdale, NJ: Lawrence Erlbaum. (*Note:* This chapter looks at the variable of the type of knowledge as it relates to transfer.)

Perkins, D, & Salomon, G. (1987). Transfer and teaching thinking. In D. Perkins, J. Lockhead, & J. Bishop (Eds.), *Thinking: The second international conference* (pp. 285-303). Hillsdale, NJ: Lawrence Erlbaum.

Sternberg, R. J., & Frensch, P. A. (1993). Mechanisms of transfer. In D. K. Detterman & R. J. Sternberg (Eds.), *Transfer on trial: Intelligence, cognition, and instruction* (pp. 25-38). Hillsdale, NJ: Lawrence Erlbaum.

Wexley, K. N., & Baldwin, T. T. (1986). Posttraining strategies for facilitating positive transfer: An empirical exploration. *Academy of Management Journal, 29*(3), 503-520.

Wiggins, G. (1989). Teaching to the (authentic) test. *Educational Leadership, 46*(7), 41-47. (*Note:* Using authentic tests to relate to real-world performance and assuring that instruction is consistent with those tests.)

Wiggins, G. (1993). *Assessing student performance.* San Francisco: Jossey-Bass. (*Note:* Does authentic assessment follow the principle of consistency?)

Yelon, S. L. (1992). M.A.S.S.: A model for producing transfer. *Performance Improvement Quarterly, 5*(2), 13-23. (*Note:* An article on the model discussed in the chapter.)

Yelon, S. L., & Berge, Z. L. (1988). The secret of instructional design. *Performance and Instruction Journal, 27*(1), 11-13. (*Note:* A brief article on consistency.)

chapter **12**

Conclusion

OVERVIEW

Powerful Instructional Principles

What Is the Power of the Principles?

Using the Principles
       Use the Principles to Create New Instructional Procedures
       Use the Principles to Justify Your Instructional Procedures
       Use the Principles to Evaluate Your Instruction
       Use the Principles to Improve Instruction by Adopting or
           Adapting Existing Instructional Procedures

An Approach for Conducting an Expository Lesson
       Introductory Section
       Core Section
       Concluding Section

Sharpen the Tools of Your Craft
       Refine Your Knowledge of Your Subject Matter and Enhance
           Your Conviction
       Sharpen Your Awareness of Students
       Improve Your Self-Awareness
       Refine Your Teaching Skills

Is teaching an art or a science? Is it a bit of both? I often think of teaching either as engineering or as a craft (Eble, 1976), where we as individual teachers translate into the daily practice of teaching what we know from our inquiry about the psychology of motivation, learning, development, group dynamics, and communication.

How does that process of translation work? Have you ever attended a craft show where you pass booth after booth of paintings and pots until they all look alike? Then, when you are about to give up and leave, you notice the clay pots in one stall. They are truly outstanding. What is the attraction? Although this potter knew the same principles and procedures for throwing, shaping, and glazing, his or her pots are different in some way. The color and pattern are unique. The work is extremely precise; you can't see the seams where the handles connect to the mugs, and there are intricate and polished carvings in the clay.

What does this have to do with you and your teaching? In your teaching, you can use the same process that the potter used to develop the craft. First, he or she used the basic principles of the field to derive an idea. Because the idea was the potter's own, it had the mark of the individual's personality. But it was only an idea, a glimmering. Then the potter took the idea and thought of the practical steps needed to carry it out. He or she followed those steps and perfected them until the result resembled the idea he or she had at the start. So, too, in the craft of teaching, you employ the basic principles of your field to derive your own instructional ideas; you convert those fragile glimmerings into firm procedures and then carry out those procedures until they produce the results you desire: student learning and motivation.

POWERFUL INSTRUCTIONAL PRINCIPLES

The ten powerful instructional principles you have read about here are some of the basic principles of your field that can help you derive your instructional ideas.

Ten Powerful Instructional Principles

1. *Meaningfulness:* To produce interest in learning a performance, help students make connections between the performance and their needs.
2. *Prerequisites:* To promote readiness to learn and to ease comprehension, assess student knowledge and help students build on what they know about the performance.
3. *Open Communication:* To guide students' efforts to improve performance, provide access to all the information they must have to achieve greater skill and knowledge.
4. *Essential Content:* To ease understanding and to speed learning, explain only the content needed to achieve the performance in a clear and organized way, or provide activities for students to acquire and organize the essential ideas themselves.
5. *Learning Aids:* To ease instruction, to speed learning, and to foster the transfer of performance, provide learning and performance aids

during instruction or provide the opportunity for students to create their own aids.

6. *Novelty:* To gain, maintain, and guide students' attention, vary the stimuli during instruction.

7. *Modeling:* To promote effective practice, fully demonstrate the performance that students are required to display in the real-world situation.

8. *Active and Appropriate Practice:* To promote the acquisition and transfer of performance, provide individual practice of the same performance as that required on the test at the end of instruction and in the real-world situation. Provide group practice if the desired real-world performance is a team skill. Provide activities other than practice purposefully.

9. *Pleasant Conditions and Consequences:* To foster interest in learning and transfer of the performance, associate pleasing circumstances with performance during instruction; and, to ensure continued practice and improvement, provide naturally rewarding valued tasks as well as reinforcement for proper performance of subskills.

10. *Consistency:* To promote transfer, coordinate the five major instructional-system components: real-world goals, objectives, contents, methods, and evaluations. Take into account the larger real-world system in which students will perform.

You may be tempted just to read and discuss this list of principles rather than put them into practice by deriving your own ideas and procedures. It is certainly easier to use a lesson plan in a teacher's edition of a textbook, or to imitate the way you were taught: Assign some readings, make an outline, and give a standard lecture. Resist those temptations to take what seems to be the easy way. Take the risk and do the creative work to unleash the power of instructional principles.

WHAT IS THE POWER OF THE PRINCIPLES?

These instructional principles are effective; they work. When you apply principles properly, you increase the likelihood that your students will be motivated to learn and will acquire the ideas, skills, and attitudes they need. Your students will be more likely to remember what they have learned and will be likely to use that knowledge. How do the principles enable you to achieve these results?

1. You can use the principles to ask yourself simple, clear questions and keep your mind on the important issues.

2. You can apply the principles to all kinds of students, subjects, contexts, and methods.

3. You can apply the principles to explain and justify your plans for teaching, to evaluate and revise instruction, to create new procedures, and to enhance established procedures.
4. You can use the principles to adapt to your circumstances.

That's powerful indeed. However, to benefit from the power of the instructional principles, you must apply them.

USING THE PRINCIPLES

Sometimes you may have the rare opportunity to apply the principles to create new instructional approaches. However, most of the time you will use the principles to creatively justify, evaluate, and improve established methods. At times, you may want to use another teacher's approach. When that teacher's procedures match your context and fulfill the principles, you may be able to adopt them exactly as you find them. But when your situation varies considerably from the other teacher's, you will have to revise the instruction to fit your class. Rather than adopt or adapt someone else's method, you can cleverly apply the principles to improve your own teaching methods.

Use the Principles to Create New Instructional Procedures

You can apply one or more principles to create a new teaching procedure. What a wonderful and creative challenge!

CREATING NEW PROCEDURES USING THE PRINCIPLES

A teacher created innovative self-study materials on gardening using interactive video, a combination of computer and video technology. He designed the system so that after watching an overview video segment on when and where to use types of gardens, students could push a button on the screen to select which type of gardening they wanted to learn (meaningfulness). For example, under special gardens, a student selected water gardening, then more specifically lily ponds. Then, the program played a videotape explaining and illustrating the choice of objectives about water gardening (open communication). After the student chose an objective, how to design a lily pond, the system provided an appropriate path through the essential content. The student was notified that he could review any major idea such as "dripstone" or "tuber," any time that it appeared by highlighting the word and pressing a review button (prerequisites). The student pushed a button on the screen to see a diagram showing where he was in the course structure. The student created, filled in, and printed out an aid to designing his lily pond with his own garden's measurements. He saw a video demonstration of a gardener making a lily pond. He selected practice to be sure he knew the steps and the standards to work in his garden.

Use the Principles to Justify
Your Instructional Procedures

As you experiment using the principles on your instructional craft, your students, colleagues, and supervisors may challenge you: Why do you play music before class? Why do you tell your students what is on the tests? Why do you spend time on reviews rather than on the lesson content? Why do you have the students doing so much? Why don't you lecture more? Why did you choose that content? Why are you using those aids? You can respond to their challenges by explaining your methods according to the principles.

JUSTIFYING INSTRUCTION USING PRINCIPLES

Dave, an elementary school teacher, ignored the prescribed lessons in the textbook for a social studies unit. He created original lessons and taught the students what they needed to learn. He told his students what they would be required to know. He explained the essentials, demonstrated how to perform, and gave the students practice in what they would do on the test without giving the test away. His students did very well on the unit test compared with the other classes where teachers followed the prescribed lessons in the text. His students did so well that the other teachers accused him of "cheating," and he was investigated by the principal and the district social studies specialist. Because Dave knew the principles of open communication, essential content, active appropriate practice, and consistency, he was able to justify his position. He wasn't cheating; he was simply doing a proper job of teaching.

Use the Principles to Evaluate Your Instruction

You can use the instructional principles to assess your instructional planning and delivery. You can use the principles and the guidelines in each chapter as a checklist to discover what you may be missing in your teaching or what principle you may be misapplying. Use the checklist in Appendix A to review your plans, to observe your own teaching by means of videotape, or to consult with colleagues about their teaching.

APPLYING THE PRINCIPLES TO ASSESS INSTRUCTION

A college teacher was reviewing and discussing a videotape of his own teaching according to the principles. When his colleague asked how he was using the principle of novelty, the teacher paused, got a puzzled look on his face, and said that he couldn't think of any use. He exclaimed, "No wonder students fall asleep!" He and his colleague spent the rest of their discussion brainstorming ways that he could apply novelty to fit his personality and his course.

Karen Lienhart was reviewing the requirements for training researchers. After her trainees learned how to find literature related to their research, she and her training team asked the trainees to write an annotated bibliography to show what the articles were about and how they could use them. Something about that assignment just didn't seem right to Karen. Using the principles of active appropriate practice and consistency, she realized that the trainees were doing an irrelevant task. As real researchers, they needed to integrate related research into the introduction of their research article, and that was what they should have been practicing.

Even though there are multiple causes for lack of learning, motivation, and transfer, you will find the principles useful for tracking down some of the main reasons for unsuccesful instruction. Each principle provides one or more hypotheses as to what may be wrong. For example, when students are not learning, apply the principles *prerequisites, open communication,* and *essential content.* Ask: Are the students not learning because they do not have the prerequisites, because they have not been given the information they need to learn, because the ideas and skills are not the essentials? When students are not motivated, think of the principles *meaningfulness, novelty,* and *pleasant conditions and consequences.* Ask: Are the students disinterested because they do not see how the task is connected to them personally, because there is not enough variation to maintain their attention, because the learning situation is unpleasant, or because they see no payoff for the task? When students are not using what they have learned, apply the principles *active appropriate practice* and *consistency.* Ask: Are students not applying what they have learned because they have not been given the opportunity to practice what they are to do in the real world, or because they don't have the motivation, awareness, skill, or support they need to perform?

DIAGNOSING INSTRUCTIONAL PROBLEMS USING PRINCIPLES

I interviewed a teacher who had been getting unsatisfactory student ratings. Students rated his instruction as dull and his tests as unfair. In this report of a small segment of our conversation, I think you will be able to tell what hypotheses I was testing as I asked him about his teaching.

I asked the teacher how he taught. He said, "I carefully reiterate in a lecture what's in the chapters I assigned." I asked if he gave examples that came from his vast experience as a farmer and scientist. He said, "No, I don't do that. I don't think that's right; that would be telling 'war stories.' " I asked if the students were interested in what he was teaching them. He said, "I don't know. But I have the feeling they are not. In this course I teach farm accounting, finance, and insurance. That is not their main interest. Growing crops and raising animals is their interest." I asked if he showed students how they could use what he was teaching them. He said, "I barely have enough time to cover the content of the course." I asked if he did anything other than lecture. He said, "If you mean do I entertain them—no, I am not an entertainer. I explain what the chapter says and I go over the problems in the book. I explain slowly and carefully. That's it." I asked what students have to do on the test. He said, "I give the students test problems different from their assignments so that the students stretch beyond what is in the book or their assignments." I asked if he gave the students practice at doing that stretching or generalizing. He said, "No, that would be spoonfeeding. I wouldn't do that." I asked if he told the students what to expect on the test. He raised his eyebrows and said, "Absolutely not! That would really be spoonfeeding. In fact, I think that's unethical."

Use the Principles to Improve Instruction by Adopting or Adapting Existing Instructional Procedures

After discovering the root of an instructional problem and seeking a solution, you may find that a magazine, a journal, a book, a video, or another teacher has just the procedure to solve your problem. But be cautious about adopting someone else's instruction. It is too tempting to adopt a slick, attractive, logical, or systematic instructional procedure and apply it even in circumstances where it is not appropriate.

Throughout this book you have seen procedures that you may have considered adopting. However, each procedure is only one example of many possible applications of a principle. If you do adopt someone else's procedure, do so thoughtfully. Be sure it applies to your circumstances and follows the spirit of the principles. If a procedure does not precisely fit your needs, apply the principles to *adapt* the procedure so that it does work for you. And, of course, give it a fair test.

To illustrate how one teacher might successfully adopt another's instruction just as it is, and how others might change it to conform to their context and varying styles of teaching, the next section describes my approach for conducting an *expository lesson,* a lesson based on explanation (Yelon & Wineman, 1987). This is what some educators call direct instruction or explicit instruction. Although it is not the only way I teach, I commonly use this approach to guide my planning and delivery of lectures. I derived this approach by using the principles to enhance my explanations. The plan comprises three main parts—introductory, core, and concluding—and the principles applied to each part are noted in parentheses under various subheadings. (See Appendix B for a more detailed chart showing how each part may be modified slightly to teach skills, facts, concepts, and principles.) The example that immediately follows the plan shows how one of my students adopted the procedure exactly. Finally, the experiences of other teachers using the approach, but modifying it to fit other styles of teaching and their circumstances, are presented.

AN APPROACH FOR CONDUCTING
AN EXPOSITORY LESSON

Introductory Section

Motivation.   By means of an attention-getting activity or statement, help students to see how the topic or task to be learned is relevant to them: why they should learn to achieve this objective; how it relates to their past, their present, and their future; where and when they will use the performance; and what the consequences of its use will be. (meaningfulness, open communication, pleasant conditions and consequences, novelty)

Objective.   In a psychologically safe environment, by means of an activity or a statement, communicate openly to students what useful, valued, real-world performance they will learn and how they will be evaluated. Show them appropriate sample final products, test instructions, and test items. (open communication, meaningfulness, pleasant conditions and consequences, consistency)

Review.   Anticipate the ideas and skills students need to be able to learn in this segment. Through a nonthreatening activity or a statement, remind students of what they have learned that they must recall and use now to be prepared to learn this performance. (prerequisites, open communication, pleasant conditions and consequences)

Overview.   Show the organization and main ideas of the essential content to come: the main parts of the content, how they are related, where the content fits into the subject matter, and where the performance fits into the real world. (essential content, open communication, learning aids, consistency)

Agenda.   State or show to the students the schedule of the activities in this instructional segment. (open communication)

Core Section

Explanation.   In a psychologically safe environment, with appropriate learning aids and course materials, explain the organized, essential information clearly, briefly, and enthusiastically. Vary the essential content according to the required facts, concepts, principles, and skills. Tell students the steps to take and the ideas needed to take each step properly. Include meaningful, accurate, clear, interesting, and generalizable examples. Use intermittent questions and puzzling events. Ask, generate, and answer questions as they occur. Direct students' attention through emphasis and various media. Vary the students' and instructor's actions, pace, style, medium, and technique. Show an attitude of professionalism and concern for the subject. (meaningfulness, open communication, learning aids, essential content, novelty, pleasant conditions, modeling, consistency)

Demonstration.   Use the four-step approach described in chapter 8 to show students how and when to do what they must during practice, on the test, and in the real world. Do so for skills, both physical and mental, and for attitudes. (meaningfulness, modeling, learning aids, consistency)

Practice.   In a psychologically safe environment, have each student perform the task that he or she will do on the test and in the real world under the most realistic conditions as described in the objective. Fine-tune practice as needed. (meaningfulness, active appropriate practice, consistency)

Feedback and Refinement.   In a timely fashion and in an appropriate medium, tell students openly what they did well, what they did poorly, and what they should do to improve. Give praise for work well done. Include more explanation, demonstration, and practice as needed. (open communication, pleasant consequences)

Concluding Section

Summary of Main Ideas.   By means of an activity or a statement, remind students of the main parts of the content and the performance, how the parts are related, and where this content fits into the subject and the performance fits into their real world. (essential content, open communication, active appropriate practice, consistency, novelty)

Integration with Other Segments.   State or show students how this performance relates to other performances already learned or to be learned. (open communication, essential content, consistency)

Reminder about Objectives.   Remind students what they have learned to do. (open communication, consistency)

Reminder about Motivation.   State again why students have learned this objective and where and when they will use it. (meaningfulness, open communication, consistency)

Test.   In a psychologically safe environment, check students' performance as called for in the objective, the practice, the explanation, and the demonstration. (meaningfulness, consistency)

Here is an example of how a teacher, Chris Reznich, adopted the procedure I use. He wanted to teach the mental skill "how to write valid test questions." He used the approach because it fit the principles and because it fit his instructional needs and style: teaching adults a mental skill in a typical classroom using an expository lesson. Here are some highlights of his lesson.

ADOPTING ANOTHER TEACHER'S PROCEDURE AS IT IS

Introduction

Motivation. "As trainers, you will write a valid test every time you teach a lesson, unit, or course. If you write a valid test, you are likely to get your trainees properly prepared to act on the job. If you don't write a valid test, you may produce people unprepared for job requirements and you may get complaints about the fairness of tests." Chris then used case examples to substantiate his points.

Objective. Chris showed an example of a valid question. "On the test and on your class project, when I give you new objectives, you will write valid test questions according to the criteria in the handout."

Overview. "Here are the main steps for writing a valid test question." Chris projected this list:

1. Read the objective.
2. Look at the contents of the objective's elements.
3. Convert the conditions to test instructions and stimuli.
4. Convert the behaviors to test instructions.
5. If the performer must be reminded of the criteria, include that reminder.

"You have already learned to recognize valid tests, and in the next session you will learn to recognize and produce reliable tests."

Review. "I want to make sure you can recall how to recognize a valid test. You will be using that idea in today's lesson. Here I have an objective and some test questions. Which is an example of a valid test?" Chris projected objectives and questions, and students responded. "I also want to make sure you can recall how to recognize the condition, behavior, and criterion in an objective: Here is an objective." Chris projected an objective and asked students to point out the condition, behavior, and criterion.

Agenda. Chris pointed to a posted agenda. "I will explain and demonstrate how to write a valid test question, and you will practice by writing some of your own."

Core

Explanation. "In a few minutes you will be writing valid test questions for given objectives. Before I demonstrate how to write valid test questions,

let me tell you the steps. Follow along on your handout. Here are the steps."
Chris projected these steps:

1. Read the objective.
   a. Isolate the conditions.
   b. Isolate the behaviors.
   c. Isolate the criteria.
2. Look at the elements of the objective.
   a. Note the givens and restrictions and their medium.
   b. Note the action and the object of the action.
   c. Note the parts and qualities of the final performance.
3. Convert the conditions to test instructions and stimuli.
   a. Rephrase the givens as "Here are. . . ."
   b. State the restrictions as "You may not use. . . ."
   c. Outline the stimuli as specified (circumstances, examples).
   d. Produce the stimuli in the medium specified.
4. Convert the behaviors to test instructions.
   a. Restate the behavior as a command: "You are to. . . ."
   b. Conclude the instruction with the object of the action.
5. If the performer must be reminded of the criteria, include that too.
   a. Add the general statement of criteria describing the parts required in the behavior.
   b. Add the general statement of criteria regarding the qualities required in the behavior.

Chris mentioned that the back of the handout had a checklist to assess a test for validity.

Demonstration. "Now let me show you how to write valid test questions, when given new objectives. I will take an objective not yet discussed and say and do each step to create a test question." Chris projected an objective and showed the process.

Practice. Chris projected new objectives. "To prepare for the test, each of you will write valid test questions for these objectives. Do so now and check your work against the checklist. Then do the same for your project objective at home."

Feedback and Refinement. "I will use the checklist based on the list of steps to check your classroom practice. Then I will use it to check your homework."

Conclusion

Summary of Main Ideas. "Once again here are the main steps for writing a valid test question." Chris projected these:

1. Read the objective.
2. Look at the contents of the objective's elements.

3. Convert the conditions to test instructions and stimuli.
4. Convert the behaviors to test instructions.
5. If the performer must be reminded of the criteria, include that reminder.

Integration with Other Segments. "In the last lesson you learned to recognize valid tests, and next you will learn how to recognize reliable tests."

Reminder of Objective. "In this lesson you have learned to write valid test questions when given new objectives according to the criteria in the handout."

Reminder of Motivation. "Now that you know how to write a valid test, you will be able to do so every time you teach a lesson, unit, or course. Remember, if you write valid test questions, your students are likely to be properly prepared to act in the real world. If you don't write a valid test, students will probably be unprepared for real-world requirements and you will probably get complaints about the fairness of your tests." Chris used more cases of successes here to illustrate.

Test. Chris handed out the test. "On this quiz write valid test questions for the objectives given."

Although Chris adopted the expository procedure because it fit his needs well, he changed parts of it when his instructional needs varied. Rather than use an expository approach, Chris wanted his students to *discover* for themselves the concept "a complete objective." In this lesson segment note how Chris changed some parts of the plan for this purpose. Those changes are indicated by bold type.

ADAPTING PROCEDURES TO ALLOW STUDENTS TO DISCOVER IDEAS

Motivation. "Here's why you need to know how to identify a complete objective. . . ."

   "Here is why you should learn how to figure out this sort of concept for yourself. . . ."

Objective. "You will learn to identify examples of a complete objective **and will learn how to learn this type of concept.**"

Overview. "**Later, you will tell me the definition of a complete objective.**"

Review. "What aspects of a test would you like to know ahead of time?"

Agenda. "**I will provide examples for you to use to figure out the definition and provide practice in identification.**"

Explanation. **"Here are a number of examples and nonexamples of a complete objective. Think aloud about the definition of a complete objective.** This is an example: Given a pot, students will brew tea, until dark brown. This is a nonexample: Students will brew tea. **What is a complete objective? (Use more examples to confirm or counter hypotheses.) How did you figure out the definition?"**

Demonstration. [not applicable]

Practice. **"Use your definition to identify examples of a complete objective.** Here are some instances that you haven't seen before. Which are examples? (1) Given wood, students will carve a duck. (2) With a choice of topics, students will write an essay according to the checklist."

Feedback and Refinement. "You said that item number 1 was an example. What was **your** definition? What attributes did you see here? **Should you refine your definition? How?"**

Your instructional needs may vary in many ways. You may want to use a method for a project on a larger scope. You may want to apply a classroom technique to independent learning. You may wish to reduce your role as an explainer. Consider changes made to the expository method to accommodate each need.

ADAPTING ANOTHER'S PROCEDURE TO YOUR NEEDS

Cameron Henry varied her use of the expository lesson introduction and conclusion for her whole-course introduction and conclusion. In her course introduction, she presented the broadest goals and objectives and the reasons for learning them. She provided an overview of all the units, a review of ideas learned in other courses, and a schedule for the whole course. For her course conclusion, she summarized the whole course, related it to future courses, and restated the broadest objectives and the reason for using what had been learned. She provided a final exam that tested all of the skills from the entire course.

Rather than using the expository lesson procedure as a teacher's script, one of my students asked her own students to use it to *guide themselves.* She asked them to find out why they should learn the task. She had them derive and state the objective. She asked them to create an overview for the course, conduct a review, and help plan the schedule of events on the basis of independent reading. She asked students to research a portion of the explanation to tell their peers. She had them provide their own practice. At the end of the lesson, she asked them to summarize and restate what they learned and state some reasons why. Together they cooperatively created the test.

When students sign up for and negotiate an independent study contract, I have them write and implement the contract themselves, including their reason for study, what they will accomplish, how they will get the information, how they will apply it, what they will present to demonstrate they have learned, and a schedule for their studies.

One of my students adapting the expository lesson procedure did not want to be speaking all the time to fulfill the principles, even to explain organized essential content. He conducted a virtually silent lesson, silent at least for him. Instead he used text, video, discussion, and activity. Physicians learning to make arm casts out of fiberglass read a short text in class, which included the motivation, objective, agenda, review, and a broad checklist of skill steps and qualities. They watched a video, which gave an overview of the process. They read another short piece and watched a continuation of the video, which filled in the details of the steps. Then they formed teams. Each team followed the guidelines to collect and prepare the materials. They reviewed their work using debriefing guidelines and the checklist in the text. They proceeded in this fashion through all the steps to produce the fiberglass cast. The teacher never said a word and yet followed the expository lesson procedure.

Do not believe you must follow a method exactly as it has been described. You cannot follow anyone else's idea exactly in any case. You can't avoid changing a method when you use it; in fact, you change it by using it. Experiment with instructional methods.

GETTING PERMISSION TO CHANGE AN INSTRUCTIONAL APPROACH

Once I watched a student teacher giving a presentation and continuously checking his notes. When I asked him what he was doing, he said he was making sure that all parts of a procedure for orienting students I had shown him were exactly in the order they were "supposed" to be. I explained that he could vary the order and even the style and still let his students know what they need to learn in an organized way. He was supposed to concentrate on fulfilling the principles of open communication and organized essential content to help his students acquire the information, not on a particular procedure or order. I asked him to develop at least three possible logical sequences for his introduction that would still fulfill the principles, one of which had to be student activity oriented. Here is what he wrote:

Sequence 1 (very similar to what I had shown him)

> *Objective.* Today we will learn how to format a letter on a computer.
> *Motivation.* Why? You will need this when sending business letters at work.
> *Overview.* You will employ these five steps to format a letter on a computer. . . .

Agenda. Here's our schedule for learning how to format a letter. . . .

Review. To understand today's explanation, recall the basic letter format. . . .

Sequence 2 (his own variation of the sequence)

Review. Recall from the last lesson this basic format of a letter. . . .

Objective. The next step is to format a letter on a computer, today's objective.

Overview. The basic steps to formatting a letter are. . . .

Motivation. You need to learn these steps to format a letter for everyday office use.

Agenda. Here's our schedule for learning how to format a letter. . . .

Sequence 3 (his own sequence, but activity oriented and student centered)

Review. What are the basic steps to create a basic letter format, and what makes the format a good one? (Students answer and responses are posted.)

Objective. Today we will learn how to format a letter on a computer like this one. . . . Look at these letters and figure out what standards we should use to judge our final performance. (Students answer and responses are posted.)

Motivation. Give me five reasons why you will need to know how to format a business letter on a computer. (Students answer and responses are posted.)

Overview. Looking at these letters and based on what you know about other letters, what do you think are the main steps to format a letter on a computer?

Agenda. Let's make a schedule for learning how to format a letter.

By understanding that he had "permission" to change the method and create his own variations, I hope this student became a bit more free and more creative in his thinking about teaching and in his application of the principles.

Use the Principles to Improve Instruction by Enhancing Your Own Procedures.   Instead of adopting or adapting someone else's procedures to improve your teaching, you may change one of your own established procedures. All you may need is an *enhancement,* a small change afforded by applying one or two principles.

ENHANCING YOUR OWN PROCEDURES

To help students learn to identify examples of plants, a teacher applied the principle of active appropriate practice to change his standard lesson: explaining the characteristics of plants. Instead he had representatives of student groups present definitions and examples of two types of plants. He showed slides of the plants in their natural environment and asked all students to identify them. The teacher asked volunteers to state the plant's name and the cues that they used for identification. The teacher continued in this way for all of the plants taught. By means of a small change to his lesson, his students became able to make discriminations among a wide variety of plants.

A few years ago a teacher consulted with me because her students were doing poorly on tests and complaining. She was in danger of being denied tenure. Recently she called me and said she had improved her teaching considerably by applying just one idea, namely, open communication. She changed one thing: At the beginning of her course and at the beginning of each class she told students what she expected them to learn. She said that now her students were doing well on tests, and reporting satisfaction.

Use the Principles to Improve Instruction by Overhauling Your Own Procedures.   Rather than borrow or buy packaged instructional procedures from others, you can apply principles to change your own instruction. In fact, you could apply the whole set of principles. For example, suppose you wanted to improve your *discussion*—having your students analyze issues or solve problems. Here is how to apply several of the principles to improve that procedure.

First, apply the principle of *organized essential content* to create well-crafted discussion questions, the essence of a discussion. In accord with the principle you may decide to structure each question so that it asks for only one idea as simply and directly as possible. You may phrase open questions, which must be answered by more than a yes or no, or by more than one or two words. Consider arranging several questions in a logical sequence on a chalkboard or a series of flipcharts, following the order of the discussion and leaving space to post students' responses.

Second, apply *open communication,* so that your students easily understand your questions and the process to be followed. Consider posting written questions as a constant, visible focus of the discussion. You may want to state an agenda showing how much time you and your students can afford for the introduction to the discussion lesson, for the dialogue on each question, and for the summary and conclusion. You may wish to explain why a discussion is the best way to proceed to achieve the objective. Furthermore, so that students can learn to participate in a focused discussion in which all participants can contribute, you may need to state ground rules (Davis, Fry, & Alexander, 1977).

Common ground rules are that all points made will be accepted and posted on the board; evaluative comments will be deferred until all contributions are posted; everyone is invited to contribute, but it is all right to remain silent; interruptions will be policed; and although disagreements are acceptable, personal attacks are not.

Third, apply the principle of *consistency* so that when students respond to the question, their answers help them to achieve the instructional objective. Fourth, apply the principle of *prerequisites* by choosing a student activity, either in or out of class, to serve as the focus for the discussion and to provide all students with something to contribute in answer to the question. It could be a short presentation, video, simulation, reading, or observation.

Fifth, apply the principle of *pleasant conditions and consequences* by creating a controlled dialogue that produces fruitful results. Think about managing the discussion so it becomes neither a bull session, nor a normal, friendly conversation. Keep the number of people in a group to about seven, enough to have varying contributions, but not so many that factions form. Plan ways to divide a larger group or to compensate for a larger number by having students take turns responding. Arrange the room so everyone can see the question, the postings, and one another.

OVERHAULING A DISCUSSION

In this example, the teacher is applying some principles to overhaul a discussion. Note how the objective, the questions, the controlled dialogue, and the agenda are used.

"We have collected and analyzed data for our research projects, and now we must be able to write a good research report. What is a good research report? [using meaningfulness to motivate by relating to experience] Remember that, using all our work so far, our objective is to write a research report that meets the criteria we set today." [open communication by linking the task to the motive.]

The teacher shows a research process diagram. "So far, we have reviewed the literature, formed questions, created methods, collected and analyzed data. We are about to enter the final phase of our research process, reporting. Last time we determined our audience and the mode for our reporting. Now we have to create our standards for reporting. [open communication and organized essential content via objective and overview]

"Last time we determined and defined overall criteria: completeness, clarity, and accuracy. Now we must discuss specific criteria for our reports. We each have prepared, either by reading one of five different sources or interviewing one of four experienced researchers. [prerequisites by means of a review]

"We agreed that we wanted to amalgamate the sources mentioned and achieve consensus to derive our standards. A discussion is a good way to do that. We will spend about 5 minutes for this introduction, 10 minutes each on three questions, and 10 minutes on a summary and conclusion. We have five ground rules today:

1. I will post all criteria suggested in the space below each question.
2. If someone mentions a suggestion you had, confirm it.
3. Wait until we summarize each question to evaluate standards.
4. Ask for explanation or elaboration if a suggestion is not clear to you.
5. Speak up. Go as fast as you want. I will police interruptions." [open communication by means of an agenda]

The teacher points to questions written in order across the top of the board and says, "Here are the three questions: What specific standards might we apply to ensure that our reports are (1) complete? (2) clear? (3) accurate? For example, you might suggest that to be clear, terms in the research question should be defined. [organized essential content as a series of questions, and an example]

"Let's take one minute for telling a partner at least two specific points we have for the question about completeness. [pleasant conditions and consequences by means of a private individual response] Now let's have your responses to the first question."

At the end of each question's discussion, the teacher reads aloud each list of ideas, then asks, "Are there any that we can group together?" The teacher numbers the groups [organized essential content as a summary]. At the end of all questions, she reads aloud the group headings. "Are there any ideas we want to add?

"Now we are a little closer to producing our research report. All our hard work will pay off when people will get a complete, clear, and accurate report. [meaningfulness and pleasant consequences by restating the objective and the motivation] Next time I will have a demonstration and have you practice how to recognize and apply these standards. [organized essential content through integration with other segments] The research report is due in 2 weeks and will be evaluated according to the criteria we derived today." [consistency by means of a "test"]

Should you use all of the principles all of the time to enhance your instruction? No, use only the principles you need. You don't purposefully have to apply every principle to every instructional experience. If the function of a principle has been fulfilled somehow, you need not attempt to fulfill it again. For example, don't apply *meaningfulness* when your students have already expressed their eagerness to learn a part of a unit. To fulfill *open communication,* you need not include an agenda in every lesson when you follow the same schedule in each presentation. Eliminate a review of *prerequisites* or reduce it to a few words when you have just finished one lesson and have moved to another.

SHARPEN THE TOOLS OF YOUR CRAFT

What are the tools of your teaching craft? They are not computers, chalkboards, notebooks, or pens. You, your feelings, and your mind are your main tools of instruction. Your love of your subject, your subject matter knowledge, your attitude toward your subject and teaching, your understanding of students, and your procedural skills are critical. You must constantly sharpen the tools of your craft; develop yourself. Here are four ways to improve yourself to teach well:

1. Refine your knowledge of your subject matter and enhance your conviction.
2. Sharpen your awareness of students.
3. Improve your self-awareness.
4. Refine your teaching skills.

Refine Your Knowledge of Your Subject Matter and Enhance Your Conviction

To be an excellent teacher and apply principles such as organized essential content, open communication, modeling, learning aids, active appropriate practice, and consistency, you need to know your subject matter (Shulman, 1987). To be able to create objectives, tests, explanations, overviews, and summaries, you must master your subject. But what does it mean to master your subject for teaching purposes? In my opinion, you can consider yourself a master of your subject matter when you are able to

- translate your subject matter into terms your students understand.
- readjust the level of content to the level of your students.
- present the same idea in various ways.
- create credible concrete examples, cases, and analogies.
- break down steps for a performance.
- point out the pitfalls in a performance.
- extract the essential content for a performance.
- structure and organize the content.
- model the desired performance.
- diagnose mistakes from an answer or from a performance.
- devise remediation on the spot.

Can you achieve perfection as a master of your subject matter? Can you perform all the skills listed without need for improvement? I think not. Half the fun of becoming a fine teacher is striving to know your subject in a way that enables you to teach better.

Did you note the second part of the application—enhance your conviction? Without conviction to the importance of your subject, you cannot sincerely apply meaningfulness, nor can you apply modeling to show a positive attitude toward the subject and the process of learning. In addition to the behaviors already listed, consider striving to

- believe what you are teaching is important for students to master.
- show the enthusiasm you feel for your subject.
- enjoy the process of learning and teaching this subject.

Sharpen Your Awareness of Students

You have to know your students to be able to apply meaningfulness, prerequisites, and pleasant conditions and consequences. But you cannot simply be aware of one set of students in one training program or in one course. Times change and students change. What they value, what they know, and how they learn differ from group to group. Find out who your learners are every time you teach. Keep an open mind. Beware of preset expectations based on rumor and bias. You must always work to

- be aware of the general characteristics of your students.
- investigate the specifics for each group you teach.
- know the motives and the concerns of your students.
- find out what your students do, under what circumstances they must apply what they learn in the real world, and what barriers they face.
- find out what students know about the performance they must learn.

Improve Your Self-Awareness

Your decisions about instructional principles are not purely logical; they are psychological as well. What you do depends on your personality. The more you know about yourself, the more you will be able to understand how and why you are making instructional decisions. The more you understand yourself, the more you may be able to improve your decision making, to the point where it will be an enjoyable use of energy.

To use the principles for all their power, to apply them in the most expansive and creative manner, to take new paths where they are needed, you have to be aware of the way your personality is affecting your thinking. Then you can be genuinely supportive and enthusiastic. You can be a sincere, confident, and self-assured model. And you can be respectful and flexible when dealing with difficult problems.

Refine Your Teaching Skills

All of the principles can be applied using any mode of instruction from text to interactive video to live instruction. But in spite of all the technology, you, as a human teacher, are absolutely necessary. Of course, information can be designed and delivered by a computer or a videotape player, but a competent instructor can have a strong positive influence by providing an intelligent and supportive human presence (Brophy & Good, 1986; Clark, 1989). There is no medium like you when you deliver instruction with concern and skill. You will be a powerful influence if you are prepared with your knowledge and experience—if you are supportive, enthusiastic, self-assured, and flexible (Maddocks & Yelon, 1986).

To apply the principles one at a time or as a set, you need excellent instructional planning and development skills. Because teaching is so wonderfully complex, you can always do better. Strive to improve your effectiveness, your efficiency, and your variety of applications. Do not adopt methods of teaching without assessing them. Take the time to revise methods as needed.

But planning is only half the battle. You also have to be a good presenter, facilitator, and tutor. Take any opportunity to improve your skills in presenting, handling groups of people, and coaching individuals. Observe the best teachers you know and consider what, how, and especially why they act as they do when they use each of these modes well.

JUST A FEW MORE FINAL WORDS

There you have it: powerful principles that will help you teach and help your students learn. Of course, there are other principles, but these can make a tremendous difference in the design of your instruction so that your students will learn well and want to use what they have learned.

Apply them one at a time or in combination, but above all *apply them.* Apply them everywhere. You can apply the principles if you teach small children, teenagers, or adults; if you teach math or science, reading or writing, managing or computing, machine operating or interviewing, problem solving or trouble-shooting. You can apply them to teaching single concepts, sets of principles and facts, groups of skills, systems of thinking, clusters of attitudes, or methods of problem solving. You can apply the principles if you teach large or small formal classes in public or private schools and colleges; if you use workshops, training programs, and seminars in professional settings, businesses, or industries; if you use lecture, discussion, expository teaching, or discovery learning; or if you use whole-class instruction or self-instruction, or teacher-centered instruction or student-centered instruction.

Apply them in every way. You can apply the principles by talking to students, or you can have your students discuss the ideas or discover them. You can have students implement the principles. You can use some principles and not others. You can use the principles for courses, units, and lessons. You can vary the kind of medium when applying principles.

Work hard to apply the principles. Some novice teachers, trainers, and college instructors often begin by thinking that you need only to "know your stuff." Then, as a subject matter expert, all you have to do to teach or train is make an outline and give a talk. You know you have to work hard to apply the principles and make use of your subject knowledge. In contrast, some teachers believe that successsful teaching requires nothing more than affection for students. They are amazed to find that when applying principles, the preparation, implementation, and follow-up of teaching and training take tremendous work.

Apply the principles in a creative manner. When methods of instruction are prescribed as part of a teacher's manual or a trainer's guide, you may find that they are mundane as well as inadequate. To compensate, you will have to practice the art of teaching and apply the principles creatively. But the practice of art is difficult, as I tried to explain in this poem I wrote in college:

> The trouble with art is . . .
> Where do you start?
> How far do you go?
> And where do you part?
> That's the trouble with art!

Apply the principles in your own way. Do not necessarily teach as you were taught. Do not necessarily teach as the people around you are teaching. Make your decisions based on principle. As a good craftsperson, use the principles and your creativity to derive the idea for an instructional procedure. Then use your logical abilities to decide exactly how to implement the procedure. As your teaching needs change, adapt your procedures.

Take the time and the effort to apply these principles with creativity and precision so that your students will learn to a high degree and will want to use what they have learned.

ACTIVITIES

Here are a number of activities that call for you to use principles flexibly. Do these by yourself, with a partner, or in a small group. You will find the practice useful when you have to justify or evaluate instruction, when you have to create, enhance, overhaul, or adapt instruction. Some exercises help you apply the principles to all forms of instruction.

1. Justify instruction. Select a procedure that you have observed or that you used to teach. State which principles apply to that procedure, as if you were explaining the procedure to a student, a colleague, or a supervisor.
2. Evaluate instruction. Choose a segment of instruction that did not go well. Perhaps students were not motivated, were not learning well, or were not applying what they learned. List questions implied by each principle to determine what might have gone wrong in the segment. Answer the questions to diagnose the nature of the instructional problem and derive guidelines or procedures to solve the problem.
3. Evaluate instruction. Use the checklist in Appendix A to observe a teacher or to look at your own instruction. Assess the presence or absence of the principles and the quality of their application. Think about what could be done to satisfy the checklist.

4. Create a new procedure. Be as creative as you can in applying the principles to instruct students to solve problems in a subject area of your choice. Use each principle to produce a unique and wild idea.

5. Enhance existing instruction. Think of a particular subject and topic. Consider a common way of teaching that topic, such as a lecture, a discussion, self-instruction, reading assignments, homework assignments, videotape, or audiotape, and apply one or two of the principles to enhance that form of instruction.

6. In collaborative learning, students work together to do a project, to learn a subject, or to study for an exam. How could you apply the principles to collaborative learning? For example, which principles could students use when studying for an exam? How? Which principles would a group of students use when working together to learn a subject? How?

7. Overhaul existing instruction. Apply each principle to create a set of instructional procedures for a common situation in which you might teach.

8. Adapt the procedures you created in activity 7, using the principles to plan two lessons, one in which you present the information to students and one in which the students discover it for themselves.

9. Adapt your method to create materials for a lesson that will stand alone. Students must be able to use the module to learn independently.

10. Select an important skill, a set of facts, a concept, and a principle in your domain and make a chart in which you would plan to teach that content. (Refer to Appendix B for guidance.)

FURTHER READING

Agne, K. J. (1992). Caring: The expert teacher's edge. *Educational Horizons, 70*(3), 120-124. (*Note:* Part of the tools of your craft.)

Clark, C. M. (1989, October). The good teacher. In *Education from cradle to the doctorate.* Plenary lecture presented to the Norwegian Research Council for Science and the Humanities Conference, Trondheim, Norway. (*Note:* Clark specifies some of the requirements of a fine teacher.)

Davis, R., Fry, J., & Alexander, L. (1977). *The discussion method.* East Lansing, MI: Instructional Media Center, Michigan State University. (*Note:* A short, clear explanation of what makes a good discussion.)

Gagné, R. M., & Driscoll, M. P. (1988). *Essentials of learning for instruction* (2nd ed.). Boston: Allyn & Bacon. (*Note:* Here is a set of procedures based on learning principles. Do they fit your circumstances? How could you adapt them?)

Gunter, M. A., Estes, T. H., & Scwab, J. (1995). *Instruction: A models approach* (2nd ed.). Boston: Allyn & Bacon. (*Note:* Many approaches to instruction. How do they use the principles?)

Hamachek, D. (1995). *Psychology in teaching, learning and growth* (5th ed.). Boston: Allyn & Bacon. (*Note:* Read chapters 11 and 12 about the psychology of effective teachers and enhancing teaching effectiveness by understanding oneself.)

Walberg, H. J. (1990, February). Productive teaching and instruction: Assessing the knowledge base. *Phi Delta Kappan,* 470-478. (*Note:* This is a summary of educational research. How do these conclusions relate to the principles and their use?)

A Checklist for Using the Ten Principles

You can use this checklist as the basis for observing, planning, or evaluating instruction.

Meaningfulness

Do the *plans* or the *instruction*

_____ help students make meaningful connections systematically?

    _____ by assessing students' motives?

    _____ by discovering the connection between the topic and the students' motives?

    _____ by creating an activity or statement that will appeal to those motives?

    _____ by helping make the connection and then checking the results?

_____ make meaningful connections continuously?

    _____ before instruction?

    _____ at the start of instruction?

    _____ throughout instruction?

    _____ at the end of instruction?

    _____ after instruction?

Prerequisites

Do the *plans* or the *instruction*

_____ show that prerequistes of required tasks were analyzed?

    _____ For complex skills, are the tasks in the objectives described explicitly?

_____ For simple objectives, are the tasks in the objectives analyzed directly?

_____ Are the objectives or the task descriptions analyzed?

     _____ to identify subskills?

     _____ to identify rules?

     _____ to identify principles?

     _____ to identify facts?

     _____ to identify concepts?

     _____ to identify attitudes?

_____ Are essential prerequisites selected from results of the analysis?

_____ Are essential prerequisites analyzed further?

_____ include an assessment of what students know?

     _____ Does the assessment balance the dangers in pretesting and not pretesting?

     _____ Is the pretest safe and nonthreatening, in either formal or informal modes?

     _____ Is the pretest strategy efficient?

_____ adjust instruction, accounting for analyzed prerequisites and students' knowledge?

     _____ Are the adjustments to pretest results appropriate choices of strategy?

     Do the adjustments involve

         _____ self-care?

         _____ individual care?

         _____ small-group direct instruction?

         _____ facilitated small-group learning?

         _____ review by whole-class instruction?

         _____ counseling to other resources?

Open Communication

Do the *plans* or the *instruction*

_____ include a student orientation?

     _____ with objectives?

     _____ with sample test items?

     _____ with sample final products?

     _____ with an overview?

     _____ with an agenda?

     _____ with a complete package of course materials?

_____ provide for feedback to students?

     _____ about students' performance?

         _____ with appropriate timing?

         _____ with appropriate statements?

         _____ with appropriate mode of feedback?

_____ about students' questions?

   _____ based on a question answering policy?

   _____ with time designated for asking and anwering questions?

_____ about students' attitudes?

_____ provide for students to give feedback to the instructor?

Do the decisions include

_____ what information the instructor needs?

_____ what method for data collection and what questions?

_____ how to collect the information after an appropriate unit?

_____ how to tally the information?

_____ how to make decisions for changes?

_____ how to report back to students?

_____ how to implement changes?

Organized Essential Content

Do the *plans* or the *instruction*

_____ show that essential content was selected from the task description?

_____ show that essential content was selected from the required facts, concepts, principles, and skills?

   _____ For facts, are there organized sets of facts and vividly illustrated examples as substantiation?

   _____ For concepts, are there definitions of the categories and a typical example or example-nonexample pairs?

   _____ For principles, are there definitions relating variables and evidence showing relationship of variables?

   _____ For skills, are there ordered, simplified steps and a demonstration?

_____ contain essential examples?

   _____ that are accurate?

   _____ that are clear?

   _____ that are interesting?

   _____ that are generalizable?

_____ show organization of essential content?

   _____ for the course content?

   _____ for the unit content?

   _____ for the lesson content?

_____ present essential content in an organized way?

   _____ with a course overview?

   _____ with transitions from one unit to another within the structure?

   _____ with simply organized presentations of lesson content?

Learning Aids

Do the *plans* or the *instruction*

_____ provide aids that fit the structure of the task?

Do aids include

_____ a flow diagram, when branching task steps?

_____ an outline, when ordering clusters of content?

_____ a chart, when comparing subtopics on multiple dimensions?

_____ a drawing, when visually simplifying complex stimuli?

_____ a mnemonic, when recalling a set of facts?

_____ a decision aid, when requiring different responses from varying situations?

_____ a decision tree, when choosing responses after a series of decisions?

_____ a narrative task description, when verbally explaining a series of steps?

_____ a checklist, when checking criteria in a process or product?

_____ an annotated model, when noting criteria for a complex, visual product?

_____ a diagram, when relating variables in complex ways?

_____ use the aids for their intended purpose?

_____ as a major teaching tool?

_____ as a small but important instructional tool?

_____ as the sole means of instruction?

_____ demonstrate anticipation of problems in using aids?

_____ Do they anticipate aids making learning too easy for students?

_____ Do they anticipate students being unable to perform without the aid?

Novelty

Do the *plans* or the *instruction*

_____ capture and maintain attention?

_____ by using varied actions?

_____ by using varied programs?

_____ by using varied techniques?

_____ by using creative teaching?

_____ by using humor, suspense, shock, and surprise?

_____ by using techniques to help stuents learn to control their own attention?

_____ direct students' attention?

by using media to direct students' attention to the _____ important cues?

_____ by stressing the important points?

_____ provoke curiosity?

      _____ with questions?

      _____ with puzzling events and demonstrations?

Modeling

Do the *plans* or the *instruction*

_____ use the four-step approach to demonstrate performance?

      _____ by telling students they will perform what will be demonstrated?

      _____ before demonstrating, by telling students what to observe in the demonstration?

      _____ by saying each step and then doing it?

      _____ by asking students to commit the steps to memory before practice?

_____ use the four-step approach to demonstrate thinking skills?

      _____ by telling students they will perform the mental skill that will be demonstrated?

      _____ before demonstrating, by telling students what to note as they watch the mental skill made observable?

      _____ by saying each general mental step and then doing it on a specific case?

      _____ by asking students to commit the mental skill steps to memory before practice?

_____ use the four-step approach to demonstrate attitudes?

      _____ by telling students they will perform the attitude as a part of performance?

      _____ before demonstrating, by telling students indicators of the attitude to watch for?

      _____ by saying each indicator of attitude and then doing it?

      _____ by asking students to commit the indicators to memory before practice?

_____ demonstrate the teacher's professional attitude continuously?

      _____ by showing an attitude of a mature, ethical professional?

      _____ by showing an attitude of concern for the subject matter, students' learning, and teaching?

      _____ by showing enthusiasm for and enjoyment of the work?

Active Appropriate Practice

Do *plans* or *instruction*

_____ provide active individual practice?

_____ provide appropriate realistic practice?

      _____ in which conditions and behaviors function realistically?

      _____ in which practice matches the test appropriately for the type of knowledge?

      _____ in which students think aloud for mental skill practice?

      _____ through a systematic choice of practice setting?

_____ provide fine-tuned practice?
      _____ Is it challenging practice?
      _____ Is it practice leading to automaticity?
      _____ Is it practice encouraging flexibility?
      _____ Is it varied practice?
      _____ Is it independent practice?
      _____ Is it clearly specified and guided practice?
      _____ Is it distributed practice?
      _____ Is it advanced practice?
      _____ Is it practice in which students are motivated to perform?
      _____ Is it practice in which students are taught about mental practice?
      _____ Is it practice in which checklists are used to monitor practice and save time?
      _____ Is it practice in which students are asked to take responsibility?
_____ use other student learning activities purposefully?
      _____ Is there purposeful selection from five types of student learning activities?
            _____ motivation activity?
            _____ orientation activity?
            _____ information activity?
            _____ application activity?
            _____ evaluation activity?
      _____ Is there thoughtful implementation of student learning activities?

Pleasant Conditions and Consequences

Do the _plans_ or the _instruction_
_____ associate pleasant conditions with learning?
      _____ before instruction?
      _____ during instruction?
_____ provide for pleasant consequences?
      _____ by teaching tasks with valued natural consequences?
      _____ by using feedback and praise as rewards for subskills?
      _____ by using a systematic approach to reward desired behavior?
      _____ by responding to undesired behavior responsibly?
      _____ by anticipating conditions and consequences to prevent undesired behavior?

Consistent Instructional Elements

Do the _plans_ or the _instruction_
_____ provide consistent instructional elements?
      _____ where the real-world performance goal is related to the terminal objective?

_____ where the content is related to the objective?
_____ where the instructional methods are related to the objective?
_____ where the tests are related to all other components?
_____ create consistency between instruction and the real world?
      _____ promoting transfer beyond the instructional setting?
            _____ by motivating students to learn and use what they have learned?
            _____ by making students aware of when to use new skills and ideas, especially when they have a wide choice of responses?
            _____ by enabling students to master and apply the skills to be used?
            _____ by promoting psychological and physical support in the real-world context in which the knowledge is to be used?

Using Principles

Do the *plans* or the *instruction*
_____ use the principles?
      _____ to create instructional procedures?
      _____ to justify instructional procedures?
      _____ to evaluate instructional procedures?
      _____ to revise instructional procedures?
            _____ by adopting and adapting existing instructional procedures?
            _____ by enhancing and overhauling your own instructional procedures?

How Instructional Elements Vary Depending on the Type of Knowledge

	Elements	Skills	Facts	Concepts	Principles
				Types of Knowledge	
I N T R O D U C T I O N	Motivation	Why learn to do the skill	Why learn to recall the facts	Why learn to identify examples of concepts	Why learn to predict and explain new cases using principles
	Objective	Do the skill	Recall the facts	Identify new examples	Predict and explain new cases using principles
	Overview	Major skill steps	Major headings of fact outline	Key attributes from definition	Major variables and relationship
	Review	Review subskills and ideas	Review concepts and facts	Review concepts in definition	Review concepts in definition
	Agenda	——— Explanation, demonstration, and practice ———			
C O R E	Explanation	Tell steps of the skill	Tell facts in an organized vivid way and substantiate	Tell definition, examples and nonexamples	Tell definition, evidence showing relationship
	Demonstration	Show how to do the skill	Show how to recall the facts	Show how to identify examples	Show how to predict and explain new cases
	Practice	Do the skill	Recall the facts	Identify new examples	Predict and explain new cases
	Feedback and Refinement	Use the skill checklist	Check the fact outline	Check the attributes	Check the variables and relationship
C O N C L U S I O N	Summary	Major skill steps	Major headings of fact outline	Key attributes from definition	Variables and relationship
	Integration	Next skill	Next ideas	Next ideas	Next ideas
	Objective	Do the skill	Recall the facts	Identify new examples	Predict and explain new cases using principles
	Motivation	Why do the skill	Why recall the facts	Why identify new examples of the concept	Why predict and explain new cases using principles
	Test	Do the skill	Recall the facts	Identify new examples	Predict and explain new cases

279

Seventeen Techniques to Make Meaningful Attention-Getters

1. Relate whatever is taught to a strong student interest.
2. Provide a real problem to start the unit.
3. Provide a simulated role within a real situation.
4. State the connection: where and when the content is used.
5. State or show the use and its payoff.
6. Use a meaningful quote.
7. Use a meaningful generalization.
8. Tell of successful applications.
9. Tell of likely problems if the ideas are not applied or understood.
10. Conduct an activity demonstrating need.
11. Ask a puzzling relevant question to show the content is needed.
12. Show a relevant puzzling event.
13. Ask which relevant idea is correct.
14. Present an unsolved case.
15. Contrast students' beliefs and students' actions with their self-view.
16. Ask students why they think the topic is important.
17. Give a case or an activity and ask students how the topic is relevant for them.

References

Aaronson, D. T. (1983). Contributions of Gagné and Briggs to a prescriptive model of instruction. In C. M. Reigeluth (Ed.), *Instructional design theories and models: An overview of their current status* (pp. 75-100). Hillsdale, NJ: Lawrence Erlbaum.

Abrami, P. C., Leventhal, L., & Perry, R. P. (1982). Educational seduction. *Review of Educational Research, 52*(3), 446-464.

Aronson, E., Blaney, S., Sikes, J., & Snapp, M. (1978). *The jigsaw classroom.* Beverly Hills, CA: Sage Publications.

Alderman, F. L. (1988). *A guide to implementing effective transfer of training strategies.* Paper presented at the 1988 National Society for Performance and Instruction Annual Conference, Denver, CO.

Ausubel, D. (1980). Schemata, cognitive structure and advance organizers: A reply to Anderson, Spiro and Anderson. *American Educational Research Journal, 17,* 400-404.

Bandura, A. (Ed.). (1977). *Social learning theory.* Englewood Cliffs, NJ: Prentice-Hall.

Bandura, A. (1986). *Social foundation of thought and action: A social cognitive theory.* Englewood Cliffs, NJ: Prentice-Hall.

Bangert-Drowns, R. L., Kulik, C., Kulik, J. A., & Morgan, M. (1991). The instructional effect of feedback in test-like events. *Review of Educational Research, 61*(2), 213-238.

Beaudin, B. P. (1987). Enhancing the transfer of job related learning from the learning environment to the workplace. *Performance and Instruction Journal, 26*(9/10), 19-21.

Berlyne, D. E. (1950). Novelty and curiosity as determinants of exploratory behavior. *British Journal of Psychology, 41,* 68-90.

Berlyne, D. E. (1960). *Conflict, arousal and curiosity.* New York: McGraw-Hill.

Berlyne, D. E. (1965). Motivational problems raised by exploratory and epistemic behavior. In S. Koch (Ed.), *Psychology: A study of a science,* Vol. 5 (pp. 284-364). New York: McGraw Hill.

Blanchard, K., & Johnson, S. (1981). *The one minute manager.* New York: Berkeley Books.

Bloom, B. S. (1984). The 2 sigma problem: The search for methods of group instruction as good as one-to-one tutoring. *Educational Researcher, 14*(6), 4-16.

Bloom, B. S., & Broder, L. (1950). *Problem solving processes of college students.* Chicago: University of Chicago Press.

Bloom, B. S., Engelhart, M. D., Furst, E. J., Hill, W. H., & Krathwohl, D. R. (1956). *Taxonomy of educational objectives—The classification of educational goals: Handbook I. Cognitive domain.* New York: David McKay.

Bottge, B. A., & Hasselbring, T. S. (1993). Taking word problems off the page. *Educational Leadership, 50*(7), 36-37.

Brick, M. (1993). When students write home. *Educational Leadership, 50*(7), 62-63.

Brophy, J., & Alleman, J. (1991). Activities as instructional tools: A framework for analysis and evaluation *Educational Researcher, 20*(4), 9-23.

Brophy, J., & Good, T. L. (1986). Teacher behavior and student achievement. In M. C. Wittrock (Ed.), *Handbook of research on teaching* (3rd ed.) (pp. 328-375). New York: Macmillan.

Browne, D. (1964). *Hagar the Horrible.* Newspaper cartoon, King Features Syndicate. November 7.

Bruner, J. S. (1960). *The process of education.* New York: Random House.

Burke, J. (1993). Tackling society's problems in English class. *Educational Leadership, 50*(7), 16-18.

Burton, W. H. (1952). *The guidance of learning activities.* New York: Appleton-Century-Crofts.

Cameron, J., & Pierce, W. D. (1994). Reinforcement, reward, and instrinsic motivation: A meta analysis. *Review of Educational Research, 64*(3), 363-424.

Canfield, J., & Hansen, M. V. (1993). *Chicken soup for the soul.* Deerfield Beach, FL: Health Communications.

Chance, P. (1992, November). The rewards of learning. *Phi Delta Kappan,* 200-207.

Chilcoat, G. W. (1989). Instructional behaviors for clearer presentations in the classroom. *Instructional Science, 18,* 289-314.

Clark, R. C. (1986). Defining the "D" in ISD: Part 1. Task-general instructional methods. *Performance and Instruction Journal, 25*(1), 17-20.

Clark, C. M. (1989, October). The good teacher. In *Education from cradle to the doctorate.* Plenary lecture presented to the Norwegian Research Council for Science and the Humanities Conference, Trondheim, Norway.

Cohen, S. A. (1987). Instructional alignment: Searching for a magic bullet. *Educational Researcher, 16*(8), 16-20.

Corno, L., & Rohrkemper, M. (1985). Self-regulated learning. In C. Ames & R. Ames (Eds.), *Research on motivation in education* (Vol. 2). Orlando, FL: Academic Press.

Covey, S. R. (1989). *The seven habits of highly effective people.* New York: Simon & Schuster.

Davis, R. H., Alexander, L. T., & Yelon, S. L. (1974). *Learning system design: An approach to the improvement of instruction.* New York: McGraw-Hill.

Davis, R., Fry, J., & Alexander, L. (1977). *The discussion method.* East Lansing, MI: Instructional Media Center, Michigan State University.

Desmedt, J. (1984). Use of force paradigm for law enforcement. *Journal of Police Science and Administration, 12*(1), 170-176.

Doig, K. (1990). Maximizing effectiveness of reading assignments. *Clinical Laboratory Science, 3*(5), 310.

Eble, K. (1976). *The craft of teaching.* San Francisco: Jossey-Bass.

Ellis, J., Wulfeck, W., & Montague, W. (1980). The effect of adjunct and test questions similarity on study behavior and learning in a training course. *American Educational Research Journal, 17*(4), 449-457.

Farnham-Diggory, S. (1994). Paradigms of knowledge and instruction. *Review of Educational Research, 64*(3), 463-477.

Festinger, L. F. (1957). *A theory of cognitive dissonance.* Stanford, CA: Stanford University Press.

Gagné, R. M. (1985). *The conditions of learning and theory of instruction.* New York: Holt, Rinehart & Winston.

Gagné, R. M., & Driscoll, M. P. (1988). *Essentials of learning for instruction* (2nd ed.). Boston: Allyn & Bacon.

Gropper, G. L. (1983). A behavioral approach to instructional prescription. In C. M. Reigeluth (Ed.), *Instructional design theories and models: An overview of their current status* (pp. 101-162). Hillsdale, NJ: Lawrence Erlbaum.

Keller, J. M. (1983). Motivational design of instruction. In C. M. Reigeluth (Ed.), *Instructional design theories and models: An overview of their current status* (pp. 383-436). Hillsdale, NJ: Lawrence Erlbaum.

Keller, J. M. (1987). Strategies for stimulating the motivation to learn. *Performance and Instruction Journal, 26*(8), 1-7.

Kobrin, D., Abbott, E., Elinwood, J., & Horton, D. (1993). Learning history by doing history. *Educational Leadership, 50*(7), 39-41.

Lakein, A. (1973). *How to get control of your time and life.* New York: Penguin.

Levin, M. E., & Levin, J. R. (1990). Scientific mnemonomies: Methods for maximixing more than memory. *American Educational Research Journal, 27*(2), 301-324.

Lewis, B. (1973, September). The British Open University: Concepts and realities. In *Productivity in higher education.* Paper presented at a symposium on educational technologies, State University of New York at Stony Brook.

Maddocks, M., & Yelon, S. L. (1986). Identifying trainer competencies. *Performance and Instruction Journal, 25*(9), 9-12.

Mager, R. F. (1962). *Preparing instructional objectives.* Palo Alto, CA: Fearon Press.

Merrill, M. D. (1983). Component display theory. In C. M. Reigeluth (ed.), *Instructional design theories and models: An overview of their current status* (pp. 279-333). Hillsdale, NJ: Lawrence Erlbaum.

Naftulin, D. H., Ware, J. E., & Donnely, F. A. (1973). The Doctor Fox lecture: A paradigm for educational seduction. *Journal of Medical Education, 48,* 630-635.

Neidermeier, F. C., & Yelon, S. L. (1981). L.A. aligns instruction with essential skills. *Educational Leadership, 38*(8), 618-620.

Palinscar, A. S., & Brown, A. L. (1984). Reciprocal teaching of comprehension fostering and comprehension monitoring activities. *Cognition & Instruction, 2,* 117-175.

Reigeluth, C. M., & Stein, F. S. (1983). The elaboration theory of instruction. In C. M. Reigeluth (Ed.), *Instructional design theories and models: An overview of their current status* (pp. 335-382). Hillsdale, NJ: Lawrence Erlbaum.

Rogers, C. R. (1983). *Freedom to learn for the 80s.* Columbus, OH: Charles E. Merrill.

Rosenshine, B., & Meister, C. (1994). Reciprocal teaching: A review of the research. *Review of Educational Research, 64,* 479-530.

Sage, G. H. (1984). *Motor learning and control: A neurophysiologiocal approach.* Dubuque, IA: William C. Brown.

Salisbury, D. F., Jacobs, J. W., & Dempsey, J. V. (1987, April). *Automaticity training: Implications for education and technology.* Paper presented at the annual meeting of the American Educational Research Association, Washington, DC.

Schack, G. D. (1993). Involving students in authentic research. *Educational Leadership, 50*(7), 29-31.

Schmidt, R. A. (1982). *Motor control and learning: A behavioral emphasis.* Champaign, IL: Human Kinetics.

Schon, D. A. (1987). *Educating the reflective practitioner.* San Francisco, CA: Jossey-Bass.

Shulman, L. S. (1987). Knowledge and teaching: Foundations of the new reform. *Harvard Educational Review, 57*(1), 1-21.

Skinner, B. F. (1968). *The technology of teaching.* Englewood Cliffs, NJ: Prentice-Hall.

Stepien, W., & Gallagher, S. (1993). Problem-based learning: As authentic as it gets. *Educational Leadership, 50*(7), 25-28.

Tyler, R. W. (1950). *Basic principles of curriculum and instruction.* Chicago: University of Chicago Press.

Whimbey, A., & Lockhead, J. (1982). *Problem solving and comprehension* (3rd ed.). Philadelphia: Franklin Press.

Wolkomir, R. (1986). "Old Jearl" will do anything to stir an interest in physics. *Smithsonian, 17*(7), 112-116.

Yelon, S. L. (1974). *Constructive evaluation: Improving large scale instructional projects.* Lansing, MI: SLY Publishers.

Yelon, S. L. (1984). How to use and create criterion checklists. *Performance and Instruction Journal, 23*(3), 1-4.

Yelon, S. L. (1985). Making decisions about pretesting: It's not a simple matter. *Performance and Instruction Journal, 24*(9), 9-14.

Yelon, S. L. (1991). Writing and using instructional objectives. In L. J. Briggs, K. L. Gustafson, & M. H. Tillman (Eds.), *Instructional design: Principles and applications* (pp. 75-121). Englewood Cliffs, NJ: Educational Technology Publications.

Yelon, S. L. (1992). M.A.S.S.: A model for producing transfer. *Performance Improvement Quarterly, 5*(2), 13-23.

Yelon, S. L. (1995). Active learning: A taxonomy of training activities. *Performance and Instruction 34*(5), 38-41.

Yelon, S. L., & Berge, Z. L. (1987). Using fancy checklists for efficient feedback. *Performance and Instruction, 26*(4), 14-20.

Yelon, S. L., & Berge, Z. L. (1988). The secret of instructional design. *Performance and Instruction, 27*(1), 11-13.

Yelon, S. L., & Berge, Z. L. (1992). Practice centered training. *Performance and Instruction, 31*(8), 8-12.

Yelon, S. L., & Desmedt, J. (1988). A performance and instructional aid for choice of appropriate action: How to create a situation by response model. *Performance and Instruction, 27*(6), 22-29.

Yelon, S. L., Desmedt, J., & Williamson, J. (1988). Integrating principle-based rules into skill instruction. *Performance and Instruction, 27*(10), 33-48.

Yelon, S. L., & Maddocks, M. (1986). Complete demonstration. *Performance and Instruction, 25*(1), 3-9.

Yelon, S. L., & Massa, M. (1987). Heuristics for creating examples. *Performance and Instruction, 26*(8), 13-17.

Yelon, S., & Reznich, C. (1991). Creating and using annotated examples. *Performance and Instruction, 30*(4), 26-30.

Yelon, S., & Reznich, C. (1992). Visible models of course organization. *Performance and Instruction Journal, 31*(6), 7-11.

Yelon, S. L., & Scott, R. (1970). *A strategy for writing objectives.* Dubuque, IA: Kendall/ Hunt Publishing.

Yelon, S. L., & Wineman, A. (1987). Efficient lesson development. *Performance and Instruction Journal, 26*(6), 1-6.

Index

Relating, consistency of
  of content to objective, 235
  of instructional methods to objective, 236
  of real-world performance goal to terminal objective, 234–235
Relevance. *See* Meaningfulness
Reporting
  back to students, 100
  of mental skill practice, requiring, 197–199
Rewards
  naturally rewarding events, sequences of, 220–221
  praise and feedback, as rewards for subskills, 222–223
  systematic approach to reward desired behavior, 224–225
Reznich, Chris, 83, 84, 89–90, 256–259
Rogers, C. R., 9
Rohrkemper, M., 35
Rosenshine, B., 179

Sage, G. H., 201, 202
Salisbury, D. F., 200
Samples, providing
  of final products, 81–83
  of test items, 78–81
Schack, G. D., 20
Schmidt, R. A., 201, 202
Schon, D. A., 88, 188, 203, 206
Scott, R., 74, 75
Secret of instructional design, 233–234, 244
Self-awareness, improving your, 266
Self-care, using, 66
Self-defense, using an activity to interest students in, 28
Self study, 250
"Sesame Street," 153, 180, 189
Setting(s), instructional
  in or out of, deciding systematically if practice should be, 199–200
  practice in all, providing, 190–192
  transfer beyond the, promoting, 241–242
Shulman, L. S., 265
Sikes, J., 154
Silent students, using eight preventative measures to avoid, 229–230
Simulation, 196–198
  maximizing practice through, 192–194

Skill(s), student
  asking students to commit the thinking-skills steps to memory before they practice, 180
  choosing essential content, for the required facts, concepts, principles, and, 108–111
  example demonstration of a simple mental, 174
  helping students in mastering and applying, 243–244
  maximizing practice through application of a, 194
  menu of, presenting a, 13
  motivating students in learning and using, 242–243
  praise and feedback, as rewards for sub-, 222–223
  simple showing of skill is unlikely to be sufficient, 167
  thinking, four-step approach for demonstrating, 173–180
Skills, of teaching. *See* Tools of your craft, sharpening the
Skinner, B. F., 218, 223
Small-group learning, 63, 67–68
Smithsonian, 155–156
Snapp, M., 154
Stein, Faith S., 85, 124
Stepien, W., 20
Symbols, poster with drawings and, as learning aid, 132

Table of contents for course package, example of, 86–87
Task(s)
  analyzing description of the, 50–55
  analyzing prerequisites of required, 45–56
  choosing essential content from the described, 107–108
  describing the, 45–50
  task description as a major teaching tool, 138–139
Techniques, varying your, 153–154
Testing. *See also* Pretesting; Objectives
  anxiety, how to create test, 212
  matching the test to the type of knowledge, designing practice for, 197. *See also* Practice, active and appropriate; Consistency
  practice tests, 80–81
  relating the tests to all other components, 236–240